THE PERMANENT DIACONATE

Its History and Place in the Sacrament of Orders

Kenan B. Osborne, OFM

Paulist Press
New York/Mahwah, NJ

IMPRIMI POTEST: Very Rev. Melvin A. Jurisich, OFM, Provincial Minister of the Franciscan Friars of the Province of Saint Barbara

June 13, 2006
Oakland, California

Cover design by Cynthia Dunne
Book design by Lynn Else

Copyright © 2007 by Franciscan Friars of California

Library of Congress Cataloging-in-Publication Data

Osborne, Kenan B.
    The permanent diaconate : its history and place in the sacrament of orders / Kenan B. Osborne.
        p. cm.
    Includes bibliographical references and index.
    ISBN 978-0-8091-4448-8 (alk. paper)
    1. Deacons—Catholic Church. I. Title.
    BX1912.O755 2007
    262'.14088282—dc22

                                                                    2006034089

Published by Paulist Press
997 Macarthur Boulevard
Mahwah, New Jersey 07430

www.paulistpress.com

Printed and bound in the United States of America

THE PAULIST PRESS DEACON'S LIBRARY

Michael E. Bulson — *Preach What You Believe: Timeless Homilies for Deacons– Liturgical Cycle B* (2005)

Michael E. Bulson — *Believe What You Read: Timeless Homilies for Deacons – Liturgical Cycle C* (2006)

Owen F. Cummings — *Saintly Deacons* (2005)

Owen F. Cummings — *Deacons and the Church* (2004)

Owen F. Cummings, William T. Ditewig & Richard R. Gaillardetz — *Theology of the Diaconate: The State of the Question* (2005)

William T. Ditewig — *101 Questions & Answers on Deacons* (2004)

Alfred C. Hughes, Frederick F. Campbell & William T. Ditewig — *Today's Deacon: Contemporary Issues and Crosscurrents* (2006)

James Keating, ed. — *The Deacon Reader* (2006)

CONTENTS

Contents

INTRODUCTION

In 1996, the National Association of Diaconate Directors (NADD) published a small volume that I had written entitled *The Diaconate in the Christian Church: Its History and Theology.* This volume served its purpose fairly well. However, as we move into the early years of the third millennium, the directors of the NADD inquired whether I had any plans to revise the small volume. I began working on a revision, and the present book is the result of that effort. In this volume, dedicated to the *permanent* diaconate, I do not address in any lengthy way the *transitional* diaconate.

This volume is more than a casual refining of the 1996 booklet. The material in this volume includes a large section of new material that analyzes in detail the conciliar and postconciliar contextualization for the permanent diaconate. The importance of the initial chapter must be stressed. The documents of Vatican II indicate clearly that *all* ecclesial ministries are interrelated, and thus an interrelational context is needed for a sharper and more accurate assessment of today's permanent diaconate. This assessment involves three dimensions of the contemporary permanent diaconate: the theological dimension, the pastoral dimension, and the self-identity dimension. These three dimensions are intrinsically interrelated. How one theologizes on the permanent diaconate affects one's pastoral approach to permanent diaconal ministry, and the theological and pastoral dimensions of the permanent diaconal ministry affect the self-identity of the permanent deacon himself. When these interrelationships are harmonious, at least to some degree, the permanent diaconate's theology, pastoral practice, and self-identity are healthy. When disharmony of any serious nature is present in any of the three dimensions—theological, pastoral, and personal—

signs of stress and confusion immediately appear. In today's permanent diaconate, particularly in the United States, there are signs of stress and confusion, and these indications affect the current theology of the deacon, the pastoral diaconal practice, and personal diaconal identity.

It is my judgment that the lack of a serious contextual interrelationship between all contemporary ecclesial ministries is one of the major causes of ministerial uneasiness today. There is a tendency on the part of some key Roman Catholic Church leaders to emphasize the radical and specific difference of each ministry over against a foundational interrelationship of all institutional church ministries. However, this stress on radical and specific differences moves away from the basic presentation of ministry that one finds in the documents of Vatican II. In many ways, this stress on radical difference is an effort to re-express a tridentine or pre–Vatican II understanding of church ministry.

As a consequence, I have focused in the initial part of this book on the interrelational contextualization of conciliar and post-conciliar ecclesial ministry. The contextual issue of ministerial interrelationality brings to center stage the key problematic factors for today's theological, pastoral, and personal problems regarding all church ministries (papacy, episcopacy, priesthood, diaconate, lay ministry, and the ministry of all baptized-confirmed believers). To ignore or minimize the problem of the interrelational contextualization of ecclesial ministry—a position that some ecclesiastical and theological leaders have taken—misinterprets the very foundation of all ministry and leadership, which the documents of Vatican II presented. The ultimate foundation of all ministry and leadership, as presented in the documents of Vatican II, exists in the *missio-ad-extra* plan of the Trinity: namely, God's sending of Jesus. The trinitarian "sending" of the Logos into the humanity of Jesus is the ultimate foundation of all ecclesial mission, ministry, and leadership. The trinitarian sending was done purposefully, that is, there was both a mission and a ministry involved in this sending. As a consequence, the actualized mission and ministry of Jesus establish the second foundation of all mission, ministry, and leadership. This foundational structure of all mission and ministry is repeated again and again throughout the documents of Vatican II. In the conciliar documents, all other specific ecclesial ministries and leadership (the ministry of all baptized Christians, papacy, episcopacy, priesthood, diaconate, lay ministry) are presented as *sharing* in the one and same mission and ministry of Jesus. This dimension of sharing in the one and same mission and ministry of Jesus is yet another basis for the interrelational contextualization of all church ministries.

Perhaps the most serious issue regarding the New Testament/ early church material on ecclesial ministry and the interrelational contextualization of church ministry has been the often deliberate ignoring and/or minimizing of the work of recent Roman Catholic biblical scholars, patrologists, and early church historians. The research of these scholars was done throughout the twentieth century, and their findings have seriously questioned the standard and dominant theology of church. This standard and dominant ecclesiology was first formulated in the apologetic atmosphere of Trent and in the immediate post-tridentine period of the Roman Catholic Church. This standard and dominant ecclesiology was and remains highly apologetic, that is, a defense against the Protestant approaches to ecclesiology. From the sixteenth century to the present day, the standard and dominant theology of church found in almost all church documents remains apologetic or anti-Protestant. Indeed, the standard ecclesiology became even more intensely apologetic, because of the defensive attitude by Roman Catholic leadership against the Enlightenment, against both the American and the French Revolutions, and against contemporary postmodern philosophy. More recently, the challenges of inculturation have also caused a retrenchment, in which one sees another defense of the standard and dominant theology of the Roman Catholic Church. An ecclesial *Prestigedenken* has been officially encouraged to ward off any and every questioning of church authority. Major twentieth-century New Testament scholars, patrologists, and early church historians began to question the structural elements of this standard and dominant theology of the church, but official church leadership has either ignored the material totally or minimized its value. Even the bishops at Vatican II barely faced up to the amount of solid research that twentieth-century scholars had gradually put together.

In the so-called standard and dominant theology of the church, the issues of ministry and leadership are key. Therefore, any major rethinking of the standard and dominant ecclesiology has been immediately considered a challenge to apostolic authority. The current interrelational and multicultural theological discussions of ecclesial ministry threaten the standard and dominant ecclesiology, even though an interrelational and multicultural theology of ecclesial ministry was stated in the documents of Vatican II.

In this volume, then, I will attempt to face these issues, but also I will indicate that there are creative and positive ways in which ecclesial ministry—especially the permanent diaconate—can enrich the contemporary Christian community. This enrichment can take place only in an interrelational way and in a way that is foundationally centered on the Trinity and the mission and ministry of Jesus. Through a trinitarian and christological foundation, both ecclesial ministry and ecclesial leadership open up to profound spiritual and theological depths, which a third-millennium world and a third-millennium church dearly need.

I am grateful to Paulist Press for the publication of this volume, and in a special way I wish to thank Kevin Carrizo di Camillo, editor, for all of his help in shaping this volume into a readable work. Over the years of my own ministry, I have been privileged to be a part of many permanent diaconal formation programs in various dioceses and to facilitate many permanent diaconal retreats and institutes. The zeal and spiritual depth of many permanent deacons are a treasure for today's Catholic Church, and I am grateful for all they have done and for letting me be a small part of their own ministries.

Kenan B. Osborne, OFM
Berkeley, California
2007

Part One

MINISTRY AND
LEADERSHIP IN THE
LATIN CHURCH TODAY:
CONTEXTUAL
CONSIDERATIONS

The theme of this volume is the theology, pastoral practice, and personal identity of today's *permanent* deacons. No theme, however, is correctly addressed in a vacuum. There is always a context within which and through which a given theme is developed and interpreted. The initial chapter, consequently, analyzes several major contextual issues that affect today's permanent diaconate in the Roman Catholic Church with a special focus on how it exists in the United States of America.

Since 1968, the Roman Catholic Church in the United States has been blessed by the renewal of the permanent diaconate. These thirty-nine years have provided permanent deacons with many joys and graces, and the Catholic Church has grown in spiritual depth because of their diaconal presence. On the other hand, the newly established diaconal ministry has had its ups and downs, its joys and pains. This mixture of dreams and tears, however, is understandable only in and through its context. My explanation of this context begins with a careful consideration of today's institutional ecclesial ministry and leadership. I do this not only because today's contextual situation of the permanent diaconate is crucial but also because today's contextual situation involves a host of major issues on the theme of institutional church ministry and leadership that range far beyond diaconal ministry itself.

The existence of the Christian Church has always coexisted with some sort of theology of church. For the first fifteen hundred years of the church's existence, however, the theological aspect of the church was not expressed in any explicit way.[1] Until the Protestant Reformation and the Council of Trent there were no fully developed "theologies of the church" (ecclesiologies). Since the sixteenth century, however, several theologies of church have

---

1. On the origins of systematic ecclesiology, see Eric Plumer, "The Development of Ecclesiology: Early Church to the Reformation," and Michael Himes, "The Development of Ecclesiology: Modernity to the Twentieth Century," in *The Gift of the Church*, ed. Peter Phan (Collegeville, MN: Liturgical Press, 2000), 23–67. Prior to the Reformation, there was no systematic formulation of ecclesiology as one understands the term today.

developed. The Roman Catholic Church has slowly but surely produced and maintained a dominant operative theology of church that remained basically unified until the end of the nineteenth century. Twentieth-century scholars continued this questioning of the standard ecclesiology, and at the Second Vatican Council (1962–1965) major changes in ecclesiology were officially advocated.

It should be noted, however, that the Second Vatican Council *itself* did not create a new ecclesiology. Rather, key theological factors had been present in the Roman Catholic Church in the decades prior to Vatican II. The positions of theologians such as Marie-Dominique Chenu, Yves Congar, Jean Daniélou, and Henri de Lubac offer excellent examples of pre–Vatican II ecclesiological themes that had enormous influence on the bishops at Vatican II.[2] Many ecclesiological issues that the conciliar bishops inherited did not correspond to the dominant and operative theology of church that had gradually become the accepted position of theologians and ecclesiastical leaders from 1600 to the mid-1950s. The conciliar bishops drew on this preconciliar material and endorsed a general structure of a theology of church. In particular, as we shall see, the bishops clearly endorsed five major changes regarding institutional ecclesial ministry and leadership. These five major theological changes in ecclesiology have played an intense role in interpreting the reinstatement of the permanent diaconate.

Since the permanent diaconate in the Roman Catholic Church is an integral and *not* simply an accidental part of the sacrament of orders, the renewal of the permanent diaconate has itself reconfigured this sacrament. When one adds to this diaconal renewal a second sacramental renewal, namely, the restoration of the episcopacy to the sacrament of orders, then an analysis of the reconfiguring of the sacrament of holy orders becomes even more pressing. These two key changes made by the bishops at Vatican II

---

2. For the pre–Vatican II theologians who wrote major essays or treatises on a theology of church, see Marie Dominique Chenu, *Une école de théologie: Le Saulchoir* (Paris: Les Éditions du Cerf, 1985); Yves M.-J. Congar, *Jalons pour une théologie du laïcat* (Paris: Les Éditions du Cerf, 1953); Henri de Lubac, *Surnaturel: Études historiques* (Paris: Aubier, 1946); Jean Daniélou, "Les orientations présentes de la pensée religieuse," *Études* 249 (1946): 5–21.

have deeply affected the contemporary contextual understanding of the sacrament of orders, as we shall see in the following pages.[3]

Is the deacon today a "full and equal order" in the Roman Catholic Church? These words are based on the title of a major book on the diaconate by James Monroe Barnett, *The Diaconate: A Full and Equal Order*.[4] Although one might quickly answer yes to the question, there is an issue that nuances such a quick affirmative reply. From an *official* standpoint, the permanent diaconate has been renewed by the highest magisterium of the Roman Catholic Church: namely, a council and the papacy. In practice, however, the permanent diaconate remains a ministry that an individual bishop may or may not establish within the diocesan structure.[5] This optional aspect of the presence of a permanent diaconate in a diocese is itself an oddity. On the one hand there is an official status for the permanent diaconate, while on the other hand there is only a possible yes-or-no status for the actualized presence of permanent deacons in a given diocese. This ambiguous situation affects both the theology and pastoral reality of the current permanent diaconate. The permanent diaconate is official in *theory* but *not required in practice*. This situation does not exist for other major ministries in the church. Both officially and in practice there is a ministry and leadership of bishop. Both officially and in practice there is a ministry and leadership of priesthood. The permanent diaconate, although a major order within the sacrament of order, is in practice *optional*. How can one theologically and pastorally deal with such an ambiguity?

In an attempt to answer such issues and questions, the following pages may seem to take us far afield, for I present a wide-ranging view of today's institutional church ministry and leadership. This wide-ranging view is, of course, the context. A context larger than one that is restricted only to the permanent diaconate offers a way

---

3. For a presentation of these two key changes at Vatican II, see my *Priesthood: A History of the Ordained Ministry in the Roman Catholic Church* (Mahwah, NJ: Paulist Press, 1988; repr., Eugene, OR: Wipf & Stock, 2000), 315–26.

4. James Monroe Barnett, *The Diaconate: A Full and Equal Order*, rev. ed. (Valley Forge, PA: Trinity Press International, 1995).

5. See the *National Directory for the Formation, Ministry and Life of Permanent Deacons in the United States* (Washington, D.C.: USCCB, 2005), 2–5.

of integrating the diverse theological and pastoral issues involved in today's diaconal situation. Indeed, it offers perhaps one of the best ways to understand the permanent diaconate today, with all its successes—and with all its problems.

Institutional church ministries and leadership positions are *all* interrelated, as we shall see, and thus one particular ministry, that is, the diaconate, is unintelligible unless it is perceived within the comprehensive interrelational framework. The documents of Vatican II clearly present an interrelational theology of institutional church ministry and leadership. Unfortunately, it is precisely this issue of *the interrelationship of all institutional church ministry and leadership* that has given rise to today's most divisive theological disagreement regarding church ministry. Given the sensitivity of today's theological discussion on the matter of interrelational church ministry, I intend to move carefully but deliberately as we study the contemporary permanent diaconate within the wider framework of today's institutional church ministry and leadership. The plan for part 1 of this book is as follows:

1. **Contextual theology and today's institutional church ministry**

2. **Characteristics of a postconciliar church**

   a. The *understanding and interpreting* of certain Vatican II texts and their respective background documents: the present reality

   b. The *acceptance or nonacceptance* of certain issues found in the text and background documents of Vatican II: the present reality

3. **The sending of Jesus and his mission and ministry**

   a. First step: The Father sends Jesus into the world

   b. Second step: The mission and ministry of Jesus himself

   c. Third step: The five major changes regarding institutional church ministry and leadership that the bishops at Vatican II established

1. The establishment of the mission and ministry of all baptized-confirmed Christians as a foundation of institutional church ministry
2. The reestablishment of the episcopacy as an official part of the sacrament of orders
   a. A lay/cleric church: the historical background for this form of ecclesiology, which became standard from medieval times to Vatican II
   b. Episcopacy and the sacrament of orders: the historical background for the nonepiscopal understanding of the sacrament of orders from medieval times to Vatican II
3. The redefinition of priesthood
4. The reestablishment of the permanent diaconate
5. The official expansion of lay ministry into the ecclesial dimensions of the *tria munera*
6. Concluding observations

4. **The sacramental mission and ministry of all Christians: The first of five major changes in ministry made by the bishops at Vatican II**

5. **The reestablishment of episcopacy to the sacrament of orders: The second major conciliar change in ministry**

6. **The redefinition of priesthood: The third major conciliar change in ministry**

7. **The renewal of the permanent diaconate: The fourth major conciliar change in ministry**

8. **An official and more inclusive recognition of specific church ministries by lay men and women: The fifth major conciliar change in ministry**

9. **The positive and negative realities of the five major conciliar changes in church ministry**

Chapter One

CONTEXTUAL THEOLOGY AND TODAY'S INSTITUTIONAL CHURCH MINISTRY

Contextual theology is a new term in the Roman Catholic lexicon.[6] *Context, contextual,* and *contextual theology* are not terms that occur in the documents from Vatican II, nor are they terms that one finds with any abundance in official Roman Catholic documents on ministry that have been written since Vatican II. Rather, theological and pastoral writers are the ones who use these terms in a generous way.[7] The writings of these authors have been of enormous service to the

---

6. See Stephen B. Bevans, *Models of Contextual Theology*, rev. and expanded ed. (Maryknoll, NY: Orbis Books, 2002), 3–15.

7. Authors who initiated the stress on the contextuality of theology include Virgil P. Elizondo, *The Future Is Mestizo: Life Where Cultures Meet*, rev. ed. (Boulder, CO: University Press of Colorado, 2000); Robert J. Schreiter, *Constructing Local Theologies* (Maryknoll, NY: Orbis Books, 1985); Jung Young Lee, *Marginality: The Key to Multicultural Theology* (Minneapolis, MN: Fortress Press, 1995); San Hun Lee, "Marginality as Coerced Liminality: Toward an Understanding of the Context of Asian American Theology," in *Realizing the America of Our Hearts,* ed. Fumitaka Matsuoka and Eleazar S. Fernandez (St. Louis: Chalice Press, 2003), 11–23; Stephen Sykes, *The Identity of Christianity* (London: SPCK, 1984); Krikor Haleblian, "The Problem of Contextualization," *Missiology* 11 (1983): 95–111; Charles Kraft, *Christianity in Culture* (1979; rev. 25th anniversary ed.; Maryknoll, NY: Orbis Books, 2002); Pyong Min Gap and Rose Kim, eds., *Struggle for Ethnic Identity: Narratives by Asian American Professionals* (Walnut Creek, CA: Alta Mira, 1999); Jane Naomi Iwamura and Paul Pickard, *Revealing the Sacred in Asian and Pacific America* (New York: Routledge, 2003); Lisa Lowe, *Immigration Acts: On Asian American Cultural Politics* (Durham, NC: Duke University Press, 1999). These last three items have impressive bibliographies. See also, Oscar Ante, *Contextual Evangelization in the Philippines: A Filipino Franciscan Experience* (Kampen: Kok, 1991).

church, since their analyses of context, both sociological and theological, have aided *all* of us to see the situation of today's institutional ministry and leadership in a much clearer perspective.

Assuredly, the terms *context, contextual,* and *contextual theology* have a plurality of meaning. They are not used in a univocal way. Different authors stress different dimensions of contextuality. Whether the focus is on a sociological, political, and economic context or on a theological, philosophical, and pastoral context, a diversity of description and usage is clearly evident. For some, context is seen as an overarching arena in which a given number of realities are analyzed. In this form of thinking, context remains more or less extrinsic and/or structural but neither internal nor permeating. This understanding of context is seen in a more-or-less spatial or temporal dimension in which other realities simply take place. One might use the example of a domed sports stadium, in which football, soccer, baseball, a track meet, or a convention might take place. The relationship of the domed stadium to the variety of activities that take place within it is for the most part external.

On the other hand, context, contextual, and especially today's contextual theology can imply a far more internal interrelationship. This is particularly evident in the writings of theologians and pastoral authors who discuss religion and culture or theology and culture or pastoral ministry and culture. In these instances, the interrelationship is not merely external. For the majority of these authors the interrelationship of context and culture is profoundly and intrinsically interrelated. However, there are some contemporary authors who present the interrelationship of context and culture in an accidental or peripheral way. Pope Paul VI presented a view of the gospel and culture, in which the culture–gospel relationship is only accidental.[8] In *Evangelii nuntiandi,* Paul VI writes in

---

8. For an understanding of culture and gospel in the writings of Paul VI, see Aylward Shorter, *Toward a Theology of Inculturation* (Maryknoll, NY: Orbis Books, 1988); Richard Cote, *Re-Visioning Mission: The Catholic Church and Culture in Postmodern America* (New York: Paulist Press, 1989); Gerald A. Arbuckle, *Earthing the Gospel* (Maryknoll, NY: Orbis Books, 1990); Arv Roest-Crollius, "What's So New About Inculturation?" *Gregorianum* 59 (1978): 721–24; Elochukwu E. Uzukwu, *A Listening Church: Autonomy and Communion in African Churches* (Maryknoll, NY: Orbis Books, 1996).

nos. 19–20: "The gospel and evangelization cannot be put in the same category with any culture. They are above all cultures." Evangelization, nonetheless, must go "to the center and roots of life." "They [the gospel and evangelization] can penetrate any culture while being subservient to none." In his view, the gospel can indeed penetrate any and all cultures, but it assiduously remains above any and all cultures. The gospel and evangelization are contextually interrelated to culture but only in an accidental or separable way. Contextual interrelationship in this aspect of Paul VI's thought is permeating, but only to a degree. The view of Paul VI has found many followers.

In this chapter, I am using the expression *contextual theology* in a way similar to that found in the writings of Robert Schreiter and Stephen Bevans.[9] Schreiter, in his volume *Constructing Local Theologies*, begins with a section entitled, "A Shift in Perspective." In this section, he mentions that "the need to adapt theological reflection to local circumstances began receiving official support with Vatican Council II, where in the Decree of the Church's Missionary Activity, *Ad Gentes*, such adaptation received explicit approbation."[10] Paul VI, in his address to the bishops of Africa (1969)[11] and in his apostolic exhortation *Evangelii nuntiandi* (1975), continued this approach of adaptation to theological discussion, but, as just mentioned, the adaptation to culture is accidental. Schreiter also commends the work of Krikor Haleblian, "The Problem of Contextualization," written in 1983, as well as the volume of Charles Kraft, *Christianity in Culture*, written in 1979 and revised for a twenty-fifth anniversary edition in 2005. Both of these works address adaptation in a permeating and integrative way.

---

9. See Schreiter, *Constructing Local Theologies*, 1–21; also his later volume, *The New Catholicity: Theology between the Global and the Local* (Maryknoll, NY: Orbis Books, 1997), 1–27. In this later volume, Schreiter deliberately speaks of contexts in the plural, indicating that contextualization is a plural-oriented reality. See also Bevans, *Models of Contextual Theology*, 3–27. Bevans speaks of contextual theology as a theological imperative, indicating that contextualization is an intrinsic element for all theology.

10. Schreiter, *Constructing Local Theologies*, 15.

11. Paul VI, "Allocution au symposium des évêques d'Afrique," *La Documentation Catholique*, 7 septembre 1969—n° 1546, 763–65.

For his part, Schreiter details two forms of contextual theology: the ethnographical form, which is concerned with cultural identity, and the liberation approach, which is concerned with social ills and the need for social change. In his later volume, *The New Catholicity*, Schreiter presents a more detailed analysis of context. In this book, he details the following: the meaning of globalization and the contexts of theology (chapter 1); intercultural hermeneutics, which brings in the contextual dimension of language (chapter 2); the various meanings of both culture itself and the cultural context (chapter 3); as well as the major problematic in contextual-cultural studies, which may involve a syncretistic approach to theological thought (chapter 4). In all of these analyses, Schreiter draws abundantly on the resources formulated in the last quarter of the twentieth century.

In 2002, Stephen B. Bevans revised and expanded his study, *Models of Contextual Theology*, which had first appeared in 1992. Bevans introduces his revision with a section on contextual theology as both radically new and traditional. Bevans states his case very strongly:

> Theology today, we can conclude, must be contextual theology....Pluralism in theology, as well as on every level of Christian life, must not only be tolerated; it must be positively encouraged and cultivated....Contextualization, therefore, is not something on the fringes of the theological enterprise. It is at the very center of what it means to do theology in today's world. Contextualization, in other words, is a theological imperative.[12]

Bevans realizes that contextual theology has major issues that must be carefully and honestly included in today's theological endeavors. Method is of major importance. Content is likewise central, and two types of theology can be found in both Roman Catholic and Protestant work today: a creation-centered theology and a redemption-centered Christology. The choice of one of these theological foci determines the model one uses in one's theological

---

12. Bevans, *Models of Contextual Theology*, 15.

enterprise. In all of this, Bevans advocates the need for clear criteria. He cites José de Mesa and Lode Wostyn:

> If there are so many diverging, and sometimes apparently conflicting interpretations, how can we be sure that our understanding of our faith is correct, that it is faithful to the Judaeo-Christian Tradition? Is it possible to recognize the one faith in the different interpretations?[13]

Contextual theology focuses, more often than not, on pluralistic issues such as cultural issues. Bevans, in developing his six models of contextual theology, is deeply concerned about pluralistic interpretations. Even the titles of his six models indicate this emphasis on how disparate issues might or might not be interrelated: the translation model, the anthropological model, the praxis model, the synthetic model, the transcendental model, and the countercultural model. Each of these models indicates a way in which the faith of the church and the regional context might or might not be best interrelated. By and large, contextual theologies center on some form of interrelationship, and thus context, as used in theology, cannot help but include the issue of interrelationality. In some instances, the interrelationality is not simply an extrinsic or accidental interrelationality, but a deeply permeating one.

My use of *contextual theology* is more modest. My focus is indeed on specific contexts: first of all, on the context in which the conciliar bishops at Vatican II interrelated all institutional church ministry. As mentioned previously, the bishops at Vatican II did not use the term *context*, but they did present an interrelational understanding of institutional church ministry that, even without calling it a context, is indeed a context. Second, my focus is on another context: namely, on the context of the acceptance or nonacceptance of conciliar interrelationality of institutional church ministry in postconciliar times. These two contexts, the one conciliar and the other postconciliar, are not identical. Postconciliar acceptance and/or nonacceptance presents the crux of the problem, but the

---

13. Ibid., 23, citing José de Mesa and Lode Wostyn, *Doing Theology: Basic Realities and Processes* (Quezon City: Claretian Publications, 1989), 86.

problem cannot be understood unless one understands the contextual ministerial theology expressed in the Vatican II documents themselves. I would like to state my thesis of this chapter as follows:

The major issues affecting the permanent diaconate today—as well as the major issues affecting the papacy, the episcopacy, the priesthood, and the lay ministry today—are unclear theologically, pastorally, and personally, because the specific issue of the interrelationality of all ecclesial ministry and leadership as expressed by the documents of Vatican II remains entrenched in a postconciliar acceptance and nonacceptance situation.

Unless one appreciates this contextual situation, no serious resolution of the major issues affecting today's church ministry and leadership can take place.

In my understanding of the term *context*, I do not mean some form of overarching framework. Such an understanding of context would be simply a spatial understanding, an accidental understanding, and a nonintegral understanding. For an understanding of the Vatican II documents regarding ecclesial ministry and leadership, a spatial interpretation of context in the dimension of a contextual theology of ministry and leadership is totally inadequate. Rather, the contextual dimension must be understood as permeating the entire reality of institutional church ministry and leadership. Schreiter and Bevans apply context to the reality of culture. Culture is not a spatial, overarching structure. Culture permeates the very life and experience of those people who belong to a given culture. So, too, contextual theology, when used in respect to institutional church ministry and leadership, has to be seen as a permeating reality deep within all institutional roles of ministry and leadership. It is precisely in virtue of this permeating reality that we find the basis for the interrelationship that the documents of Vatican II express. Contextual interrelationship is not an extrinsic, structural, or spatial object; contextual interrelationship has an intrinsic and permeating dimension.

Today, however, to speak of a contextual theology of institutional church ministry is to some degree ambiguous, since the interrelationship of the two—the context and the institutional ministry—is presented by today's writers in a variety of intensities. The texts and documents of Vatican II, though not using the terms *con-*

text, *contextual*, and *contextual theology*, nonetheless do present a strong interrelationship of the many aspects of church ministries that they develop. We will consider this Vatican II documentary interrelationship in detail, since it is only on the basis of ministerial interrelationality that the meaning of today's permanent deacon can become clear.

In the Roman Catholic Church today there have been and there remain several serious issues on the meaning of ecclesial, institutional ministry. These issues have as yet found no accepted resolution. The unresolved issues on the meaning of ecclesial, institutional ministry affect all six major institutional ministries in the contemporary Roman Catholic Church:

1. The ministry of all baptized-confirmed Christians

2. The ministry of the papacy

3. The ministry of the episcopacy

4. The ministry of the priesthood

5. The ministry of the diaconate

6. The ministry of lay men and women

The documents of Vatican II, in different ways and with different emphases, contain major statements on all six of these institutional ecclesial ministries. Key statements in the conciliar documents constitute, on the one hand, a major *positive source* for an understanding of institutional ministry and leadership in the contemporary Latin church. Some of the same key conciliar statements, on the other hand, affect today's unsettled or *negative issues* on the theme of church institutional ministry and leadership. This latter conclusion needs careful consideration. Such a careful consideration is the major focus here. In order to help us understand this positive/negative repercussion of Vatican II, let us first consider the characteristics of a postconciliar church, since it is precisely within the current postconciliar church that we find these positive/negative issues in heated competition.

Chapter Two

CHARACTERISTICS OF A POSTCONCILIAR CHURCH

Today's Roman Catholic Church is a church that exists in a postconciliar period. A postconciliar period is a very special time in itself. It has its own distinct characteristics. After every major council of the Christian church, a prolonged time of uncertainty has inevitably occurred. Church history is very clear on this matter.[14] A postconciliar uncertainty was present after the Councils of Nicaea (325), Constantinople I (381), Ephesus (431) and Chalcedon (451)—four major councils of the early church. A postconciliar uncertainty was also present after the councils of Lateran IV (1215), Constance (1414–1418), Trent (1545–1563) and Vatican I (1869–1870)—four major councils during the thousand years preceding Vatican II. On the basis of historical research, one can say that a postconciliar time of uncertainty is, in many ways, both normal and needed. The present postconciliar time after Vatican II resembles other postconciliar times, but it is also a time with its own unique dimensions.[15]

The uncertainty in the current postconciliar time after Vatican II follows a pattern that one finds in almost all of the above-mentioned councils. The uncertainty focuses on two distinct divisive situations:

---

14. See Chris Bellitto, *The General Councils* (Mahwah, NJ: Paulist Press, 2003).

15. See Giuseppe Alberigo, "The Christian Situation after Vatican II," in *The Reception of Vatican II*, ed. Giuseppe Alberigo, Jean-Pierre Jossua, and Joseph A. Komonchak; trans. Matthew O'Connell (Washington, DC: Catholic University of America Press, 1987), 1–24. Alberigo provides a brief overview of postconciliar reception and its variations from Nicaea to Vatican II.

- **Understanding and interpreting certain conciliar texts**
  There exists today a divisive situation over the *understanding and interpreting* of certain Vatican II texts and their respective conciliar background documents.
- **Acceptance or nonacceptance of certain conciliar texts**
  There exists today a divisive situation over the *acceptance or nonacceptance* of the contents of these same texts and their respective background documents.[16]

Let us consider each of these two situations in a brief way, pointing out the major issues that are currently taking place.

The Understanding and Interpreting of Certain Vatican II Texts and Their Respective Background Documents: The Present Reality

The first focus indicates that there is a necessary time and space in which church officials, theologians, and ordinary Catholic Christians come to a common understanding and interpretation regarding particular accomplishments of Vatican II. The present postconciliar period has certainly been a time for both extensive learning about and intensive evaluating of Vatican II. During this period, which is still going on, there have been and still are various understandings and interpretations regarding the exact meaning of

---

16. In this paragraph I am using the two terms, *text* and *documents* differently. *Text* refers to the approved and final statements of the Second Vatican Council. The term *documents* refers to the many earlier drafts for the final texts, as also the many reports by committees, theologians, interventions, and so on. In a postconciliar period of uncertainty, scholars may agree on the text itself but disagree on the interpretation of the historical documentation, which can only be determined by a thorough study of the synodal documents. For Vatican II, one of the most prominent instances of this interpretative disagreement concerns *Lumen gentium* 8: "This church, constituted and organized in the world as a society, subsists in the Catholic Church, which is governed by the successor of Peter and by the bishops in union with that successor." In the aftermath of Vatican II, no one challenges the text itself, but the exact meaning of *subsists in* has become a matter of major discussion.

several key issues in the conciliar texts and documents. These varying understandings and interpretations arise for a number of reasons. Three such reasons are of particular importance.

- The council texts or documents themselves are not crystal-clear.
- The historical discussions of the respective background documents describing the final and official conciliar statements have as yet not been adequately analyzed or presented.
- Either the texts or the conciliar background documents of Vatican II have been read from a particular interpreter's view rather than from the council's view.

In all of these different forms of interpretation, which have been publicly made by church officials and reputable theologians, one finds both objective and subjective aspects; that is, one finds in these presentations discordant interpretations of the council's texts and synodal documents as regards all three of the above reasons. In the above listing, the first two tend to be more objective, while the third tends to be more subjective. In all fairness, it must be admitted that almost all the major divergent interpretations that have been made by official church leaders and by reputable theologians represent sincere efforts. Even the interpretations, which are more subjective than objective, represent strong positive personal views. None of the above three reasons should be seen as the main problematic issue in and of itself. Such objective/subjective divergence of interpretation is part and parcel of a normal and needed postconciliar period of time.

During this normal postconciliar process, calling one or the other opposing view "heretical" or "contrary to church doctrine" is, more often than not, a sign of frustration rather than a correct evaluation. In our church today, we have at times heard the call of "heresy" and "contrary to church doctrine." In a postconciliar period of divergent understanding and interpretation, church leaders and church people generally need to be far more restrained than some church leaders and church people presently are. Tolerance and dialogue are far more important than name-calling and condemnation. John Paul II himself, in a public letter to Cardinal Joseph Ratzinger, emphasized the need for openness and tolerance.[17] John Paul II wrote:

> In the period since the Council we are witnessing a great effort on the part of the Church to ensure that this *novum* constituted by Vatican II correctly penetrates the mind and conduct of the individual communities of the People of God. However, side by side with this effort there have appeared tendencies which create a certain difficulty in putting the Council into practice. One of these tendencies is characterized by a desire for changes which are not always in harmony with the teaching and spirit of Vatican II, even though they seem to appeal to the Council. These changes claim to express progress and so this tendency is given the name "progressivism."
>
> The opposite tendency, which is usually called "conservatism" or "integralism," stops at the past itself, without taking into account the correct aspiration towards the future which manifested itself precisely in the work of Vatican II. While the former tendency seems to recognize the correctness of what is new, the latter sees correctness only in what is "ancient," as such, or what is "new" *per se*, which corresponds to the correct idea of tradition in the life of the Church....The Church, like that householder in the Gospel, wisely brings "from the storeroom both the new and the old" (Mt 13:52), while remaining absolutely obedient to the Spirit of truth.

This is a lengthy citation. However, John Paul II wrote this in an open letter to Ratzinger. He wanted Ratzinger to read this letter, but he also wanted to make sure that others in the church were aware of the contents of this communication. Unfortunately, few theologians ever cite this letter. For its part, the letter reminds all of us that both the new and the old are of profound value. One

---

17. John Paul II, Letter to Cardinal Ratzinger, *L'Osservatore Romano*, April 18, 1988, n. 16:2.

without the other is non-real. In a postconciliar church situation, any quick demand for an end of discussion is myopic.

The Acceptance or Nonacceptance of Certain Issues Found in the Text and the Background Documents of Vatican II: The Present Reality

The second focus is on the acceptance or nonacceptance of particular conciliar issues. In the histories of the major church councils, as we have noted above, an acceptance of key conciliar provisions was never an automatic reality. The historical aftermath of every major church council has had groups who accepted some aspects from a given council and groups who rejected certain aspects from the same council. Let me simply list some of the more salient instances of slow acceptance of both conciliar texts and conciliar background documentation.

- At the Council of Nicaea (325) the term *homoousios* (ομοουσιος) was selected to indicate the divinity of Jesus. This term was not readily accepted by many bishops and theologians at that time. In fact, one has to move to the Council of Chalcedon (451) before the term was widely accepted, and even then the christological issues involved in *homoousios* (namely, did Jesus have a human will and a divine will) required three additional councils before the term was almost unanimously accepted.
- At the Fourth Lateran Council (1215) a rule was made that Catholics should receive holy communion once a year and that this should be preceded—if needed—by the reception of the sacrament of penance. This regulation did not automatically take hold. Three hundred years later the Council of Trent (1545–1563) had to reinforce these sacramental practices because they were neglected by many Catholics.
- The Council of Trent used the term *transubstantiation*, but in the aftermath of the council reputable theologians continued to argue about its meaning. In 1947

Emmanuel Doronzo mentioned twenty-five different views by such major and reputable theologians as: Francisco Suarez, Robert Bellarmine, Leonard Lessius, John de Lugo, Otto Pesch, Johann Baptist Franzelin, Aemilius de Augustinis, Giles de Coninck, Gregorio de Valencia, Alexis H. M. Lépicier, L. Labauche, Adolphe Tanquerey, Florence D. Cohalan, Nicholas Gihr, Wilhelm Diekamp, G. Van Noort, Maurice De la Taille, Aldémar D'Alès, G. Mattiussi, M. T.-L. Penido, Nicholas Cachia, J. M. Hervé, Jean Baptiste Gonet, Édouard Hugon, and Louis Billot.[18] If there was a single defined understanding of the term *transubstantiation*, there could not possibly have been so many Catholic theologians offering different definitions of what the term *transubstantiation* meant.

• Not only were doctrinal issues not immediately accepted, but also reform issues caused problems. From Trent, once again, a reform directive was issued for the establishment of a seminary system for the training of priests. By and large, however, it was not until roughly 1700—two hundred years later—that a seminary system was in place in the majority of dioceses.[19]

The renewal of the permanent diaconate, when considered from a worldwide dimension, has not been uniform. Many dioceses and some conferences of bishops have preferred not to establish a permanent diaconate in the territories under their jurisdiction.[20]

---

18. Emmanuel Doronzo, *De Eucharistia*, vol. 1, *De Sacramento* (Milwaukee: Bruce, 1947), 225–314.

19. See Kenan Osborne, "Priestly Formation: The Council of Trent and the Second Vatican Council," in *Trent and Vatican II: Change and Renewal*, ed. Raymond Bulman and Frederick Parrella (Oxford: Oxford University Press, 2007); see also Hermann J. Pottmeyer, "A New Phase in the Reception of Vatican II: Twenty Years of Interpretation of the Council," in *Reception of Vatican II*, 27–43.

20. The reasons for this hesitation are uneven. In some areas of the world a permanent diaconate does not fit in culturally, since for centuries it has been a priest who provides the sacramental and pastoral life. In a few instances, bishops have decided not to establish a permanent diaconate since this diaconate was not open to women (e.g., earlier on in New Zealand and the Archdiocese of Seattle).

The United States and Canada have the largest number of permanent deacons, but neither the Canadian bishops nor the bishops of the United States were champions of this renewal during Vatican II. The major champions came from the bishops in developing countries, but Catholic leadership in developing countries, for the most part, has not fostered the renewal of the permanent diaconate.

From all of this we can see that today's struggle of acceptance or nonacceptance of certain conciliar issues has been and is a normal reality of a postconciliar period.[21] The divergence regarding today's acceptance or nonacceptance of certain conciliar positions should, therefore, not surprise us. The texts of Vatican II introduced both new and deeply significant material and also new and deeply significant terminology, as we shall see. Many church leaders and many church people are by nature extremely hesitant when it comes to "new" material and "new" terminology, especially when this "new" material and wording affect major church realities. In many instances of nonacceptance the reasons are not totally objective. Popes and bishops have, at times, voiced their own subjective positions in official documents, and at times they have acknowledged that a plurality of views is legitimate.[22] This does not mean that their subjective positions need to be accepted by other Catholic Christians; it means only that their subjective view should be honored for what it is worth.

I am not saying, however, that all subjective positions must be honored. I am simply saying that, by themselves, subjective reasons cannot be preemptively dismissed. The issue of newness at times raises a negative, subjective reaction. The negative reaction is at

---

21. See Elmar Klinger and Klaus Wittstadt, eds., *Glaube im Prozess: Christsein nach dem II Vatikanum* (Freiburg im Br.: Herder, 1984); J. Zizioulas, "The Theological Problem of 'Reception,'" *Centro Pro Unione Bulletin* 26 (1984): 3–6; W. Siebel, *Katholisch oder Konziliar: Die Krise der Kirche heute* (Munich: Langen-Müller, 1978); G. Alberigo and A. Melloni, "L'allocuzione *Gaudet Mater Ecclesia* di Giovanni XXIII (11 Ottobre 1962)," in *Fede, Tradizione, Profezia: Studi su Giovanni XXIII e sul Vaticano II* (Brescia: Paideia, 1984), 187–283.

22. In the encyclical *Fides et ratio*, John Paul II lists major philosophical thinkers from India and China along with the great philosophers of Greece (1, 3) and mentions a "legitimate plurality of positions" (5). He also states: "The Church has no philosophy of her own nor does she canonize any one particular philosophy in preference to others" (49).

times based on the love and respect for the traditional. Care must, therefore, be taken to distinguish—as Congar once described it—tradition from traditions. There is in the Roman Catholic Church a "tradition" that we do not wish to jettison. There are also traditions that may be personally comforting and piously persuasive, but objectively these traditions may have served their wider usefulness.

When we look at the more objective reasons for acceptance or nonacceptance, we often see that the reality principle arises. In the multicultural and multireligious world of today, certain wishes of a given council do not necessarily coincide with what is actual and possible in many cultures and in many multireligious regions. The wishes of a council might be very applicable in the Euro-American world. However, they can be inconsequential or even counter-productive for the third world. Accordingly, certain conciliar issues are, for realistic and objectively valid reasons, not regionally accepted. The renewal of the permanent diaconate certainly exemplifies this aspect of acceptance/nonacceptance.

There are, however, subjective positions that have played a harmful role in the present expressions of acceptance or nonacceptance. The wishes of a given council regarding certain matters are simply not accepted, because the particular conciliar material is not in accord with someone's personal stance or a group's stance. The liturgy has been and continues to be the current lightning rod for this kind of subjective nonacceptance. Acceptance or nonacceptance of some postconciliar liturgical instructions has been based on personal or subjective interpretations. Clear examples of this manner of reaction are: to kneel or not to kneel at the reception of the Eucharist, to offer or not to offer the kiss of peace at the stated time, and to allow or not to allow the permanent diaconate in a given diocese. These decisions to accept or not to accept are made, more often than not, on the personal preferences of a bishop, a pastor, or even of an individual Catholic Christian. Eucharistic kneeling/not kneeling, offering/not offering of a kiss of peace, the presence and/or nonpresence of a permanent diaconate are not matters of church dogma. These kinds of traditions have nothing at all to do with the fundamentals of one's faith. On the other hand, these kinds of issues can be the lightning rod for traditionalists to raise, without adequate basis, the judgment of heresy and schism.

For those who have studied the histories of major church councils, none of the above material is surprising. Major councils have consistently engendered the need for a postconciliar space-time that allow a measured and respectful time of divergent interpretations and divergent acceptance/nonacceptance. In the case of Vatican II, the issue of nonacceptance as regards certain specific matters appeared almost from the very start of the council itself. Commentaries on the texts and documents of Vatican II make mention of the "majority" and the "minority" positions of the attending bishops. This division, however, does not mean that all individual bishops who can be classified as being in a "majority" position on one issue remained in a "majority" position on all issues. Nor does it mean that those bishops who can be classified as being in a "minority" position on some issues remained in the "minority" position on all issues. The same is true for the labels: *liberal* and *conservative*. Bishops were at times liberal on certain issues and conservative on other issues. The conciliar bishops moved back and forth on the issue of majority/minority or liberal/conservative, and they did so for a variety of reasons.[23] The phrases majority/minority and traditional/conservative are ambiguous.

A few trends among their staunch adherents, however, did remain fairly steadfast throughout the entire conciliar process. Alberigo expresses the situation in a delicate way:

> Above and beyond the positions taken by individuals, a mute institutional resistance built up in wide circles of the Curia during the years of the [Second Vatican] Council. This resistance found expression not only in acts of hostility to John XXIII but subsequently also in opposition to the Secretariat for Christian Unity and the commission for liturgical reform as being creations of the Council and means whereby it was influencing the

---

23. Paul VI from the beginning was well aware of the minority presence of bishops at the council. Time and time again he took steps so that the minority view would be honored by the council. See Paul Lakeland, *The Liberation of the Laity: In Search of an Accountable Church* (New York: Continuum, 2002), 113–20; Peter Hebblethwaite, *The Runaway Church: Postconciliar Growth or Decline?* (New York: Seabury, 1975).

Church. Paul VI's plan to change this situation by internationalizing the Curia was based on an insufficient analysis of the Curia's institutional structure, and its inadequacy soon became clear [in the years following the conclusion of the council itself].[24]

Some key members of the Roman Curia worked hand in hand with certain major conciliar bishops, and on many occasions the problems at the council that the bishops faced were the result of the political machinations of these members of the papal Curia and certain important but conservative bishops. Even the position of Paul VI, which on many occasions was inconsistent in itself, created enormous tensions among the conciliar bishops.[25]

One of the issues that tended to galvanize this kind of minority/majority division in a fairly permanent way during the council itself was the issue of institutional church ministry. This same galvanizing issue, producing its own minority/majority stance, has continued throughout the entire postconciliar period. This oppositional stance is highly significant for the theme of this present volume, the renewal of the permanent diaconate. In some parishes there is friction between the permanent deacon and the priest-pastor. The issue is not only liturgy but also leadership of the parish community. It is an issue not only of pastoral leadership but also of social concerns affecting the parish. Permanent deacons today in the United States live in a postconciliar church, and it is not easy to do so. Acceptance or nonacceptance and the understanding of the conciliar texts and underlying documentation are simply part and parcel of today's church and therefore of today's living situation of permanent deacons.

---

24. Alberigo, "Christian Situation after Vatican II," 9, n. 26.

25. See Daniele Menozzi, "Opposition to the Council (1966–1984)," in *The Reception of Vatican II*, 330–36; in this section Menozzi carefully discusses the role of Paul VI during the council.

Chapter Three

THE SENDING OF JESUS AND HIS MISSION AND MINISTRY: THE FOUNDATION OF ALL CHURCH MINISTRIES

The overarching thesis of part 1 of this volume can now be more clearly explained, namely, that the institutional church ministry in today's Latin church can be understood only within and through a contextual theology. The issue of institutional church ministry and leadership, both during Vatican II itself and throughout the post–Vatican II period, has continually galvanized church leaders and theologians as well as ordinary Catholic Christians into a majority/minority stance. Sides have clearly been taken. The taking of sides is part and parcel of today's postconciliar period of divergence. The presence of a minority/majority stance is the reason why I said in chapter 1: "Some of the same key conciliar statements, on the other hand, affect today's unsettled or *negative issues* on the theme of church institutional ministry and leadership."

The sometimes strident voices of the minority group on the issue of institutional church ministry have affected both foci of the current postconciliar time of divergent views. These voices have affected the first focus regarding the *understanding and interpreting* of conciliar texts and documents, and they have affected the second focus regarding the *acceptance/nonacceptance* of conciliar positions. Nonetheless, as I mentioned above, polarizing divergences on a conciliar issue is part of a normal and even needed postconciliar situation. The fact of polarizing differences by itself is not the deepest issue. The issues that I wish to pursue center on a major tendency of the nonaccepting group, namely, their tendency to "define" the individual forms of institutional church ministry in a nonrelational way. These authors want to define the "radical difference" between one particular institutional church ministry over and against all others. We find this, for instance, in the efforts of Jean Galot, who attempts to delineate the precise difference between the priesthood of the faithful and the ministerial priesthood. He writes:

> In conclusion, the difference between the universal and the ministerial priesthood is *a radical one* with respect to both consecration and mission. We can well understand why Vatican II declares that it is one of nature, not of degree.[26] [Italics added; the allusion to Vatican II as stated by Galot refers to *LG 10*.]

Galot's reference to *Lumen gentium* is correct, but his interpretation misinterprets the conciliar text. *Lumen gentium* reads:

> Though they differ from one another in essence and not only in degree, the common priesthood of the faithful and the ministerial or hierarchical priesthood are nonetheless interrelated. (10)

> Sacerdotium autem commune fidelium et sacerdotium ministeriale seu hierarchicum, licet essentia et non gradu tantum differant, ad invicem tamen ordinantur. (10)

It is clear from the Latin text that the main sentence reads: they are nevertheless interrelated: *ad invicem tamen ordinantur*. The statement on the separation is contained in a relative clause beginning with *licet* ("although"), which means that the statement on the separation is only secondarily related to the main sentence. In other words, the text states that one cannot have a distinction, *licet essentia et non gradu tantum differant*, unless there is an underlying and

---

26. Jean Galot, *Theology of the Priesthood*, trans. Roger Balducelli (San Francisco: Ignatius Press, 1984), 119.

more basic interrelationship. Throughout his volume, Galot does not indicate in any detailed way what this underlying and more basic relationship truly is. Rather, he continues to emphasize the radical difference between the two. The Vatican II text, on the other hand, unambiguously states that there is a radical interrelationship of the two. Only on the basis of this "root or radical interrelationship" can one make a secondary distinction between the two priesthoods. Galot simply misinterprets the conciliar text in order to advance his position on radical difference.[27]

Galot's presentation is only one example of many in which today certain theologians focus on radical difference and omit the primordial radical interrelationship. In the following pages, we will see how extensively the texts of Vatican II portray a fundamental interrelationality of ecclesial ministry and leadership. The argument I present is not based simply on parsing paragraph 10 of *Lumen gentium*. It is based on an overabundance of texts found in the conciliar documents. An exclusive focus on a definitional difference for a specific ecclesial institutional ministry misses the *contextual basis* for the divergences. It is only within a contextual dimension that one finds the underlying, basic interrelationship. The interrelational contextual theology of institutional church ministry and leadership as found throughout the documents of Vatican II and throughout post–Vatican II official texts is the major theme of the following pages.

What I wish to argue even further is that the sensitive issues that have confronted today's institutional church ministry and have caused deep divisions in the Catholic community *contextually constitute part and parcel of the problem in institutional church ministry and leadership today.* In other words, the divisions themselves are part of the problem and part of the context. They are part of the problem

---

27. Galot even asserts: "There is a difference as to the mission assigned to the two priesthoods in the Church" (*Theology of the Priesthood*, 118). However, both priesthoods share in one and the same mission and ministry of Jesus. Galot's position states that each priesthood shares in a different mission and ministry of Jesus himself. Such a view cannot be substantiated from the conciliar texts, nor do the passages from the New Testament that he cites substantiate such a different mission and ministry. Galot interprets the New Testament passages by reading into them his own preconceived ideas. His interpretation is not exegesis but eisegesis.

because they are divisive. They are part of the context, because divisions of acceptance/nonacceptance are part and parcel of a postconciliar church. Nonetheless, one could say that those who focus singly on a specific institutional ministry and attempt to offer a radical definition of such a ministry completely miss the context. Many contemporary books and articles on priesthood, episcopacy, diaconate, and lay ministry have focused on specific issues for each ministry and have argued that a precise definition or description of the conciliar and postconciliar understanding of bishop, priest, deacon, or lay minister removes the problematic issues.[28] These books, rather than resolving the issue through their focus on a single, precise definition of a particular institutional church ministry, have only created a much more troublesome situation.

A prime example of this definitional and specific focus by some church leaders, ecclesiastical as well as theological, is their effort to define the priest as a "representative of Christ the head." Through such a definition they imply that all major issues on priesthood are taken care of. Even the *Catechism of the Catholic Church* moves in this direction (see 875, 1548–51). The focus on Christ the Head as the definition of priesthood becomes so central in these explanations that the priest's relationship to all other institutional church ministries is either overlooked or given only a casual cross-reference. In the efforts of these authors to emphasize Christ the Head, the *context* of ecclesial institutional ministry is either ignored completely or alluded to in only an incidental way. The broader and more significant contextual understanding of priesthood is simply not a major part of their writings on the definition of priesthood with its exclusive view of priest as representative of Christ the Head. Such a definitional goal is not mine, nor is such a procedure the one I wish to take. In my view, such a pinpointing goal—the clear formulation of a definition—is counterproductive during this present postconciliar time. Focus on a single

---

28. The desire to define the exclusive nature of the priest is evident in J. Lécuyer, *Le Sacerdoce dans le mystère du Christ*, Lex Orandi 24 (Paris: Les Éditions du Cerf, 1957); A. Del Molino, "Identidad teológico del ministerio ecclesiástico," *Claretianum* 12 (1972): 5–175; Justin Rigali, *I Call You Friends* (Chicago: Liturgy Training Publications, 2004).

detail with little or no focus on the overarching context distorts the single detail itself.

My thesis, then, focuses on the *contextual theology of institutional ministry and leadership in the Roman Catholic Church today.* The following pages must therefore be seen as *contextual* theology, not as *definitional* theology. Admittedly, a study of the context will not take away the argumentative situation, but it does provide, as all contextual theologies attempt to do, a clearer horizon in which the individual issues concerning institutional church ministry and leadership can be discussed more intelligently and more comprehensively.

Institutional Roman Catholic Church ministry and leadership, in conciliar and postconciliar theology and practice, have major comprehensive and contextual dimensions that cannot be set to one side. The bishops at Vatican II discussed institutional ministerial issues, developed reports on these same issues, and voted on final texts that touched on every level of institutional church ministry: the papacy, the episcopacy, the priesthood, the diaconate, the lay ministry, and the priestly ministry of all baptized-confirmed Christians. The bishops did this in a contextual way. Any ignoring or belittling of this contextual fabric as central to an understanding of today's institutional ecclesial ministry and leadership leads nowhere. Such ignoring and belittling only bring about misunderstanding.

The *institutional dimension* is only one part of ecclesial ministry and leadership; there is also another major dimension—the *charismatic dimension.* The bishops at Vatican II focused on charismatic leadership and ministry, which in the Roman Catholic Church is not identical with institutional leadership and ministry. There have been studies of the Vatican II documents and texts on this matter of charismatic leadership.[29] Charismatic church ministry and leadership, however, are not the focus of this present study. They are not

---

29. On the issue of charismatic leadership, see Ernst Käsemann, "Amt und Gemeinde im Neuen Testament," in *Exegetische Versuche und Besinnungen,* 1/2 (Göttingen: Vandenhoeck & Ruprecht, 1967), 109–34; Hans Küng, "The Charismatic Structure of the Church," *Concilium: Ecumenism* 1 (1965): 23–33; Gérard Philips, *La Chiesa e il suo Mistero* (Milan: Jaca Books, 1975), 159–63, in which he analyzes paragraph 12b of *Lumen gentium* on the issue, "I doni carismatici del popolo di Dio."

part of the contextual theology of *institutional* church ministry and leadership. Charismatic ministry and leadership are, however, part of the *contextual theology of all church leadership and ministry*. At the end of this study, I will come back to the charismatic dimension. Since the current institutional ecclesial ministry and leadership are bogged down by a minority's demand for a definitional theology, I simply acknowledge at this juncture the valid presence and necessary existence of charismatic leadership and ministry in the church. Since charismatic ecclesial ministry and leadership, however, are not the source of today's problems with institutional church ministry, they do not constitute the precise focus of my thesis.

To understand the contextual fabric of *institutional ministry and leadership* in today's Roman Catholic Church, I want to argue my thesis in a step-by-step way. This procedure brings clarity to the intricate contextual interrelationship of all contemporary church ministries. For those in the permanent diaconate these steps may seem far from their own ministry and vocation. However, if the theology of ministry itself is not clear, then the theology of the permanent diaconate will also not be clear, and this unclarity will have serious effects on the way in which a permanent deacon understands his ministry and the way in which he spiritually appropriates his own personal sense of ministerial worth.

First Step:
The Father Sends Jesus into the World

In the texts and documents of Vatican II, the bishops did not formulate a *summa theologiae*. In an occasional way, however, the bishops do indicate both trinitarian elements and christological elements, which are of keen significance for their teaching. Nonetheless, their focus remained primarily on the theology of church itself; with the result that trinitarian and christological issues are mentioned in an *obiter dictum* way. On the issue of institutional ecclesial ministry and leadership, however, the bishops went out of their way to stress both the trinitarian and christological base. That God sent Jesus with a mission and a ministry is stated

31

by the bishops as **the foundational element of all institutional church ministry and leadership**. We read:

> The Son, therefore, came on mission from His Father. It was in Him, before the foundation of the world, that the Father chose us and predestined us to become adopted sons, for in Him it has pleased the Father to reestablish all things. (*LG* 3)

> When the work which the Father had given the Son to do on earth (see Jn 17:4) was accomplished, the Holy Spirit was sent on the day of Pentecost in order that He might forever sanctify the church continually and thus all believers would have access to the Father through Christ in the one Spirit. (*LG* 4)

> By an utterly free and mysterious decree of His own wisdom and goodness, the eternal Father created the whole world. His plan was to dignify men with a participation in His own divine life....All the elect, before time began, the Father "foreknew and predestined to become conformed to the image of his Son, that he should be the firstborn among many brethren" (Rom. 8:29). (*LG* 2)

> The Lord Jesus "whom the Father has made holy and sent into the world" (Jn. 10:36) has made his whole mystical body share in the anointing by the Spirit with which he himself had been anointed.
> (*Presbyterorum ordinis* [*PO* 2])

The phrases in the above passages: namely, *sent by the Father,* the work which *the Father gave the Son* to do, *the holy Spirit was sent,* God *has willed,* and the *Father sent Jesus into the world,* all indicate the primordial or foundational action of God. Institutional church ministry and leadership are fundamentally established by God's action alone. There is a basic relationship or, better, a basic interrelationship between God's sending and all institutional ecclesial ministry and leadership. At its very roots, ecclesial ministry and leadership are interrelational to the divine Trinity's initiative.

I have not set up an exhaustive list of Vatican II passages on this issue. Many other passages could be added to the few mentioned here. The above citations are typical of all other references. These citations speak of God's primordial action: the trinitarian sending of Jesus. This sending is the proto-relationality for all mission, ministry, and leadership.

The *Catechism of the Catholic Church* repeats in a very clear way this position of the Vatican II bishops. In the following citations, I have placed the key phrases indicative of God's primordial action in italics. The passages are taken from the section of the *Catechism* that is deliberately entitled: "On the church's origin, foundation and mission." The title alone speaks volumes: the very origin of the church and its mission, as well as the very foundation of the church and its ministerial leadership, lies in the trinitarian sending of Jesus. At its origin and its foundation the church is relational; its mission is relational; its ministry is relational; and its leadership is relational. All of these ecclesial dimensions are primordially related the mission and ministry of Jesus.

> We begin our investigation of the church's mystery by meditating on *her origin in the Holy Trinity's plan* and her progressive realization in history. (758)

> The gradual process of development takes shape "in keeping *with the Father's plan.*" (758)

> There is a *"plan of God's loving kindness,* conceived by the Father before the foundation of the world."…"This plan is a grace which was given to us in Christ Jesus before the ages began, stemming immediately from Trinitarian love." (257)

> The Lord's missionary mandate is *ultimately grounded in the eternal love* of the Most Holy Trinity. (830)

These citations indicate that God, from creation onward, planned for and guided the people of God for a mission and ministry that God alone had established. The primordial action of

God, God's plan, is stated unequivocally. It is unequivocally the foundation for all mission, ministry, and leadership. We creatures do not tell God what mission and ministry God can do. Rather, God tells us during all periods of human history what *our* mission, ministry, and leadership are and what this mission, ministry, and leadership *mean*. The ultimate and most profound understanding of mission, ministry, and leadership is found only in God, and this founding trinitarian grace of mission and ministry determines all subsequent missions and ministries, including that of Jesus, of the people of Israel, and of the new people of God. There is, therefore, a basic, foundational and unquestionable interrelationship of God's plan and action for all forms of ecclesial mission and ministry. At its very root, ministry is interrelational: that is, related to God's own initiative. God's action is relational and foundational for all institutional ministries. In God's founding mission and ministry we have *the ultimate basis for the contextual theology of all institutional ministries and leadership*. This divine context cannot be left to one side when we discuss specific institutional ecclesial ministries, missions, and leadership. This divine context establishes the primary interrelationality of all institutional church ministry and leadership.

Nor can this divine sending be seen as *external* to the theology of institutional church ministry. The divine sending cannot be seen as a structural and spatial context, similar to the example of the sports arena mentioned above. This sending by the Holy Spirit, according to the texts cited above, *permeates* all institutional church ministry, mission, and leadership. Nor is the divine sending simply a causal relationship; that is, the trinitarian action simply got the process of church ministry started. The trinitarian sending is a *constitutive and ongoing element* at the depths of all institutional church ministries. It is the foundational reality of what ministry and leadership are all about. In other words, *the trinitarian sending is a deeply interrelational and contextual issue without which institutional church ministry and leadership have no meaning whatsoever.*

The position of Vatican II, as repeated in the *Catechism of the Catholic Church*, is accepted by contemporary Roman Catholic leaders and writers who discuss institutional church ministry. Indeed, this trinitarian context of institutional ministry is generally presented by all of these writers as the major foundational context

for all church ministries. They even agree that this major foundation is continually at work in the ministers and in the ministries of
the church. The interrelationship of God's action and the church's
ministry is ongoing, permeating, and intrinsic. What is often not
carried through to its full implication is the all-pervasive interrelationality of ministry, mission, and leadership which the position of
Vatican II expresses. Authors will write of this trinitarian foundational relationship, but they do not integrate it into a specific ministry. We will see this particularly in the following chapter.

Second Step:
The Mission and Ministry of Jesus Himself

The conciliar bishops clearly addressed the mission and ministry of the incarnate Jesus and taught in carefully worded but
deftly expressed terms that Jesus' own mission and ministry constitute the second foundational basis for all institutional church ministries and leadership. Again, the wording of the Vatican II texts is
crystal-clear. Next to the trinitarian sending of Jesus, the incarnate
Jesus' own mission and ministry form the underlying contextual
basis for all other ecclesial institutional missions and ministries. We
read:

> The mystery of the holy Church is manifest in her very
> foundation, for the Lord Jesus inaugurated her by
> preaching the good news, that is, the coming of God's
> Kingdom....The Church, consequently, equipped with
> the gifts of her Founder and faithfully guarding His pre-
> cepts of charity, humility and self-sacrifice, receives the
> mission to proclaim and to establish among all peoples
> the Kingdom of Christ and of God.   (*LG* 5)

> Inspired by no earthly ambition, the Church seeks but a
> solitary goal: to carry forward the work of Christ
> Himself under the lead of the befriending Spirit.
>   (*Gaudium et spes* [*GS*] 3)

35

Christ the Lord, the Son of the living God, came that He
might save his people from their sin and that all men
might be made holy. Just as He Himself was sent by the
Father, so He also sent His apostles. Therefore, He sanc-
tified them, conferring on them the Holy Spirit.

(*Christus Dominus* [*CD*] 1)

Christ gave the apostles and their successors the com-
mand and the power to teach all nations, to hallow men
in the truth, and to feed them.   (*CD* 2)

The *Catechism* is equally clear on this matter:

It is from God's love for all men that the church in every
age receives both the obligation and the vigor of her missionary dynamism, for the love of Christ urges us on. (851)

The apostolic ministry is the continuation of Christ's
mission....Jesus unites them [the apostles] to the mission
he received from the Father. (859)

The whole church is apostolic...in that she is sent out
into the whole world. All members of the church share
in this mission [of Christ], though in various ways. (863)

It is Jesus who gives the mission and ministry to the church.
The church does not establish what the mission and ministry of
Jesus are or can be, nor does the church, in all its dimensions,
determine what the church's mission and ministry are. Ecclesial
ministry and leadership are totally and fundamentally dependent
on Jesus. Jesus is not dependent on the church. Church leaders,
both ecclesiastical and theological, must continually purify their
presentations of Jesus' mission and ministry by a return to the
gospels. On various occasions in the past and even in the present,
some church leaders have claimed that x is part and parcel of Jesus'
own mission and ministry. However, this so-called x is more their
subjective interpretation than the expression of Jesus' ministry and
mission as found in the New Testament itself. In every generation

and in every local church, church members—and this surely includes permanent deacons—must ask themselves in an honest and humble way: Are our mission, ministry, and leadership a reflection of Jesus' own mission and ministry? At times there is indeed convergence. At times, however, there is unquestionable divergence. This humble soul searching can be stated more bluntly: Do our institutional church ministry, mission, and leadership reflect the mission, ministry, and leadership of Jesus or not? This question bluntly indicates the contextual role that the very mission and ministry of Jesus have for any and every understanding of ecclesial institutional ministry and leadership. It also indicates the interrelational dimension of ministry and leadership. There are no ecclesial ministry, mission, and leadership that are not related to the mission, ministry, and leadership of Jesus himself. The bishops at Vatican II and subsequently the *Catechism of the Catholic Church* have stressed this secondary foundational and contextual presence of Jesus' own mission and ministry.

In *Lumen gentium* we read: "It was for this reason that God sent His Son, whom He appointed heir of all things that He might be Teacher, King and Priest of all, the Head of the new and universal people of the sons of God" (13). With this citation, Bonaventure Kloppenburg introduces his chapter entitled "New Theological Portrait of the Bishop" in Vatican II. He writes:

> According to a traditional terminology which was systematically adopted in the documents of Vatican II, we can distinguish three essential functions of Christ: teaching (prophet, teacher, light), sanctifying (priest, mediator, pontiff), and ruling (shepherd, king, lord, head). All the baptized without exception share in these three functions of Christ.[30]

Kloppenburg goes on to state: "This is a fundamental starting-point on which a great deal of stress must be laid, a backdrop that

---

30. Bonaventure Kloppenburg, *A Eclesiolgia do Vaticano II* (Rio de Janeiro: Editora Vozes, 1971); Eng. trans. by Matthew J. O'Connell, *The Ecclesiology of Vatican II* (Chicago: Franciscan Herald Press, 1974), 220.

needs constantly to be rediscovered: the Church has no other teachers besides Christ, no other prophets, priests, mediators, pontiffs, shepherds, lords, kings and heads [other than Christ]."[31] Our human vocabulary, he argues, is limited, and thus we may use all of these terms and titles for our church ministers, but they are not used in a univocal way. We have but one teacher, Christ; we have but one priest, Christ; we have but one leader, Christ.[32] All others to whom we apply these names and titles are sacraments of the one teacher, the one priest, and the one leader. More fundamentally, there is a common and an equal sharing in this threefold sacramental ministry by all the baptized and confirmed. To repeat Kloppenburg's statement: "This is the fundamental starting point." And this starting point is profoundly interrelational.

Once again, the mission and ministry of Jesus are not accidentally a part of institutional church ministry and leadership. They are not external to institutional church ministry. They are the very substance of institutional church ministry and leadership. There is a contextual and interrelational dimension that permeates a true and valid institutional church ministry at every level. It is abundantly clear that the bishops at Vatican II did not present the mission and ministry of Jesus as something external to the institutional ministry of the church itself. It is abundantly clear that the bishops at Vatican II saw the mission and ministry of Jesus himself as the operative reality in the very depths of institutional church ministry and leadership. It is a permeating interrelational and contextual reality, not an external, merely causative or exemplary reality.

I think it is fair to say that there are few, if any, Roman Catholic authors, who do not accept the above interrelational and contextual presence of the trinitarian sending and of Jesus' own mission and ministry as a continuing foundational reality in institutional church ministry. On this matter, there is a common agreement and a common acceptance. It is the third step, however, that

31. Ibid.

32. This way of theologizing on Jesus the only teacher, only priest, and only leader is found in one of St. Bonaventure's most famous sermons, "Christus unus omnium magister," in *S. Bonaventurae Opera Omnia*, vol. 5 (Quaracchi: Typographia Collegii S. Bonaventurae, 1891), 567–74.

engenders the problems in today's struggle for the meaning of institutional church ministry.

The glory of the permanent diaconate is to realize that the permanent deacon's main objective is *to reflect Jesus* in his own ministry and mission. Along with every other church minister, the permanent deacon *shares* in the very same mission and ministry of Jesus himself. This foundational position of both Vatican II and the *Catechism of the Catholic Church* offers the permanent deacon a powerful *theological* base for his ministry, a powerful *pastoral* focus for his ministry, and a powerful *personal* base for his diaconal spirituality. Although I have spent time on this fundamental theme, I also have noted that there are some major figures in church leadership who bypass these issues in both the documents of Vatican II and the *Catechism* and stress a radical individualized definition of the different church ministries. In doing so, these church leaders ignore what the documents of Vatican II clearly state and what the *Catechism*, in turn, clearly repeats. In the next chapter I will consider in depth the five major changes regarding church ministry that were instituted by the Second Vatican Council.

Chapter Four

THE SACRAMENTAL MISSION AND MINISTRY OF ALL CHRISTIANS: THE FIRST OF FIVE MAJOR CHANGES IN MINISTRY MADE BY THE BISHOPS AT VATICAN II

The bishops at Vatican II established five major changes regarding institutional church ministry. These five major changes are the following:

- The establishment of the mission and ministry of all baptized-confirmed Christians as a foundation of institutional church ministry
- The reestablishment of the episcopacy as an official part of the sacrament of orders
- The redefinition of priesthood on the basis of the *tria munera*
- The reestablishment of the permanent diaconate
- The official expansion of lay ministry into the ecclesial dimensions of the *tria munera*

Whenever a serious change is made in one major area of church ministry and leadership, all the other major forms of ministry and leadership are affected. This is true because all ministry and leadership in the Catholic Church are interrelated. For a permanent deacon, then, it is necessary today that he understand why a change in episcopacy or priesthood needs to be studied, since episcopal and presbyteral changes affect his own standing as a deacon minister. This chapter cannot help but be lengthy, and I hope that the permanent deacon remains patient as the changes made by Vatican II are delineated in some detail. We begin with the establishment of the mission and ministry of all baptized-confirmed Christians as a foundation of all other institutional church ministry.

The First Major Change
Made by the Bishops at Vatican II

The establishment of the mission and ministry of all baptized-confirmed Christians as a foundation of institutional church ministry is the first major change. Many commentators on Vatican II have noted the significance of placing the material on the "people of God" in the second chapter of *Lumen gentium*.[33] A minority of bishops wanted, in a very strong way, to place the material on "hierarchy" in the second chapter. The first chapter, which had dealt with the church as mystery, was meant to provide the foundation for all the chapters of *Lumen gentium*. In the first chapter the christological base was clearly presented, the emphasis on the mystery of the church was stressed, and the multiple aspects and biblical descriptions of the church's mystery were established. Chapter 1 presented a comprehensive statement on the church as mystery. The question arose: What should be the next ecclesial theme? To make the next ecclesial theme that of "hierarchy" would place the hierarchy in a dominant position. To make the next ecclesial theme that of the "people of God" would place the common unity and equality of all Christians in a dominant position. After heated arguments pro and con, the bishops finally voted to place the "people of

---

33. See Canon Charles Moeller, "History of *Lumen Gentium's* Structure and Ideas," in *Vatican II: An Interfaith Appraisal*, ed. John Miller (Notre Dame, IN: University of Notre Dame Press, 1966), 123–52; also R. Sugranyes de Franch, "Apostolado Laical," in *Estudios sobre el Concilio Vaticano II* (Bilbao: Mensajero, 1966), 341–46. For Sugranyes de Franch a key moment in the council was the day on which the bishops decided to place the chapter on the people of God prior to the chapter on the hierarchy. Sugranyes de Franch was an official lay observer at the council.

God" issue in second place. This decision in itself marked a major turning point for the ecclesiology of Vatican II.

As regards the specific issue of institutional church ministry and leadership, the inclusion of the *tria munera* in chapter 2 marks an even more resounding change as regards the placement of the people of God rather than the hierarchy as the theme of chapter 2. The phrase *tria munera* (three tasks), unites the mission and ministry of Jesus with the mission and ministry of all baptized-confirmed Christians. All Christians share in the mission and ministry of Jesus. All Christians continually relate to the threefold mission and ministry of Jesus.[34]

	1. Jesus' teaching and preaching	= prophet
All Christians *share* in:	2. Jesus' sanctifying	= priest
	3. Jesus' leading and administrating	= king

The texts of Vatican II, as we shall see, not only indicate that all Christians share in Jesus' own threefold mission and ministry; they also indicate in clear terms three major aspects of this sharing.

God Calls and Commissions All Christians for This Threefold Mission and Ministry.

The calling and the commissioning of all Christians to share in Jesus' threefold mission and ministry are the prerogative of Jesus himself—or at times we read, a prerogative of God. The calling and the commissioning come from God. It is *not* the pope, the bishops, or the priests who call and commission Christians for this sharing in the ministry and mission of Jesus. Consequently, the hierarchy of the church is not the ultimate basis for either the calling or the commissioning of all Christians to this threefold ministry and mission. *God alone* is the ultimate basis.

---

34. The documents of Vatican II use the terms *prophet*, *priest*, and *king*. On this threefold description of ministry, see Y. Congar, "Sur la trilogie: Prophète-Roi-Prêtre," *Revue des sciences philosophiques et théologiques*, 67 (1983): 106–12; also Thomas F. O'Meara, *Theology of Ministry*, rev. ed. (New York: Paulist Press, 1999), 265–66.

This Sharing of All Christians in the Mission and Ministry of Jesus Is Institutional.

If Jesus' own threefold mission and ministry are the basis for the institutional leadership in the church, then all who share in his own mission and ministry share in it in an institutional way. The bishops never speak of this participation of Christians in Jesus' own mission and ministry as "charismatic." They *do* speak of personal gifts that are charismatic; but as regards the people of God as sharers in Jesus' own mission and ministry, the bishops are speaking of a structural element of the church, and structure is institutional, interrelational, and sacramental.

This Sharing of All Christians in the Mission and Ministry of Jesus Is Sacramental.

There have been some theologians who refer to the priesthood of all believers as spiritual, while the ministerial priesthood is sacramental.[35] Such a view contradicts the texts of Vatican II. Time and time again the bishops indicate that the basis for the sharing by all Christians in Jesus' own mission and ministry are the sacraments of baptism and confirmation. We call the hierarchical mission and ministry of bishops, priests, and deacons *sacramental* because of the sacrament of orders. In a very clear way, the conciliar texts base the mission and ministry of all Christians on a sacramental foundation as well. Therefore, all Christians are sacramentally part of the mission and ministry of Jesus.

These three factors regarding the interrelationship of Jesus (God) and the people of God are a major part of the first change that the conciliar bishops made. In chapter 2 of *Lumen gentium*, we read that through the sacraments of baptism and confirmation all Christians are given a share in the threefold mission and ministry of Jesus himself (the sacramental aspect). All Christians are given this privilege of participating in Jesus' own mission and ministry by God (the calling and commissioning aspect). Moreover, all Christians

---

35. See Kenan Osborne, *Ministry: Lay Ministry in the Roman Catholic Church— Its History and Theology* (New York: Paulist Press, 1993; repr., Eugene, OR: Wipf and Stock, 2003), 535–40.

are called and commissioned by God to an institutional and sacramentally based mission and ministry (the institutional aspect). These factors also indicate that the *tria munera* mission and ministry of all Christians are interrelational. The mission and ministry of all Christians are *intrinsically related* to the mission and ministry of Jesus himself. Christians share in Jesus' own mission and ministry, and therefore they, too, share in the trinitarian sending of Jesus. Trinity, Jesus, and the mission and ministry of Jesus are all interrelated in this second chapter of *Lumen gentium*. The contextual framework for an understanding of the mission and ministry of all Christians is interrelational. Take the interrelational context away and the mission and ministry of Christians make no sense.

All Christians share in the *tria munera* mission and ministry of Jesus himself, and because of that they share in the trinitarian sending mission and ministry of Jesus. They receive this mission and ministry sacramentally through their baptism and confirmation. Their sharing in the mission and ministry of Jesus has as it goal the building up of the institution we call church. The following conciliar citations leave no doubt that there is an *intrinsic interrelation* involving the trinitarian sending of Jesus, Jesus' own mission and ministry, and the sharing in this same mission and ministry by all baptized-confirmed Christians.

> The baptized, by regeneration and the anointing of the Holy Spirit, are consecrated into a spiritual house and a holy priesthood. Thus through all those works befitting Christian men they can offer spiritual sacrifices and proclaim the power of Him who has called them out of darkness into His marvelous light. (*LG* 10) [This passage stresses that all Christians share in the priestly mission and ministry of Jesus.]

> The common priesthood of the faithful and the ministerial or hierarchical priesthood are nonetheless interrelated. (*LG* 10) [Again, the passage stresses that all Christians share in the priestly mission and ministry of Jesus.]

The holy People of God shares also in Christ's prophetic office. It spreads abroad a living witness to Him, especially by means of a life of faith and charity and by offering to God a sacrifice of praise. (*LG* 12) [Here the stress is this: all Christians share in the prophetic mission and ministry of Jesus.]

The body of the faithful as a whole, anointed as they are by the Holy One, cannot err in matters of belief. (*LG* 12) [All Christians share in the prophetic and teaching ministry and mission of Jesus.][36]

These citations as well as many others from the texts of Vatican II indicate clearly that all baptized-confirmed Christians in virtue of baptism and confirmation share in the *tria munera* of Jesus' own mission and ministry. It is also clear that it is Jesus or God who calls Christians to this mission and ministry and who also confers on them a share in the mission and ministry of Jesus. Fundamentally, it is not the hierarchical church leadership that either calls or commissions Christians for this threefold mission and ministry. It is God who calls and commissions. In other words, the hierarchical church plays no definitive role in the conferral and commissioning of the baptized-confirmed Christians. Both the conferral and the commissioning are God's actions. Church leaders have only a discerning role, on the one hand, and an ecclesiastical-jurisdictional role, on the other. Without any doubt, I am repeating myself here, but I am doing so deliberately, since it is precisely in this critical area of interrelational ministry that today's acceptance and nonacceptance have created the current problematic. The major crux of the problems regarding ministry in the Roman Catholic Church today lies first of all in the very acceptance or nonacceptance of the statements of Vatican II that have just been cited. Second, the crux of the problems regarding today's ecclesial

---

36. Other passages from the Vatican II documents could also be listed: from *LG*, see 12, 31, 33, 34, and 35; from *Apostolicam actuositatem (AA)*, see 2, 3, and 10; from *Sacrosanctum concilium (SC)*, see 48. For a full listing, see Bonaventure Kloppenburg, *The Ecclesiology of Vatican II*, 263–64.

ministries appears whenever the interrelationship just described is interpreted in a minimalistic way. As regards a current ecclesial theology of mission, ministry, and leadership, it is precisely this conciliar change that brings us to the heart of the matter. Let us consider the serious ramifications of these citations.

God calls and commissions all Christians through the sacraments of baptism and confirmation. In standard Roman Catholic theology, this action of God is designated by the phrase *vi sacramenti*. In the standard theological terminology of pre–Vatican II theology, the phrase *vi sacramenti* (through the power of the sacrament) means that the action of God is accomplished in and through a sacrament itself, not through the work of the priest or minister. The opposite of *vi sacramenti* is *vi delegationis* (through the power of delegation), which means that someone—a hierarchical person in many instances—delegates someone for a given task. He who delegates can also take the delegation away. If, however, it is through a sacramental action, then only God can make a change. *Vi sacramenti* theologically states that the action of calling and commissioning is God's work alone. At best, hierarchy has a secondary and nonessential role.[37]

The inclusion of the *tria munera* and their relationship to the ministerial life of all Christians is generally not contested and has been accepted as a major part of the teaching of Vatican II. The *Catechism of the Catholic Church* repeats the Vatican II position:

> The Christian faithful are those who, inasmuch as they have been incorporated in Christ through Baptism, have been constituted as the people of God; for this reason, since they become sharers in Christ's priestly, prophetic and royal office in their own manner, they are called to

---

37. At this juncture, some theologians might argue that the hierarchy acts in an instrumental efficient way, similar to the instrumental efficient causality found in Thomistic sacramental theology. This view is only a theological opinion. The Franciscan intellectual tradition has never accepted instrumental efficient causality in its sacramental theology. To insist on an interpretation that involves instrumental efficient causality places a particular theology on a par with the defined teaching of the church. See Kenan Osborne, *Sacramental Theology: A General Introduction* (Mahwah, NJ: Paulist Press, 1988), 49–68.

exercise the mission which God has entrusted to the Church to fulfill in the world, in accord with the condition proper to each one. (871) [This is a direct citation from the *New Code of Canon Law*, canon 204; the *Catechism* makes an additional reference in the footnote to *LG* 31.]

Even though the *Catechism* cites verbatim the *New Code of Canon Law*, the presence of this paragraph in the *Catechism* as its opening paragraph for the entire section, which is entitled "Christ's Faithful—Hierarchy, Laity and Consecrated Life," indicates that this sharing by all Christians is foundational. This particular section of the *Catechism* (871–933), moreover, is the precise locus in which the authors of the *Catechism* have gathered together a detailed theology of institutional church ministry. To start the detailed theology of institutional ministry with this citation was certainly deliberate. The authors wanted to establish a foundational position for the *tria munera* of all the baptized and confirmed Christians.

This is further clarified and stressed by the second paragraph in this same section, which again is a verbatim citation from the *New Code of Canon Law*. We read:

In virtue of their rebirth in Christ there exists among all the Christian faithful a true equality with regard to dignity and the activity whereby all cooperate in the building up of the Body of Christ in accord with each one's own condition and function. (872) [This too is a direct citation from the *New Code of Canon Law*, canon 208; the *Catechism* makes an additional reference in the footnote to *LG* 32.]

Since this is the second paragraph of the *Catechism*'s major discussion on the mission and ministry of the church, its opening position is also indicative of its importance. The equality of all Christians is stressed, and it is an equality with regard to the dignity and the activity in the building up of the body of Christ. In other words, there is an *institutional* ministry of building up the church, in which all Christians have an equality of dignity and action. The calling and commissioning by God of all baptized and confirmed Christians is not presented as a charismatic ministry or a personal ministry. Rather, it is presented as an institutional church ministry.

In the third paragraph of this section of the *Catechism* (873) we find the citation from the Vatican II text mentioned above, in which all "share in the priestly, prophetical and kingly office of Christ." In this paragraph, the authors of the *Catechism* without any detailed explanation simply state that there is a connection of the *tria munera* between the nonhierarchical members of the church and the hierarchical members of the church. The text does this by stating that all Christians share in one and the same foundational calling and commissioning by God: namely, all share in Jesus' mission and ministry.

A summary of the first major change in institutional ministry and leadership made by the conciliar bishops leads us to the following conclusions. From the texts of Vatican II, we hear that the foundation for all mission and ministry in the church lies **first of all** in God's sending of Jesus himself. **Second,** the texts state unequivocally that the foundation for every mission and ministry in the church lies in Jesus' own mission and ministry. We hear, **finally,** that the foundation for all mission and ministry in the church lies in the *common sharing* of the mission and ministry of Jesus by all baptized and confirmed Christians.

The *Catechism*, as seen above, presents this same ecclesiology of ministerial foundation in its own direct and clear way. It deliberately starts its major section on institutional church ministry with two key paragraphs of the ministry and mission of all Christians. In the third opening paragraph, the *Catechism* cites verbatim the council's statement from *Apostolicam actuositatem (AA)* 2. It is only on this basis that the *Catechism* then turns to the other forms of institutional church ministry: the hierarchy, the laity in special ministries, and religious life. Contextually, then, the sharing in the *tria munera* of Jesus' own mission and ministry by all Christians is the *third foundation for all other institutional church ministry and leadership.*[38]

---

38. The first foundation is the sending of Jesus by the trinitarian God; the second foundation is the very mission and ministry of Jesus.

The majority of writers on church ministry today present the same general re-imaging of the Vatican II statements.[39] On this issue, there appears to be common acceptance. However, when it comes to the issue of specifically interrelating the mission and ministry of the *tria munera* of the baptized and confirmed to hierarchical ministries, namely: papacy, episcopacy, priesthood, and the diaconate, there is on the part of many writers a strong resistance and reluctance to identify this foundational interrelationship in a clear way. We see this resistance and reluctance in the efforts of scholars who radically distinguish the priesthood of all believers from the hierarchical priesthood. There has been an appreciable amount of theological literature attempting to explain the difference, and in this body of literature some major scholars overwhelmingly tend to distinguish the two rather than interrelate the two.[40] The citation from Vatican II, as we saw above, presents the key statement.

> Though they differ from one another in essence and not only in degree, the common priesthood of the faithful and the ministerial or hierarchical priesthood are nonetheless interrelated. Each of them in its own special way is a participation in the one priesthood of Christ. (*LG* 10)

The term *interrelated* has become the major sticking point. The phrases "differ essentially and not only in degree" and "each in

---

39. See Jon Nilson, "The Laity," in *The Gift of the Church*, ed. Peter Phan (Collegeville, MN: Liturgical Press, 2000), 395–413; Giovanni Magnani, "Does the So-Called Theology of the Laity Possess a Theological Status?" in *Vatican II: Assessment and Perspectives: Twenty-five Years After (1962–1987)*, ed. René Latourelle, 3 vols. (New York: Paulist Press, 1988), 1:568–633; Paul Lakeland, *The Liberation of the Laity: In Search of an Accountable Church* (New York: Continuum, 2004); O'Meara, *Theology of Ministry*; Edward Schillebeeckx, The Mission of the Church (New York: Crossroad, 1973).

40. For the distinction of the two priesthoods, see Jean Galot, *Theology of the Priesthood*, trans. Roger Balducelli (San Francisco: Ignatius Press, 1984), 105–28, for one view; and Gérard Philips, *La Chiesa e il suo Mistero* (Milan: Jaca Books, 1975), 129–53, for a differing view. On p. 131, Philips includes a lengthy bibliography on the issue.

its own way" are given a priority emphasis over the phrase "are...interrelated." Some authors have attempted to clarify the conciliar statement on the interrelationship between the priesthood of all believers and the special priesthood, but generally they attempt this by first distinguishing the two rather than by first relating the two.[41]

On this matter, a caution is necessary. The issue of interrelationship cannot be limited to the priestly ministry of the *tria munera*. The issue of interrelationship must also be explained for an understanding of the prophetic mission and ministry as well as for an understanding of the leadership or regal mission and ministry. Theological material on these two interrelationships is negligible. The statement from *Lumen gentium* itself focuses only on the priestly ministry. It is evident that the statements presented in *Lumen gentium* and in the *Catechism* go out of their way to indicate interrelationship and difference as regards the *priestly munus*. However, there are *tria munera*, not just a single *munus*. Nowhere in the documents of Vatican II do we find a paragraph similar to the one cited above on the priestly *munus* which focuses in a similar way on the prophetic *munus* (teaching-preaching) or on the regal *munus* (leadership). Naturally, all three *munera* are mentioned in many areas of the conciliar texts, but nowhere do the bishops take as much care to specify interrelationship and distinction for the prophetic ministry and the regal ministry as they do for the priestly ministry. The same pattern of singling out priestly ministry is found in the abundance of literature on priesthood that has developed since Vatican II. The focus on the priestly function and the nonfocus on the prophetic and regal functions in such a detailed way indicate that the priestly issue itself is far more sensitive than the other two.

Whether the focus is on the teaching-preaching mission and ministry, or on the sanctifying mission and ministry, or on the lead-

---

41. Galot's *Theology of the Priesthood* is a major example of this procedure. However, the *Catechism of the Catholic Church* also focuses more on the distinction than on explaining the relationship (784, 901–3, 1268, but esp. 1546–53). In both of these sources, the interrelationship of the two priesthoods is readily acknowledged; however, there is little explanation of the interrelationship and a great deal of explanation of the difference.

ership mission and ministry, it is the contextual theology of the interrelationship of the *tria munera*, foundationally present in all Christians, with the two foundational elements stated above—the trinitarian and christological—that is central. The documents of Vatican II express forthrightly that the foundation for all mission and ministry in the church lies **first of all** in God's sending of Jesus himself. God's primordial sending of Jesus is contextually not some sort of domed structure. God's sending of Jesus *permeates* the spiritual depths of Jesus' ministry and of all church ministries. The same can be said of the **second foundation** of all institutional church ministries, which again the documents of Vatican II clearly express, namely: the foundation for all mission and ministry in the church lies in Jesus' own mission and ministry. Jesus' mission and ministry spiritually permeate the very mission and ministry of the institutional church. The same manner of permeating that is attributed to the sharing by all Christians in the *tria munera* of Jesus' own mission and ministry, is the **third foundation** of all institutional church ministries. All Christians are spiritually inspired and energized by Jesus' own mission and ministry. When a given Christian becomes a member of the hierarchy, that same deep, profound, basic permeation that a Christian received by God's grace at baptism and confirmation and that has permeated the Christian's life year after year remains foundationally within his newly accepted position in the hierarchy. It is precisely at this stage—when one is both part of the prophetic, priestly, and leadership people and also part of the hierarchy—that a relationship of the two is not maintained, and terms such as *radical difference* begin to appear.

In order to indicate how this threefold foundation relates to specific institutional church ministry, it may help if we consider briefly another threefold interrelationship: namely, the interrelationship in institutional church ministry of theology, pastoral practice, and the personal self-identity of the minister. This threefold interrelationship—theological, pastoral, and personal—is also part of the context of contemporary institutional ecclesial ministry. The contemporary context is not simply an academic or intellectual issue (the theological dimension). The theological dimension deeply affects the pastoral dimension and vice versa. As both Paul VI and John Paul II have said, evangelization lies at the very heart of the church and evangelization is pastoral. Theology that is not pastoral is meaningless theology. Finally, in today's world, one of the key issues that arises time and again has been the person: What is the self-identity of a bishop? Of a priest? Of a deacon? Of a lay minister? Personal identity of a specific minister has become one of the most telling needs today. In fact, it is often the most powerful problem of the so-called crisis of contemporary ministry. Whatever I say in the following pages and what I have said above have profound implications for theology, for pastoral practice, and for personal self-identity. The context of institutional ecclesial ministry permeates theological understanding, pastoral life, and the personal self-identity of the institutional minister. These three interrelated dimensions of institutional ministry are present in all institutional church ministries: baptismal-confirmational, papal, episcopal, presbyteral, diaconal, and special lay ministries. Because of this particular threefold interrelationship, institutional church ministries are again contextually and intrinsically interrelated to each other. A preliminary diagram of this all-inclusive permeating context indicates the depth and breadth of the contextual interrelationship.

| Theological issues
Pastoral issues
Self-identity issues | > in < | Papal ministry
Episcopal ministry
Priestly ministry
Diaconal ministry
Lay ministry | **all of which**
> **are based** <
on | • the baptism-
confirmation
mission ministry
of all Christians
• the mission and
ministry of Jesus
himself
• who was sent and
commissioned by
God. |

In this diagram, one sees all the major realities of the context for today's institutional church ministry:

- the three dimensions—theological, pastoral, and person
- the five special areas of institutional church ministry from papacy to special lay ministry
- the three foundational levels—God sending Jesus, Jesus' own mission and ministry, and the sharing in

Jesus' mission and ministry by all baptized-confirmed
Christians

In the above diagram, the context cannot be seen *only* as identified by the framing lines in which all these elements have their
own noninterrelated existences. Such a view would make context
only a spatial arena in which ministry takes place. Rather, the context is identified by *both* the framing lines and the shading in the
above diagram. The shading in particular permeates, unites, and
interrelates each of the realities. It is precisely the presence or inten-
sity of this all-inclusive interrelationship among institutional church
ministries that is disputed today. Interrelationship means the following: to speak of one aspect you are also speaking to some degree
of all the aspects mentioned in the diagram. Institutional church
ministry and leadership are by their very nature interrelational.

The interrelationship of the priesthood of all believers to the special priesthood is, without any doubt, the main area in which we currently find antagonistic differences. The antagonism is based on a
desire by some authors and officials to maintain a definition of a particular ministry, which, so these authors argue, does not depend on
interrelationship at all, or depends on an interrelationship that is more
nominal than real. In all of this we see that in one way or another *the
contextual issue of ministerial interrelationship is at the heart of the matter.*

An interrelational and contextual ecclesiology is clearly different from the ecclesiology which one finds in theological textbooks
on a theology of church written prior to Vatican II. The ecclesiology of Vatican II in major ways has changed pre–Vatican II ecclesiology. These changes in ecclesiology have produced an immediate
domino effect on the theological understanding of all institutional
church ministries. Any and every serious change affecting one of
the institutional church ministries cannot help but affect all other
institutional church ministries.

The following diagram, which needs to be read from the bot-
tom up rather than from the top down, presents the contextual
interrelationship in a more detailed way.

ALL OTHER INSTITUTIONAL MINISTRIES IN THE CHURCH
PAPACY
EPISCOPACY
PRIESTHOOD
DIACONATE
LAY MINISTRY
ARE BASED ON THE BAPTISMAL AND CONFIRMATIONAL
MINISTRY

∧

∧

ALL BAPTIZED AND CONFIRMED
CHRISTIANS
ARE CALLED AND COMMISSIONED BY GOD
TO SHARE IN THE *TRIA MUNERA* OF JESUS

∧

∧

THE *TRIA MUNERA*
MISSION AND MINISTRY
OF JESUS CHRIST

∧

∧

GOD'S SENDING
OF
JESUS CHRIST

By and large, there is today a commonly accepted *general understanding* of this conciliar teaching. By and large, there is even a commonly agreed on *general interpretation* of this conciliar approach to ecclesial institutional ministry and leadership. By and large, therefore, there is a *general acceptance* of the conciliar position. In other words, church officials and theologians are in agreement if this ecclesiology is expressed *in a general and abstract way*. Where, then, is the problem? Why are there identity problems among lay ministers? Among deacons? Among priests? Among bishops? Why are there today, in the aftermath of Vatican II, major theological, pastoral, and personal-identity problems regarding lay ministers, deacons, priests, bishops, and even popes? The problematic issue can be stated most sharply in a negation rather than in anything positive:

> Many key church officials and theologians have not interrelated all of the elements of institutional church ministry and leadership into a contextually unified continuum upon which they base their theology of specific and individualized ministries.

What is lacking today in most official and/or theological explanations of individual church ministries is an integrating contextual theology of institutional ministry. Such an intrinsic interrelationship is either ignored completely or is only minimally stated. In the view of many current church officials and theologians, context is simply a framework within which the real institutional ministries operate. Such a context remains external, accidental, and one-dimensionally spatial. There is a nonacceptance of a context that *permeates* all the respective realities of institutional church ministry. Vatican II, however, moved in a *permeating* contextual manner.

A permanent deacon must, indeed, regard his vocation as a special grace for mission and ministry. But he must also regard his baptismal-confirmational vocation as a founding basis for the diaconal calling. This basic interrelational unity nourishes the deacon's theological, pastoral, and personal identity in a profound way.

Chapter Five

THE REESTABLISHMENT OF EPISCOPACY TO THE SACRAMENT OF ORDERS: THE SECOND MAJOR CONCILIAR CHANGE IN MINISTRY

It was the conciliar bishops' reestablishment of the episcopacy as part of the sacrament of orders that can be seen a second major change. The precise texts in the documents of Vatican II which present a major change for a theological, pastoral, and personal understanding of a Roman Catholic bishop are the following:

> The sacred Synod teaches that by episcopal consecration is conferred the fullness of the sacrament of orders, that fullness which in the Church's liturgical practice and in the language of the holy Fathers of the Church is undoubtedly called the high priesthood, the apex of the sacred ministry. (*LG* 21)

> In the first place, the shepherds of Christ's flock ought to carry out their ministry with holiness, eagerness, humility and courage, in imitation of the eternal High Priest, the Shepherd and Guardian of our souls....Those chosen for the fullness of the priesthood are gifted with sacramental grace enabling them to exercise a perfect role of pastoral charity through prayer, sacrifice, and preaching, as through every form of a bishop's care and service. (*LG* 41)

Rarely, in the documents of Vatican II, do the bishops begin a statement with the words: "The sacred Synod teaches...." When this occurs, it is clear that a major statement is being made.[42] Gérard Philips helps us understand the depth of this section of *Lumen gentium*, for the phrasing of the material was very carefully constructed. He notes that the paragraph in which the first citation above is found (*LG* 21) moves beyond the solemn declaration— "The sacred Synod teaches"—and expresses a strong christological base of episcopal sacramentality. We read:

> In the bishops, therefore, for whom priests are assis-
> tants, our Lord Jesus Christ, the supreme High Priest,
> is present in the midst of those who believe and yet Jesus
> is also not absent from the gathering of His high priests.
> (*LG* 21)

This remarkable sentence is followed immediately by the presence of Jesus in a threefold manner in and through the bishops.

> Above all through their excellent service He [Jesus] is
> *preaching* the Word of God to all nations, and constantly
> *administering* the *sacraments* of faith to those who
> believe. By their paternal role (cf. 1 Cor 4:15) He *incor-*
> *porates* new members into His body by a heavenly regen-
> eration, and finally by their wisdom and prudence He
> [Jesus] *directs and guides* the people of the New Testament

---

42. In the initial draft on the church, which was rejected and then replaced with *Lumen gentium*, the position that bishops were part of the sacrament of holy orders was already included. There were a large number of theologians and church offi-cials who wanted a magisterial statement on this issue. See Bonaventure Kloppenburg, *The Ecclesiology of Vatican II*, 218–62, for a detailed presentation of the theology of bishop in the conciliar texts. See also, Joseph Komonchak, "The Significance of Vatican Council II for Ecclesiology," in *The Gift of the Church*, ed. Peter Phan (Collegeville, MN: Liturgical Press, 2000), 86–88; also *History of Vatican II*, ed. Giuseppe Alberigo and Joseph Komonchak, 4 vols. (Maryknoll, NY: Orbis Books, 1995–2004), particularly Giuseppi Ruggieri, "Beyond an Ecclesiology of Polemics: The Debate on the Church" (2:281–357); and Jan Grootaers, "The Drama Continues between the Acts: The 'Second Preparation' and Its Opponents" (2:259–314).

in its pilgrimage toward eternal happiness. (*LG* 21; emphasis added)

How is Jesus present in the person of the bishops? The paragraph follows the *tria munera*: it is primarily through their service of *preaching* the word of God to all people; it is through their administration of the *sacraments of faith;* it is through their *direction and guidance.* Prophet, priest, and king—and in this precise order—are the three dimensions of Jesus' own ministry and mission, which Jesus continues to accomplish in and through the service ministry of bishops. The quality of service for episcopal ministry is strongly stated: bishops are "servants of Christ and stewards of the mysteries of God. To them has been assigned the bearing of witness to the gospel of God's grace and to the ministration of the Spirit and of God's glorious power to make men just" (*LG* 21).

If today's theology, pastoral practice, and self-identity are not interrelated with the *tria munera* of Jesus' own mission and ministry, then the presentation of the conciliar bishops means nothing. To be a bishop is to be in relation to the triune God and to the mission and ministry of Jesus. If the mission and ministry of a bishop do not reflect in a foundational way this presence of Jesus' own mission and ministry of the *tria munera*, then a bishop's activity has little to no value.

The second paragraph (*LG* 21.b) officially (i.e., magisterially) changes the meaning of bishop. The paragraph begins with the words: "For the discharging of such great duties *[tria munera]*...." The document then describes how Christ endowed the apostles with a special outpouring of the Holy Spirit and how the apostles in turn conveyed their own gift of the Spirit to their collaborators: "It has been transmitted down to us in episcopal consecration."[43] All of this material leads up to the words:

---

43. Throughout the documents of Vatican II the standard approach regarding Jesus' historical institution of the church is repeated. None of the research by Roman Catholic biblical scholars, patrologists, and early church historians that took place in the first sixty-years of the twentieth century plays a role in the conciliar bishops' presentation on the institution of the church. Nor does the *Catechism of the Catholic Church* deviate from the standard position or make mention of this research (857–65).

This sacred Synod teaches that by episcopal consecration is conferred the fullness of the sacrament of orders, that fullness which in the Church's liturgical practice and in the language of the holy Fathers of the Church is undoubtedly called the high priesthood, the apex of the sacred ministry. (*LG* 21.b)

These words cannot be interpreted without the preceding *tria munera* and the Jesus-centered context (*LG* 21.a). Philips, at this juncture of his commentary, turns to the issue that these words clearly express: *L'Episcopato è un sacramento*,[44] "episcopacy is a sacrament." Philips presents a lengthy historical digression on the issue of episcopacy as part of the sacrament of holy orders. In the paragraphs below, I will do the same thing, though in a slightly different way. In Philips's digression he stresses the sacramentality of the bishop by citing John Chrysostom from the Eastern tradition and Ambrosiaster from the Western tradition. He even cites Thomas Aquinas, who did not accept episcopal sacramentality, but Philips uses Thomas's statement that the grace of Christ and the Holy Spirit constitute episcopacy.[45]

In the above passage from *Lumen gentium*, episcopacy is called the "high priesthood." In other sections found in the Vatican II texts the phrase used is the fullness of the priesthood. This summit of sacred ministry is immediately explained in *Lumen gentium* by a reference, once again, to the *tria munera*. "But episcopal consecration, together with the office of sanctifying, also confers the offices of teaching and of governing. (These, however, of their very nature, can be exercised only in hierarchical communion with the head and the members of the college)" (*LG* 21.b).[46] Episcopal office and activity are interrelational; they are collegial. No bishop, if he follows the presentation of Vatican II, acts alone. He acts by the very nature of episcopacy as a collegial bishop. Even more impor-

---

44. Philips, *La Chiesa e il suo Mistero*, 223ff.

45. Ibid., 224.

46. See ibid., 226; after the citation from *LG*, Philips immediately adds: "Non si tratta affatto di una innovazione dottrinale, se non per un certo numero di teologi occidentali, soprattutto dei secoli xix e xx. In realtà, la dottrina qui proclamata è antichissima e non fu mai contestata prima di una data molto recente."

tantly, a bishop acts only in union with the mission and ministry of Jesus himself.

The text of *Lumen gentium* 21.b immediately mentions sacramental character: "and the sacred character [is] so impressed" on the bishop who is being ordained. For centuries the theology of sacramental character has been described, disputed, redescribed and redisputed. Even today, theologians have abundant freedom to continue their theological analysis of what sacramental character means. No one view has ever been mandated by the magisterium of the Catholic Church.[47] The bishops at Vatican II had no intention of resolving the theological discussions on the meaning of sacramental character. In a very generalized way, they state: "and the sacred character [is] so impressed, that bishops in an eminent and visible way undertake Christ's own role as Teacher, Shepherd, and High Priest, and that they act in His person" (*LG* 21.b). A variety of theological interpretations on sacramental character can be cited to explain—differently of course—the relationship between the impression of the character and the activity of a bishop. *LG* 21.b gives no theological view of sacramental character the upper hand.

In the paragraphs above, I have parsed *LG* 21 rather carefully. It was necessary to do this, since we need to begin with the text itself. The text with its official statement on the sacramental nature of a bishop needs, however, a wider context if it is to be clearly understood. We must read this statement first of all in conjunction with a major discussion that took place at Vatican II one year before *Lumen gentium* was finally promulgated. When the initial draft or position paper on the church was given to the conciliar bishops, a majority of the bishops were less than supportive. They found to their dismay that the initial draft on ecclesiology only repeated the standard Roman Catholic operative ecclesiology as it had developed from the aftermath of the Council of Trent to the early years of the twentieth century. The standard ecclesiology of that long period of time was overly apologetic in nature and defended the

---

47. In an earlier book, *La Nature du Caractère Sacramentel* (Paris: Desclée de Brouwer, 1956), 231, Galot wrote: "Le concile définira l'existence comme certaine, mais refusera de se prononcer sur la nature du caractère." However, in his volume on the priesthood, Galot presents a very outspoken and focused interpretation of the nature of sacramental character.

Roman Catholic Church against Protestant thinking by means of a magnified role of the pope.[48] The initial position paper conveyed the idea that bishops were simply vicars of the papacy. Bishop Fernando Gomes dos Santos, speaking in the name of sixty Brazilian bishops, denounced the position paper when, in the first session of the council, it came under discussion. In a plenary session, Gomes dos Santos stated that the paper "makes the bishops simply vicars not only of the pope but even of the Roman Congregations on which the bishops are to depend in the least detail."[49] This statement was made on November 8, 1963, at the sixty-first general meeting. His denunciation of the position paper helped bring about its eventual rejection. When the initial position paper was officially rejected, the bishops were then free to formulate *de novo* an ecclesiology that eventually became the conciliar interrelational ecclesiology. They accomplished this rewriting of ecclesiology by making definite major changes.

Philips, who does not mention the intervention of Gomes dos Santos, nonetheless says clearly that the stress on sacramental character as used in *Lumen gentium* relates the bishops to Christ, not to the pope. Bishops are *not* vicars of the papacy, nor are they vicars of the congregations. In other words, the sacramentality of bishops is based on God's sending of Jesus and the bishop's sharing in Jesus' own mission and ministry. The sacramentality of bishops is theological and christological; it is not papal.[50]

The implications of this major change with regard to sacramental episcopacy seriously affect a contemporary bishop's relation to the papacy, his own self-identity, and his relationship to the priests, deacons, and the lay men and women who have special official ministries within his diocese. The reestablishment of sacramental episcopacy, therefore, has far-reaching, highly sensitive, and multi-interrelational dimensions, each of which needs careful

---

48. See the insightful presentation of post-tridentine ecclesiology by Michael J. Himes, "The Development of Ecclesiology: Modernity to the Twentieth Century," in *Gift of the Church*, 45–67.

49. For the intervention of Gomes dos Santos, see Kloppenburg, *The Ecclesiology of Vatican II*, 218–19.

50. See Philips, *La Chiesa e il suo Mistero*, 223–33.

explanation. These dimensions affect the *theology* of episcopacy, the *pastoral practice* of episcopacy, and the *self-identity* of a bishop.

From a theological standpoint, paragraph 21 in *Lumen gentium* is monumental. For the first time since 1150, the magisterium of the Western church officially acknowledged episcopacy as part of the sacrament of orders. For a theologian this magisterial statement is very telling. Most authors on the history of the sacrament of orders admit that from Trent to Vatican II a large number of theologians did indeed advocate that episcopacy was a part of that sacrament. However, the theologians had no magisterial statement on which they could base their argument, not even statements from the Council of Trent. From 1150 to the eve of Vatican II, the teaching on episcopacy as part of the sacrament of orders was simply a theological opinion held by a large number of eminent theologians, and the value of their opinion relied solely on the theological argumentation they assembled. What the bishops at Vatican II accomplished in a monumental way was this: *they made the theological opinion of episcopal sacramentality a matter of magisterial teaching.*

Since this major change has had repercussions on all of the institutional church ministries including the papacy, some historical background is needed. A full presentation of all the details that led up to this magisterial approval of the sacramental nature of episcopacy is beyond the limits of this present work. Therefore, I will focus briefly on two historical issues that constitute the background for the change made at Vatican II.

Some permanent deacons who are reading these pages might say: "Why do we have to go through all this historical and theological material on bishops? Isn't the theme of this book the renewal of the permanent diaconate?" These are excellent—and valid—questions, and I want to reply as follows. Whenever one ministry is substantially changed within a tightly interrelated understanding of church mission, ministry, and leadership, all the other key ministries will be affected. In an interrelational network of ministry, one cannot change in a major way one solitary ministry without affecting all the other key ministries. Second, all the key ecclesial ministries have indeed changed over the centuries. The view that an understanding of bishop, priest, or deacon has remained theologically and practically identical since the time of

Jesus himself is a chimera. Change in these ministries has taken place, and this means for us today that ministerial changes now and in the future can also be made. History gives us freedom, and this is why we need to reconsider the histories of these various ministries. The present permanent diaconate needs to move with freedom into its own future.

The Historical Background for a Lay/Cleric Church That Became Standard from Medieval Times to Vatican II

In the middle years of the twelfth century, Gratian [d. ca. 1180], a Camaldolese monk and an Italian jurist, taught church law at the University of Bologna. He compiled a brilliant book entitled *Concordia Discordantium Canonum* [Concordance of Discordant Canons]. Gratian's book, which gained the new title *Decretum Gratiani*, eventually became *the* leading textbook for doctoral students of law in almost all the medieval European universities. In his book, Gratian emphasized a twofold canonical distinction of the entire institutional church: namely, the clerics on the one hand, and the laity on the other. As his book gradually became the common textbook, Gratian's twofold distinction (cleric/lay) also became the common *canonical* understanding of ecclesiology. In a short time, this common canonical position was taken over by medieval theologians, and the twofold distinction of the institutional church became a theological as well as a canonical position. However, the dual distinction cleric/lay did not remain in academic halls. It rapidly became a major part of the dominant and operative pastoral life of the Roman Catholic Church. By the fourteenth century, a lay/cleric division of the church was part and parcel of the dominant, operative theology of the Western church. From Gratian's time down to the Council of Trent there were *no* books that focused exclusively on a theology of church. None of the great thirteenth- and fourteenth-century theologians, such as Alexander of Hales, Albert the Great, Thomas Aquinas, Bonaventure, and John Duns Scotus, wrote a book or a section of a book on *De ecclesia* [On the church]. When the Protestant Reformation began and during the years of the Council of Trent, both Protestant and Roman Catholic theologians had basically no theological texts on ecclesiology.

It was only *after* the Council of Trent that the first books on ecclesiology began to appear. In the Roman Catholic world, the books that dealt with a theology of the church made the dual distinction of lay/cleric an essential part of their presentation. They did this because the ecclesiologies written from the end of the Council of Trent down to Vatican II were by and large apologetic. The treatises on the church stressed the position that *only* the Roman Catholic Church—in clear distinction from any and all Protestant churches—was apostolic. *Only* the Roman Catholic Church went back to the apostles, whom Jesus himself had selected as the founding leaders of his church. These apostles, in turn, selected bishops as their successors, and the bishops, as successors of the apostles, subsequently chose priests to be their own helpers. In these books on ecclesiology it was argued that the Roman Catholic Church is apostolic because of its apostolic succession, which included both the apostolic succession of popes and the apostolic succession of bishops. Clergy, therefore, as a distinct class was presented in these books on ecclesiology as a foundational dimension of the apostolicity of the Roman Catholic Church.

Protestant churches emphasized the priesthood of all believers. Both Luther and Calvin had written some very critical pages on popes and bishops. There appeared to be an anticleric tendency in Protestant thought, and Roman Catholic writers, therefore, challenged the lay tendencies and the anticleric tendencies of Protestant thought with a strong defense of the lay/clergy division of the church. This lay/cleric division, these authors wrote, goes back to Jesus and the apostles. Consequently, in the ecclesiologies apostolic succession became the clearest identification of the only true church of Jesus Christ.

The defense of the lay/cleric division was strongly reformulated after the American and French Revolutions, when once again there was a tendency to stress, on the one hand, the equality of all people, which was found in the Declaration of Independence of the United States of America. On the other hand, the French motto, *Liberté, Egalité, Fraternité*, with its own anticlericalism as expressed during the French Revolution, caused the Roman Catholic Church, particularly in Rome itself, to defend in no uncertain terms the lay/cleric division of the one true church. Later in the nineteenth century, the inroads of the Enlightenment contributed to this challenge of anticlericalism in Europe, and the defense of the lay/cleric church from 1840 to the eve of Vatican II was made over and over again. Even Vatican I (1869–1870) stressed the lay/cleric church in a defensive way.

However, the church as essentially divided into lay and cleric is only a part of the historical background. A second historical issue that contributed to the clerical emphasis dominated the Roman Catholic Church from 1200 to the eve of Vatican II.

The Historical Background for the Nonepiscopal Understanding of the Sacrament of Holy Orders from Medieval Times to Vatican II

Peter Lombard (ca. 1100–1160) lived at the same time as Gratian. In 1150, Peter Lombard published his own book, *Libri IV Sententiarum* [The Four Books of Sentences]. By 1200 his book was well on the way to becoming the common textbook for doctoral theology students in the medieval universities. In his book, Peter Lombard considered the various traditional positions on the sacrament of orders. One of the key issues focused on the question: Which church orders belong to the sacrament of orders? At that time, there were many minor orders (porter, lector, acolyte, exorcist) as also major orders (subdiaconate, diaconate, and priesthood). In the traditional teaching, Peter Lombard noted that some scholars included episcopacy as one of the major orders. Peter Lombard, along with many other renowned theologians, did not favor the view that episcopacy was part of the sacrament of orders. Peter Lombard subscribed to the view that there were only *two* orders that belonged essentially to this sacrament: diaconate and priesthood. In the course of time, Peter Lombard's position that only two orders constituted this sacrament became the common tradition. Thomas Aquinas, Bonaventure, and John Duns Scotus followed

Peter Lombard's view, and their influence became very strong from the thirteenth to the sixteenth century.

If episcopacy was *not* part of the sacrament of orders, what was it? Medieval and Renaissance theologians considered episcopacy an institutional office and an institutional dignity in the church. The reasons for excluding episcopacy from this sacrament continued to be based on Peter Lombard's arguments: namely, priesthood was the highest order since *only* the priest could change the bread and wine into the body and blood of Christ in the sacrament of the Eucharist, and only the priest was able to take away sin, especially mortal sin, in the sacrament of reconciliation. The diaconate was a major order of this sacrament since in that period of time deacons were eucharistically centered. Episcopacy added nothing to this highest order and therefore was not regarded as part of the sacrament of orders.[51]

The Council of Trent did not change this theological presentation of the sacrament of orders.[52] From the Council of Trent down to the eve of Vatican II, a defense of sacramental episcopacy became only a theological opinion. No magisterial statement of the church could be found to defend sacramental episcopacy. This situation is evident in one of the best theological textbooks produced in the twentieth century. In 1962, the Jesuit theologian Francisco

---

51. It has been argued that only a bishop could ordain a person to major orders. However, in the fifteenth century there are papal bulls allowing priests (usually an abbot) to ordain to the priesthood. See Osborne, *Priesthood*, 262–63. Moreover, in the fourth century, a few deacons were placed in charge of rural communities, and it appears that these deacons celebrated the Eucharist. At the Council of Arles (314) and the Council of Ancira (314) such eucharistic celebrations by deacons were on the agenda. See also Edward Echlin, *The Deacon in the Church, Past and Future* (New York: Alba House, 1971), 54.

52. In the various manuals of theology, the presentation of the Council of Trent on episcopacy as sacramental varies from author to author; see Ludwig Ott, *Das Weihesakrament* (Freiburg: Herder, 1969), 119–27. From September 18, 1562, to July 14, 1563, the tridentine bishops heard and read arguments for and against the source of a bishop's power and jurisdiction. At the center of this argumentation was the role of the pope vis-à-vis bishops. A complete resolution of this issue was not attained. The order of priests culminated in the power to celebrate the Eucharist and to forgive sins. There is, Trent notes, a hierarchy in the Roman Catholic Church that consists of bishops, priests, and lesser ministers. Bishops are superior to priests hierarchically, but sacramentally bishops and priests are equal.

Solá, in the four-volume *Sacrae Theologiae Summa*, defended the thesis: *Episcopus est verum Sacramentum Novae Legis* (Episcopacy is a true sacrament of the New Law).[53] The year 1962 is, of course, the same year in which the opening session of Vatican II took place. Solá, just prior to the section on episcopacy, had presented two other theses: (1) *Ordo est verum Novae Legis Sacramentum* (Order is a true sacrament of the New Law); and (2) *Ordo Presbyteratus habet veram et propriam rationem Sacramenti* (The order of the presbyterate has a true and proper reality of sacrament). His first thesis on holy order itself has a dogmatic value: *De fide divina et catholica definita* (of divine and catholic defined faith). Solá cites the Second Council of Lyon (1274) and the Council of Trent (1545–1563) to establish the defined nature for the theological evaluation.[54] His second thesis on the priesthood as a true sacrament has a similar dogmatic value: *de fide divina et catholica definita*. Solá cites the Council of Florence (1431–1445) and especially the Council of Trent for a basis for the defined status of his thesis.[55]

For the third thesis on sacramental episcopacy, the dogmatic value is entirely different: "The thesis, insofar as it is understood as referring to episcopacy in opposition to the presbyterate, is certain and common" *(Thesis, prout intelligitur de episcopatu per oppositione ad presbyteratum, est certa et communis)*. These are telling words. Solá can only cite major theologians who help substantiate the "certain and common position": Robert Bellarmine, Pedro Soto, Heinrich Lennerz, Adolphe Alfred Tanquerey, and Pietro Gasparri.[56]

A discussion of the dogmatic value of theological positions undoubtedly must sound very pedantic. However, the issues of dogmatic value are extremely important from a theological standpoint. Solá is simply one Roman Catholic theologian among many, and I cite him only because his work, written in the very same year as the opening of Vatican II, is so thorough. Solá, together with many other Roman Catholic theologians prior to Vatican II, could argue for episcopacy as a part of the sacrament of orders only on

---

53. Francisco Solá, "De sacramento ordinis," in *Sacrae Theologiae Summa* IV (Madrid: Biblioteca de Autores Cristianos, 1962), 596.
54. Ibid., 578.
55. Ibid., 591.
56. Ibid., 598–99.

the basis of a common theological view. The argument for the presbyter as part of the sacrament of orders was made on the basis of
the magisterium, especially the clear statements found in the documents of the Council of Trent. Besides Solá and the theologians
he mentions, many other Roman Catholic theologians prior to
Vatican II had also argued the case for episcopacy as one of the
orders in this sacrament, and they argued their position in exactly
the same way Solá does. The view of sacramental episcopacy was
common among many theologians, but the view was based on theological reasoning. From 1150 to Vatican II there is *no* statement by
the magisterium that definitely indicates that episcopacy is an integral part of the sacrament of orders. Priesthood and diaconate were
the integrating orders in this sacrament.

In other words, officially from 1150 to Vatican II, the popes
and the papal Curia never magisterially endorsed episcopacy as
sacramental. For the official church, episcopacy was a major institutional office *(officium)* and a major institutional dignity *(dignitas)*.
The relationship of papacy to episcopacy was through office and
dignity, not through sacramentality. It is precisely this relationship
that Bishop Fernando Gomes dos Santos challenged. Bishops are
not vicars of the papacy, and, even more emphatically, they are *not*
vicars of the congregations.

When, therefore, the bishops at Vatican II made the following
statement, a foundational and monumental change took place.

> This sacred Synod teaches that by episcopal consecra-
> tion is conferred the fullness of the sacrament of orders,
> that fullness which in the Church's liturgical practice and
> in the language of the holy Fathers of the Church is
> undoubtedly called the high priesthood, the apex of the
> sacred ministry. (*LG* 21)

With Vatican II, the Roman Catholic Church had expressed
for the first time since 1150 a magisterial statement on the sacramentality of episcopacy. Theologians no longer needed to say: *certa
et communis*—common and certain in theology. Theologians can
now cite a magisterial statement, made in an official way by bishops at an ecumenical council. This conciliar statement, however, is

not an infallible, *de fide definita*, statement, but it is a statement of the magisterium. Episcopal sacramentality is no longer simply one among several theological opinions. The magisterium has officially endorsed the view of episcopal sacramentality, although they did not do so via an infallible decree.

A statement, however, is one thing; actual acceptance of a statement and an acceptance of its implications is another thing. In the postconciliar process, episcopal sacramentality has been accepted. The implications of episcopal sacramentality have, as yet, not been accepted. The cause for this hesitation to accept the theological and practical implications rests squarely on the issue of interrelationship. Let us consider some of the major interrelational issues that have immediately arisen over the inclusion of episcopacy into the sacrament of orders. To do this, I will use conciliar material that explains what the bishops meant when they taught that episcopacy was the fullness of priesthood in the sacrament of orders.[57]

Bishops are now part of the sacrament of orders, and the documents of Vatican II emphasize this by saying that bishops enjoy the "fullness of the priesthood." What does this phrase "fullness of the priesthood," mean? Nowhere in the texts and documents of Vatican II is there a clear definition of the phrase, "fullness of the priesthood." Its use in conjunction with episcopal sacramentality indicates that the sacramental ordination of a bishop *cannot* be considered an eighth sacrament. For the bishops at Vatican II, episcopal sacramentality is part of one of the seven sacraments, the sacrament of orders.[58] In other words, episcopacy and priesthood are *not* separate even though the names are different. However, the bishops also wanted to say that episcopacy is not totally identical with priesthood. To indicate this difference, the phrase "fullness of priesthood" was chosen. It was left to further theological work to clarify its meaning.

---

57. Philips, *La Chiesa e il suo Mistero*, 224–25.

58. Some theologians from Trent to Vatican II had even suggested that episcopal sacramentality was an additional sacrament of the church. This was not a common opinion, and the bishops at Vatican II taught that episcopal sacramentality is part of the sacrament of orders, not a new and different sacrament. See Philips, *La Chiesa e il suo Mistero*, 218–25.

However, the phrase has caused theological, pastoral, and personal problematic issues. If the bishop is the fullness of the priesthood, what is the theological, pastoral, and personal-identity meaning of the presbyter? In what way is the presbyter a "lesser" priest? What are the borders between "fullness of the priesthood" and "less-than-fullness of the priesthood"? If the episcopacy constitutes the fullness of priesthood, what is the self-identity of a "less-than-full" priest? The same type of argument holds for the meaning of the deacon, permanent and transitional, as far as the sacrament of orders is concerned. Is the sacrament of orders greater and more eminent in a bishop than in a deacon? Is the diaconate only a lesser sacrament of orders? All the issues that this undefined phrase has engendered have a strong focus on interrelationality. How can one theologically, pastorally, and personally interrelate "fullness of priesthood" with "less-than-fullness of priesthood"? Or, in the case of a deacon, an interrelationship of "fullness of a sacrament" with "less-than-fullness of sacrament"? The answer to this remains a task for future theologians.[59]

A second implication arises. Episcopal sacramentality can be understood only on the basis of the Roman Catholic teaching on sacramentality itself. In the standard theology on sacraments, the phrase *vi sacramenti* plays an essential role. The phrase *vi sacramenti*—by the power of the sacrament itself—is related to several other sensitive sacramental issues. One of these is the distinction between *ex opere operato* and *ex opere operantis*. Another issue is the causality of the sacraments, for the sacramental causality is attributed to the sacramental reality *vi sacramenti*. Another issue to which *vi sacramenti* is closely allied is the church's teaching on sacramental character. Since the character is impressed on the soul *vi sacramenti*, it can never be taken away. Other serious issues are also connected to the phrase *vi sacramenti;* these serious issues focus on the intention of the minister and on the faith and moral character of the minister. Does an imperfect intention falsify a sacramental act? Does a minister's lack of Christian faith falsify a sacramental act? Does the

---

59. In many dioceses in the United States, the morale of the priests is at low tide. One of the issues that causes this low morale is priestly identity. To be a "lesser priest" or a not "fully priest" cannot help but cause identity issues.

sinfulness of a minister falsify a sacramental act? In all three cases, the answer is negative, since the sacrament's effect does not come from a minister's totally proper intention, nor does it come from a minister's faith, nor does it depend on a minister's moral qualifications. Rather, *vi sacramenti* indicates that those involved in the sacramental action, even when a priest is subjectively deficient, are indeed blessed with God's loving grace.

When we apply *vi sacramenti* to episcopal sacramentality, then we must say that a man becomes a bishop not because of papal selection. Rather, it is precisely in the sacramental act itself, that is, *vi sacramenti*, that God and God alone calls and commissions a person to be a bishop. Sacramentally ordained bishops are bishops in their own right; they are not delegates or vicars of the pope. At Vatican II, the interrelationship between pope and bishop was changed. The complaint that Bishop Gomes dos Santos had made in 1963 focused directly on the issue of papal vicar. Gomes dos Santos had stated that the initial position paper "makes the bishops simply vicars not only of the pope but even of the Roman Congregations on which the bishops are to depend in the least detail." What is, today, the correct relationship of a bishop to the pope? Some might say: papal appointment. However, the papal appointment of bishops is simply a juridical act. It is *not* a sacramental act.

No bishop, however, is an *episcopus nullius*, a bishop with no specific community.[60] God calls and commissions a bishop to be a bishop for an existential community. By establishing the bishop within the sacrament of orders, the question of the relationship of the existential community to its bishop reemerges. Does a community have a say as to who its bishop should be? If the bishop is simply a vicar of the pope, he is sent by the pope. If the bishop is called and commissioned by God and this call and commissioning are celebrated in a sacrament, then the long church history of a community's election of its own bishop, of choosing its own bishop, and of selecting its own bishop gains momentum. Until roughly AD 1000, an ecclesial community played in one way or another a major role in the selection process of its own bishop. Even after AD 1000, many

---

60. In the history of the church, a few men were *episcopi nullius*, bishops with no specific community. This situation was condemned again and again.

kings and princes continued to have a major voice in the selection process of bishops for their particular countries. History clearly indicates that bishops have *not always* been appointed by the pope. Papal appointment of bishops on a large scale is a part of Catholic life only from later times onward. Papal appointments of bishops cannot be historically validated as an unchanging situation in the Western church. Even today, the bishops of the Eastern churches are recognized by the Roman Catholic Church as true sacramental bishops, yet not a single one of them has been appointed by a pope. Papal appointment of bishops is simply a matter of a late tradition in the church. Without any doubt current discussion on this issue makes the papacy uneasy. Nonetheless, lay involvement in the selection of hierarchy has had a long, long history in the Roman Catholic Church. The lengthy span of lay involvement is yet another indication of the interrelationship of all institutional church ministries. The questions of interrelationality will not go away. Rather, the questions will only become more pointed and pressing, because interrelationality is an integral part of all church ministries.

In summary, we can say that the conciliar bishops at Vatican II made a major, even monumental, change in the theological, pastoral, and personal understanding of episcopacy. The texts are abundantly clear on this issue of major change. The acceptance of the change has taken place in a generalized way. Collegiality of bishops has been accepted, but for some the acceptance is minimal. The relationship of bishop as fullness of priest to the ordinary priest has been accepted, but no effort has officially been made to clarify what fullness of priesthood means. More egregious, however, is the unspoken and unwritten nonacceptance that ministerial priesthood in its totality, that is, both bishops and presbyters, is intrinsically related to the priesthood of all Christians. Any meaningful or foundational interrelationality between the two remains, for the most part, unaccepted. The role of a permanent deacon in the sacrament of orders has also been challenged by the inclusion of episcopacy into this sacrament, but the inclusion means that the "fullness of the sacrament" is found in a bishop, leaving a permanent deacon in some undefined "less-than-fullness" situation.

Chapter Six

THE REDEFINITION OF PRIESTHOOD: THE THIRD MAJOR CONCILIAR CHANGE IN MINISTRY

The third major change for a theology of institutional ecclesial ministry made by the bishops at Vatican II focused on the redefinition of priesthood. The history of the conciliar documents has been traced in detail in several works; it is not my purpose in this volume to readdress this history, but a brief overview is in order.[61] In the responses to the initial questionnaire sent out to the bishops of the world by Pope John XXIII, shortly after his announcement of the council on January 25, 1959, the life of priests was considered too important a topic to treat only in a passing way.[62] The responses to this inquiry were compiled by a special commission in book form, the very size of which indicated the worldwide concern for priestly life. Most of the responses were largely juridical in nature. On June 5, 1960, John XXIII established a Commissio de Disciplina Cleri et Populi Christiani, which prepared a number of drafts that would later be given to the conciliar bishops. In November 1963, the conciliar bishops changed the name of this compendium of drafts to *De Sacerdotibus* (On Priests). A commission of bishops was appointed to consider the compendium. Further changes were made, and the document was reduced to ten principles and a *relatio* (explanatory statement) describing the history of

---

61. Osborne, *Priesthood*: 308 n. 1.
62. Ibid., 309.

the document and rationale of its structure. On September 14, 1964, the council officially took up this draft and made substantial changes in it. The name was also changed to *De Vita et Ministerio Sacerdotali* (On the Life and Ministry of Priests). From October 13 to November 14, forty-one bishops spoke on the subject of the priestly document. The dissatisfaction of the bishops was clearly and strongly stated. A new revision was mandated, and from February through May 1965, the commission, now chaired by Bishop François Marty, studied all the *modi* (suggested revisions) that the conciliar bishops had submitted. On October 14, 1965, the revised document was discussed in a plenary session. On December 2, 1965, the final text was voted on, and on December 7, 1965, the text was promulgated by Pope Paul VI.

In one of the key plenary sessions of the bishops at Vatican II, Bishop Marty spoke very forthrightly on the meaning of priest that the vast majority of the bishops wanted. His words are of major importance.

> The commission cannot agree with those Fathers who think the position paper should have followed the scholastic definition of priesthood, which is based on the power to consecrate the eucharist. According to the prevailing mind of this Council and the petition of many Fathers, the priesthood of presbyters must rather be connected with the priesthood of bishops, the latter being regarded as the high point and fullness of priesthood. The priesthood of presbyters must therefore be looked at, in this draft, as embracing not one function, but three, and must be linked with the Apostles and their mission.[63]

Marty's words were deliberately chosen. A nonscholastic definition of priesthood had been developed by the council and the traditional scholastic definition of priesthood was not endorsed. A number of factors redefined the meaning of priest in a major way:

1. The priesthood of holy orders *includes the bishop as the fullness of priesthood*. The phrase "fullness of priesthood" was

---

63. Ibid., 318.

left undefined, as we have seen, and because of this nonde-
finition difficulties have arisen.

2. The priesthood of holy orders is *to be defined by the tria
munera*, not by the power to consecrate bread and wine into
the body and blood of Christ in the Eucharist and by the
power to forgive sin in the sacrament of reconciliation.

3. The priesthood of holy orders is *defined interrelationally*. The
term *collegial* was not used for priestly interrelationality.
Rather, the phrase "the priesthood of presbyters" must
include the "priesthood of a bishop." The interrelational
word for this connection is *presbyterium*, and a *presbyterium* of
a diocese includes *de iure* both the ordained priests and the
ordained bishops of a diocese.

Since the third issue has caused the most difficulties for
acceptance of this new definition of priesthood, it will be necessary
to focus more strongly on this issue. The starting point for this is
the rejection of the former scholastic definition of priesthood.
Kloppenburg describes the situation in a stark and preemptive way:
"The Commission which worked on the *Decree of the Ministry and
Life of Priests* called such a definition the scholastic definition of
priesthood, and Vatican II abandoned it once and for all."[64]

One can legitimately ask: In the postconciliar church has the
once-and-for-all abandonment of the scholastic definition of
priesthood been accepted or not? Given the writings on priesthood
by several church officials and theological scholars, the answer
appears to be negative. These writers apparently have not accepted
the Vatican II abandonment of the scholastic definition of priesthood. Rather, these authors continue to state that the scholastic
definition of priesthood remains *the Roman Catholic definition of
priesthood*. In a recent volume written by Cardinal Justin Rigali entitled *I Call You Friends: The Priesthood—Merciful Love*, one reads the
following in the opening paragraphs: "You received your mission
from our Lord Jesus Christ."[65] By itself, this sentence relates well to
Vatican II. However, ten lines further on one reads: "You were

---

64. Kloppenburg, *The Ecclesiology of Vatican II*, 267.
65. Rigali, *I Call You Friends: The Priesthood: Merciful Love*, 2.

being called above all to become ministers of the Eucharist," and on the very next page the text reads: "In the very act of the Eucharist, you are the ministers of forgiveness." The text continues: "This ministry of forgiveness will be applied to individual hearts by the Sacrament of Confession."[66] Remarkably, there is no mention of preaching the Word of God, which Vatican II over and over again presented as the primary task of a priest, nor is there any mention of the *tria munera*. Instead, we are faced with a scholastic view of priesthood, centered in the power to consecrate the bread and wine and the power to forgive sin. This is what the priest, in Rigali's words, is called on to do. In chapter 9, mention *is* made of preaching the Word of God: "The content of evangelization hence takes on for us in our a ministry a great significance."[67] However, there is a world of difference between his statement that a priest has been called above all to be a minister of the Eucharist and the position of John Paul II in *Pastores dabo vobis*, namely:

> Thanks to the insightful teaching of the Second Vatican Council, we can grasp the conditions and demands, the manifestations and fruits of the intimate bond between the priest's spiritual life and the exercise of his threefold ministry of word, sacrament and pastoral charity. The priest is first of all *a minister of the Word of God*. (26; emphasis original)

The *tria munera* understanding of priesthood was neither the scholastic view of priesthood nor the view found in the Council of Trent. Eucharist and confession are not at the center of the *tria munera*; they are at the center of the scholastic and tridentine definition of priest. In the documents of Trent we read that priests receive *potestatem consecrandi, offerendi et ministrandi corpus et sanguinem Domini Nostri Iesus Christi, necnon et peccata dimittendi et retinendi* (the power of consecrating, offering, and ministering the body and blood of our Lord Jesus Christ and also the power of forgiving and retaining sin) (Denzinger 957). In this scholastic view, only the priest is able

---

66. Ibid., 2–3.
67. Ibid., 37.

to perform these sacred mysteries. The power is given *vi sacramenti* and is therefore a *potestas ordinis* not a *potestas iurisdictionis*. In the scholastic view, this is what defines the priest. It is a definition of priest that radically separates the priest from all other Catholic Christians.

As we have seen above, Bishop Marty clearly told the conciliar bishops that this scholastic definition was not the definition that the majority of the bishops at Vatican II wanted to use. Rather, the majority of the bishops wanted the *tria munera* to define priesthood. The scholastic definition of priesthood is limited to a sacramental focus; the *tria munera* witness to the mission and ministry of Jesus himself. Therefore, any definition or description of today's Roman Catholic priest must center on the *tria munera*, that is, an understanding of today's priesthood that is founded on the sharing of the *tria munera* of Jesus himself, which all Christians have, and that is even more deeply based on the *tria munera* of Jesus' own mission and ministry, which was given to him by the Triune God. Any definition of priesthood today that is not clearly elaborated within this framework is a definition that the Second Vatican Council has clearly rejected.

The issue, however, goes further. Most authors who stress an isolated, radically different type of definition for priests do mention the *tria munera* of all Christians. After mentioning such a relationship, however, they make no effort to integrate it into their presentation of priest. The conciliar bishops made a deliberate change in the construction of *Lumen gentium* when they placed the material on the people of God in the second chapter and the material on the hierarchy in the third chapter. There was a very solid ecclesiological reason for this change. Only on the basis of a total vision of the church can a hierarchical structure make sense.

> Il populo di Dio no è altro in realtà, che la manifestazione terrestre del mistero della chiesa....Una seconda considerazione sottolinea che nella Chiesa vi sono *diverse categorie* di cui non si potrebbe valutare esattamente e pienamente la funzione se si trascura di situare questi gruppi subordinati *nell'insieme del Populo di Dio*.[68]

---

68. Philips, *La Chiesa e il suo Mistero*, 120–21.

> The people of God is in reality nothing other than the earthly manifestation of the mystery of the church.... A second consideration stresses that in the church there are *diverse categories* whose functions cannot be exactly and fully defined unless the subordinate group is *situated within the people of God*. (emphasis original)

Context and interrelationship play a major role for the understanding of each and every institutional ministry and leadership role in the church. On the issue of the context and interrelationship of priesthood, *Pastores dabo vobis* is categorically clear. As far as context is concerned, the very word *contextualize* is used by John Paul II to describe the subtitle of the exhortation.

> For this reason the Synod desired to "contextualize" the subject of priests, viewing it in terms of today's society and today's Church in preparation for the third millennium. This is indicated in the second part of the topic's formulation: "The formation of priest in the circumstances of the present day." (5)

As far as interrelationship is concerned, the exhortation provides numerous citations. The following simply offer a small indication of priestly interrelationality.

> The priest's identity [described by the Synod Father], like every Christian identity, has its source in the Blessed Trinity. (12)

> The priest, by virtue of the consecration which he receives in the Sacrament of Orders, is sent forth by the Father, through the mediatorship of Jesus Christ,...in order to live and work by the power of the Holy Spirit. (12)

> Consequently, the nature and mission of the ministerial priesthood cannot be defined except through this multiple and rich interconnection of relationships which arise

from the Blessed Trinity and are prolonged in the communion of the church. (12)

In this context the ecclesiology of communion becomes decisive for understanding the identity of the priest, his essential dignity, and his vocation and mission. (12)

Jesus thus established a close relationship between the ministry entrusted to the Apostles and his own mission. (14)

The priest's fundamental relationship is to Jesus Christ, Head and Shepherd. (16)

By its very nature, the ordained ministry can be carried out only to the extent that the priest is united to Christ. (17)

The ordained ministry has a radical *communitarian form* and can only be carried out as a collective work. (17; emphasis original)

In no. 26, John Paul II presents the priest within the *tria munera* framework which the bishops at Vatican II endorsed. He places the ministry of the Word as the first *munus* of the priest. The second *munus* is the work of sanctification, and the third *munus* is the encouraging and leading of the ecclesial community. In all of these statements from *Pastores dabo vobis*—and many more could be cited—we hear the basic orientation of the conciliar bishops regarding institutional ecclesial ministry and its application to the ministry of the presbyter.

The ecclesiology of Vatican II parts company with the apologetic ecclesiologies that dominated Roman Catholic thought prior to the council. In the apologetic ecclesiologies, the stress on apostolicity dominates. The ecclesiology of Vatican II takes a holistic view. If one does not understand the contextual and interrelational nature of the church, one will never understand the meaning of institutional church ministry and leadership in its specific categories. Joseph Komonchak's essay "The Local Realization of the Church" offers a well-stated context of today's Roman Catholic

Church, which finds itself in a minority situation worldwide and in areas that are overwhelmingly non-Christian and are multicultural in a global way. Komonchak's presentation makes one realize more clearly that today's global context for the Roman Catholic Church differs enormously from preceding contexts.[69] In the same volume, Giuseppe Ruggieri offers us an essay entitled "Faith and History." In this essay, Ruggieri opens up a different context, namely, that of church history. Since the Council of Trent and the subsequent, one-sided, apologetic theology of the church, most Roman Catholic leaders remained complacent in a context that pictured only a small segment of the rich and diverse history of the Christian community.[70] These leaders became comfortable in the cocoon of this small segment, and Vatican II clearly invited us to see the wider and transcending horizons of Christian history. In a cocoon existence, the issues of nonacceptance seem so easy; in a larger horizon, the issues of nonacceptance are far more complex.

Jean Galot, in his volume *Theology of the Priesthood*, represents one of the leading authors who is very uneasy about a redefinition of priesthood based on the texts and documents of Vatican II. He begins his argument with a chapter on a "mystery" of the priestly character.[71] Such a beginning repeats the pre–Vatican II textbook theology of priesthood such as one finds in the writings of Francisco Solá.[72] Galot writes: "What distinguishes the priestly character from the character impressed by baptism and confirmation is that man's being is conformed to Christ the Shepherd."[73] A page later, Galot unites his understanding of Christ the Shepherd to Christ the Head. It is precisely this distinction, produced by the sacramental character, that gives the true definition of the priest: the priest acts "in the person of Christ the Head." Galot rightly cites *Presbyterorum ordinis* 2,

---

69. Joseph Komonchak, "The Local Realization of the Church," in *The Reception of Vatican II*, 77–90.

70. Giusseppe Ruggieri, "Faith and History," in *The Reception of Vatican II*, 91–114.

71. Galot, *Theology of the Priesthood*, 201.

72. Solá, 683–88.

73. Galot, *Theology of the Priesthood*, 207.

where this position is stated. However, Marty's statement above does not move in the same direction that Galot takes, and Marty was the chair of the committee that wrote the document on priesthood. Marty told the plenary session that the scholastic definition is no longer dominant; the dominance now comes from the *tria munera*. Marty makes no mention of a theology of priesthood based on sacramental character. For Galot, however, the sacramental priestly character is not only the radical and distinctive characteristic of the priest, but it is also the basis for the *tria munera* mission of a priest. This priestly mission is "essentially" (Galot's terms are *ontologically* and *radically*) different from the *tria munera* ministry and mission of the baptized and the confirmed. Galot is certainly free to make theological statements, just as all theologians can do. What Galot cannot do is make his theological statements the teaching of Vatican II.

Nowhere in his volume does Galot attempt to interrelate the priesthood of all the baptized with the priesthood of the clergy. Rather, his effort is to separate them. The sixth chapter of his book is entitled "The Priesthood of the Faithful and the Ministerial Priesthood."[74] In this chapter, Galot's major issue is to indicate the total difference between the two; he shows no interest in their foundational interrelationship. He writes as we noted above: "In conclusion, the difference between the universal and the ministerial priesthood is a *radical* one with respect to both consecration and mission."[75] It is helpful to read the lengthy section in Gérard Philips's *La Chiesa e il suo Mistero* on this issue of the distinction between the priesthood of all believers and the priesthood that we celebrate in the sacrament of holy orders.[76] Philips was intimately connected to the actual writing of *Lumen gentium* and was privy to all the discussions on this issue of distinguishing the two priesthoods. Galot, on the other hand, does not indicate any details of the lengthy discussions by the bishops at Vatican II nor their hesitancy to clarify the distinction. Even the phrase the bishops finally used, "essentially and not only in

---

74. Ibid., 105–28.
75. Ibid., 119 (emphasis added).
76. Philips, *La Chiesa e il suo Mistero*, 129–39.

degree," was intended to leave the doors of theological research open, since the massive amount of material from the fathers of the church indicated to the bishops that the distinction could move in several directions. Galot, on the other hand, presents his clarification as the only correct one.

The *Instruction on Certain Questions Regarding the Collaboration of the Non-Ordained Faithful in the Sacred Ministry of Priests*, issued by six congregations and two pontifical councils on August 15, 1997, does not resolve the theological issue regarding the distinction between the priesthood from baptism-confirmation and the priesthood from holy orders. In its opening section on "Theological Principles," we find some key statements:

> Thus the essential difference between the common priesthood of the faithful and the ministerial priesthood is not found in the priesthood of Christ, which remains forever one and indivisible.[77]

> Nor is the difference found "in the sanctity to which all the faithful are called. 'Indeed the ministerial priesthood does not of itself signify a greater degree of holiness with regard to the common priesthood of the faithful.'" [The instruction cites John Paul II, *Pastores dabo vobis* 17.][78]

Both of these initial principles are negative, but they are profoundly important. They tell us not to go in these two directions. In what directions, then, should we go? On the positive issue, the *Instruction* does not present a convincing position. The ministerial priesthood, the *Instruction* states, is:

> Rooted in the apostolic succession and vested with *"potestas sacra"* consisting of the faculty and the responsibility of acting in the person of Christ the Head and the

---

77. *Instruction on Certain Questions Regarding the Collaboration of the Non-Ordained Faithful in the Sacred Ministry of Priests* (Washington, DC: USCCB, 1998), 6.
78. Ibid.

Shepherd.[79] [The instruction cites *Pastores dabo vobis* 15 and the *Catechism*, 875.]

It is a priesthood which renders its sacred ministers servants of Christ and of the church by means of authoritative proclamation of the Word of God, the administration of the sacraments and the pastoral direction of the faithful.[80]

The mere stating of these two positive principles does not present a convincing argument. First of all, the two statements are based not on the texts of Vatican II documents but rather on an encyclical and a catechism. Second, in the USCCB edition of the English text of the *Instruction*, only six small pages are devoted to "Theological Principles," and in six pages it is impossible to settle all the issues that have arisen in the postconciliar church on the matter of this distinction. Because of the brevity, the six pages present not an overview but a particular view. The particular view lacks depth of presentation, for it simply states one position but does not delve into the ramifications and objections that are found in the abundant contemporary literature on the issue of this distinction. Third, the introductory material—and the authors meant it to be only introductory—is theologically thin and noncompelling. The main issues with which the *Instruction* deals are found in the lengthy second section, "Practical Provisions," which covers twenty pages of the booklet. Most of these main issues are canonical rather than doctrinal or theological.[81]

---

79. Ibid., 7.

80. Ibid., 8.

81. After this *Instruction* appeared, several dioceses asked me to come and review the instruction with the presbyterium and in some instances also with the diaconate and the laity. I analyzed each of the paragraphs in my preparation for these conferences and presented as best I could the intent and meaning of the *Instruction*, but also noting the limitations of the *Instruction*. The brief section on "Theological Principles" (6–12) makes no effort to indicate the current biblical, historical, and theological questioning of the positions presented; the larger section on "Practical Provisions" (13–31) is basically a restatement of canon law.

Collegiality of priests is also part of today's identification or definition of priesthood.[82] As we have seen above, collegiality affects the papacy and its relationship to bishops. It affects bishops and their relationship to the pope. However, collegiality also affects the relationship of priests to bishop and bishop to priests, as well as priest to priest. In the documents of Vatican II, the term *collegiality* was generally used in reference to bishops. For priests, the term that has become commonplace is *presbyterium*. This word emphasizes the collegial nature of both diocesan bishop and the priests of the diocese. The diocesan bishop is not above the presbyterium; he is an integral part of it. A convocation of the priests of a diocese should never take place if the diocesan bishop does not attend the convocation from start to finish. Collegiality is a two-way street that includes communication from bishop to priest as well as from priest to bishop. Theologically, pastorally, and personally, neither the diocesan bishop nor the priests of a given diocese have a nonrelational self-identity.

In some dioceses bishops hear the priests' interventions (e.g., at a priest senate, convocation), but they do not have to follow what the priests indicate unless canon law expressly requires it. In episcopal synods, the papacy and the congregations hear what the bishops have to say and then they move in their own direction.

A collegial understanding of bishop and priest indicates that one cannot have a theological, pastoral, or personal [self-identity] view of priesthood that is nonrelational. The older scholastic view, which was based on the power to consecrate and to forgive sin, was individualistic. A priest individually had this self-defining power, and no one could take it away. The issue of collegiality has become a major factor in why there are theological, pastoral, and personal problems for today's priests, since contextual interrelationship—another name for collegiality and presbyterium—is minimalized or at times even set to one side as irrelevant. John Paul II, however, speaks of relationship as necessary not minimal. He states: "The ministry of priest is above all communion and a responsible and necessary cooperation with the bishop's ministry, in concern for the universal Church and for the individual particular Churches, for whose service they form with

---

82. See John Paul II, *Pastores dabo vobis* (Post-synodal exhortation, March 25, 1992), Eng. trans. (Washington, DC: USCCB, 1992), 17.

the bishop a single presbyterate."[83] No wonder that the morale of many priests has plummeted downward. When the communion aspect of priestly ministry is minimalized, the individual priest is marginalized.

The following series of diagrams brings out the interrelational aspect of church ministry: papacy, episcopacy, priesthood, diaconate, and lay ministry. Each diagram places one of these institutional ministries in the center as its focus, and from this focus we see foundational relationships and ministerial relationships.

The foundational context

\\/

GOD'S SENDING OF JESUS—THE DIVINE PLAN
JESUS' OWN MISSION AND MINISTRY
THE MISSION AND MINISTRY OF ALL BAPTIZED-
CONFIRMED CHRISTIANS

\\/

The specific church ministries
THE MISSION AND MINISTRY OF PAPACY

   /   /   \\   \\

BISHOP   PRIEST   DEACON   LAY MINISTER

The above diagram is meant to indicate the total interrelational context of institutional church ministry with a focus on the institutional church ministry of papacy. Let us change the focus of the diagram from *papacy* to *episcopacy*.

The foundational context

\\/

GOD'S SENDING OF JESUS—THE DIVINE PLAN
JESUS' OWN MISSION AND MINISTRY
THE MISSION AND MINISTRY OF ALL BAPTIZED-
CONFIRMED CHRISTIANS

\\/

The specific church ministries
THE MISSION AND MINISTRY OF EPISCOPACY

   /   /   \\   \\

POPE   PRIEST   DEACON   LAY MINISTER

---

83. Ibid.

Let us change it again so that the *presbyterate* is in the central focus:

The foundational context
\\/
GOD'S SENDING OF JESUS—THE DIVINE PLAN
JESUS' OWN MISSION AND MINISTRY
THE MISSION AND MINISTRY OF ALL BAPTIZED-
CONFIRMED CHRISTIANS
\\/
The specific church ministries
THE MISSION AND MINISTRY OF PRIEST
/   /   \\   \\
POPE   BISHOP   DEACON   LAY MINISTER

Let us change it once more, placing the *diaconate* in the focal center:

The foundational context
\\/
GOD'S SENDING OF JESUS—THE DIVINE PLAN
JESUS' OWN MISSION AND MINISTRY
THE MISSION AND MINISTRY OF ALL BAPTIZED-
CONFIRMED CHRISTIANS
\\/
The specific church ministries
THE MISSION AND MINISTRY OF DEACON
/   /   \\   \\
POPE   BISHOP   PRIEST   LAY MINISTER

And a final change takes place when *specific lay ministry* is put into the centering focal position:

```
┌─────────────────────────────────────────────────────────┐
│              The foundational context                     │
│                        \/                                 │
│       GOD'S SENDING OF JESUS—THE DIVINE PLAN              │
│         JESUS' OWN MISSION AND MINISTRY                   │
│       THE MISSION AND MINISTRY OF ALL BAPTIZED-           │
│              CONFIRMED CHRISTIANS                          │
│                        \/                                 │
│            The specific church ministries                 │
│     THE MISSION AND MINISTRY OF LAY MINISTERS            │
│        /         /         \          \                   │
│      POPE    BISHOP    PRIEST    DEACON                   │
└─────────────────────────────────────────────────────────┘
```

This series of diagrams indicates that all the institutional ministries of the church are interrelated and that one cannot be defined in isolation of the others. If we add to this the understanding that each individual ministry is interrelated theologically, pastorally, and personally, then we begin to see what the contextual theology of institutional ministry is all about. The lack of this permeating and interrelational contextual reality has been and remains one of the major reasons why there are problems with every one of the institutional church ministries today.

One might surely ask: Why is there such hesitation to utilize a contextual, interrelational theology for ecclesial institutional ministry? The answer comes down to the following:

- **A noninterrelational theology of institutional church ministry** continues the isolated definitions of pope, bishop, priest, deacon, and lay minister that were dominant prior to Vatican II.
- **A relational theology of institutional church ministry** discontinues the isolated definitions of pope, bishop, priest, deacon, and lay minister that were dominant prior to Vatican II.

1. The Theological Dimension

Many church leaders, both ecclesiastical and theological, are still, on the one hand, stressing the essential difference between lay

87

and cleric, between priest and bishop, and between deacon and priest; on the other hand, they are minimizing the interrelational foundation of all these specified institutional church ministries. In the minds of those who move in this way, "essential difference" is absolutely necessary, and essential in their presentations means nonrelational. For these writers, *essential difference* and *radical difference* are phrases that are difficult to integrate into an interrelational context. The conciliar interrelational context is accepted but only in a generalized way. It is precisely the nonacceptance of a permeating and interrelational theology of institutional ministry that exemplifies the negativity of their stance. I have often mentioned the three aspects that affect institutional church ministry: the theological, the pastoral, and the personal. To conclude this description of the major change on priesthood that is found in the documents of Vatican II, let us look more carefully at each of these three dimensions of priestly life.

Priesthood is interrelational in a profound way. Theologically, the priesthood is united to God's sending of Jesus and to the very life and ministry of Jesus. Priesthood makes sense only on the basis of the baptismal-confirmational sharing of all Christians in God's sending of Jesus and Jesus' own life and ministry. Priesthood, theologically, is not individualistic but interrelational, and this interrelational dimension includes a collegial or presbyteral relationship with the bishop as fullness of the priesthood, with fellow priests and with all fellow ministers. These are some of the positive theological issues of today's priesthood.

There are also negative aspects. Theologically, bishops often do not relate to priests except in a juridical or authoritative way. In other instances, the priest is seen theologically by his bishop as a vicar of the bishop, and this has major effects on the priest's personal self-identity. Priests themselves do not bond with one another and therefore do not support one another. This is because priests themselves remain theologically individualistic and not interrelational in their own understanding of priesthood. Similarly, there is in the United States a bombardment by conservative elements in the Roman Catholic Church that priests should follow a pre–Vatican II understanding of priesthood, which, in the mind of these conservative elements, represents the true Roman Catholic tradition. There is in the air a clash of theologies, which leads to theological confusion.[84]

2. The Pastoral Dimension

In the pastoral dimension of priesthood, the *tria munera* present a view of mission and ministry that moves beyond the sacramental priest. The priest has a ministry in teaching and preaching and in the area of leadership far beyond Eucharist, reconciliation, baptism, marriage, and anointing of the sick. The richness of the mission and ministry of Jesus himself is meant to inspire and permeate all that a priest does. This, too, is a positive understanding of priesthood, and one that helps the priest live a deep and meaningful life in today's multicultural world.

Negatively, this *tria munera* vision of the priest creates a situation in which the priest, now alone in his ministry and without other priests in a parish, finds himself stretched to the limit. There is no team of priests in an ordinary parish to provide all that the people of God need. The presence of deacons and lay ministers within a parish structure helps and hinders. It helps since many issues are clearly taken care of; it hinders because the priest sees aspects of what he thinks is "his work" being done by permanent deacons or by lay men and women. Respect for borders becomes a frictional part of pastoral life, and the friction is a negative reality day after day after day. Pastorally, there are many frustrations for the ordinary parish priest today, and the bishop offers in many locales a very limited support. Some bishops, for their part, are called on by the conference to be away from the diocese and unavailable to the ministry going on in the diocese. However, the conference by itself is not the only cause for this absence of bishops from a diocese. Some bishops find personal honor in being called away to help out the needs of the conference. Their time,

---

84. In 2004, a book entitled *Priest, Where Is Thy Mass? Mass, Where Is Thy Priest?* (Kansas City, MO: Angelus Press, 2004) was sent out free of charge to all priests. It contains interviews with certain priests. It is a book that is outspokenly anti–Vatican II. It is clearly an example of nonacceptance of certain reforms mandated by Vatican II. There is no name of an editor of this volume.

allegiance, and interest are focused on the conference issues, not on the local issues.

3. Personal Identity Dimension

In the *tria munera* theology of priesthood, the closeness to Jesus is foundational. In my book on the priesthood I mention that in the *Summa IV Liber III*, qq. 34–40, Thomas Aquinas mentions Jesus only when he says: *corpus Christi, plebs Christi and corpus Christi mysticum* (body of Christ, people of Christ, and the mystical body of Christ). There is no mention of Jesus as model for those who receive the sacrament of holy orders. Bonaventure's presentation of the sacrament of orders is very much the same. Jesus is not central to his theology of priesthood. Scotus, likewise, is no different. Today, however, Jesus and his mission and ministry are at the heart of priesthood. Jesus' mission and ministry are placed before the priest as the operative model for his own self-identity as priest. This christological, not ecclesiological, base is marvelous and gives a depth to priesthood that the scholastics did not offer. For the scholastics, the priest was fundamentally a church person; for the *tria munera* theology of priesthood, the priest is fundamentally a Jesus person. For priestly self-identity, Jesus enriches the meaning of priest; church constricts the meaning of priest.

However, the self-identity of a priest today is a matter of no little concern. The morale of priests has indeed suffered in the postconciliar church, and the moral life of a few priests has become an issue of major scandal. When people in some public places see a priest dressed in his blacks, often the thought arises: is this man one of "those" priests? The sexual scandal has spread a shadow over all priests, and it will take at least two or three generations of priests before this shadow is no longer dominant. Seminarians are, today, often restricted in their outside contacts. They wear the cassock; they focus on church; and in their curriculum there are many reviews and discussions of sexual issues. Will such inward-looking seminaries produce better priests? It is hard to say, but the majority of those priests who have been involved in the current scandals came from pre–Vatican II seminaries that were equally restrictive and equally church oriented. In some ways, the self-identity of a priest today depends not on priestly identity but on human identity. Human issues, not church issues, need to be addressed in a major way.[85]

---

85. See Howard Bleichner, *View from the Altar* (New York: Crossroad, 2004).

Chapter Seven

THE RENEWAL OF THE PERMANENT DIACONATE: THE FOURTH MAJOR CONCILIAR CHANGE IN MINISTRY

The bishops at Vatican II called for the reestablishment of the permanent diaconate as a major part of the sacrament of orders (*LG* 29; cf. *AA* 16). In the conciliar text itself, the concrete details of such a reestablishment were deliberately left to competent local episcopal conferences, whose decisions needed the approval of the Holy See. Many episcopal conferences in the Roman Catholic Church took up the issue of reestablishing the permanent diaconate, and several—though *not all*—such conferences eventually did reestablish the permanent diaconate. Even though in some dioceses and within the limits of certain episcopal conferences no reestablishment of the diaconate took place, enough dioceses and enough conferences moved to a formal reestablishment. Because of this adequate numerical base, permanent deacons today, therefore, are officially recognized in our current Roman Catholic Church as an intrinsic part of the church's clerical leadership, and the diaconate is a true, actual, and constitutive order within the sacrament of sacred orders. Both theologically and canonically, diaconal ministry is today an official leadership ministry.

The reinstatement of the permanent diaconate by the bishops at Vatican II (*LG* 29) constituted a major moment in the life of the contemporary Roman Catholic Church. Paul VI, in both the apostolic letter *Sacrum Diaconatus Ordinem* (June 18, 1967) and his subsequent *motu proprio, Ad pascendum* (August 15, 1972), established the basic source of legislation on the permanent diaconate. On June 17, 1968, the Apostolic Constitution, *Pontificalis Romani Recognitio,* established official rites for diaconal ordination. In 1971 the United States bishops' committee on the permanent diaconate published an official document, *Permanent Deacons in the United States: Guidelines on Their Formation and Ministry;* and in 1985, a revised edition under the same title was issued by the USCCB. In 1974 the bishops' committee on the liturgy issued its own statement, *Study Text III: Ministries in the Church.* In 1979, the bishops' committee on the liturgy published an updated *Study Text VI: The Deacon, Minister of Word and Sacrament.* In 1981, the USCCB issued a review of the permanent deacon in the American Catholic Church, entitled: *A National Study of the Permanent Diaconate in the United States.* This, too, was updated by the USCCB publication in 1996, *A National Study of the Permanent Diaconate of the Catholic Church in the United States.* In 2005 the USCCB published the *National Directory for the Formation, Ministry, and Life of Permanent Deacons in the United States.* Moreover, the 1983 promulgation of the revised *Code of Canon Law* (1031–37 and 1039) provided even more juridical material on the permanent diaconate. All of this material indicates that the reestablishment of the permanent diaconate has been and remains a major theme of the renewal of clerical leadership in today's Roman Catholic Church.

We must keep in mind that a *permanent diaconate* had not existed in the Western Catholic Church for over twelve hundred years.[86] To reestablish a nonexistent permanent diaconate after such a lengthy period of time can only be seen as a monumental step. From AD 800 onward, traces of permanent deacons became an increasing rarity in the early medieval world.

> Sixth-century inscriptions on towers and some literary references record that deacons died in Gaul at sixty, seventy or eighty years. Alcuin, who had been ordained deacon when about 35 years old and who died in the year

---

86. A transitional diaconate had, of course, continued during this same period of time.

804 at about 75, was never ordained priest. But such men increasingly become the exception.[87]

Pope Gregory VII (1020–1085) was ordained a deacon and spent most of his early diaconal life in Rome as assistant to Gregory VI. While he was still a deacon, he was elected pope. Only in the subsequent months was he ordained to priesthood. In other words, while he was a deacon he was already acclaimed juridically as pope. Of course, this instance at the beginning of the second millennium was unique, just as the case of Alcuin was unique.

We have no historical data indicating that there was an official edict revoking the permanent diaconate. Historical data simply indicate that a permanent diaconal ministry from AD 800 onward became the exception and eventually disappeared. The conciliar bishops, therefore, had little historical data, beyond that of the early patristic church, for the actual implications regarding a revised permanent diaconate.

Consequently, the bishops at Vatican II were well aware of the historical significance of their injunction on the issue of the diaconate. They were also well aware that it is one thing to reinstate the permanent diaconate by a written fiat and quite another thing to actualize the permanent diaconate in concrete diocesan and parish structures. Paul VI's *motu proprio* provided some assistance to the reinstatement, but again a written *motu proprio* is measurably different from an actual and existential reinstatement. As a result, the actual diaconal reinstatement since 1964 has not been without serious problems.[88] An abundance of richness has indeed taken place for church life with the reestablishment of the permanent diaconate, since the presence of deacons on a permanent basis within the clerical leadership of the church has brought new gifts and new talents to church leadership. However, the reestablishment of the permanent diaconate has engendered some major *theological*, pastoral, and *personal* issues of a conflictual nature. Theological and

---

87. Barnett, *The Diaconate: A Full and Equal Order*, 110.

88. USCCB, *A National Study on the Permanent Diaconate of the Catholic Church in the United States*, (Washington, DC: USCCB, 1996) lists some major problems (13–15).

pastoral material appeared in the United States, and these writings were very helpful. On the other hand, these writings also reflect a large spectrum of positions on diaconal ministry.[89]

The importance of the permanent diaconate and the structural difficulties of the permanent diaconate, in my view, cannot be assessed correctly without all the material on context. Without this larger context, neither the importance nor the difficulties of today's permanent diaconate can be truly analyzed, resolved, and maintained. I realize that some of the material in this present work seems to take us far afield. However, only within the larger context of ecclesial institutional ministry and leadership can the main features of diaconal ministry be comprehensively understood. To the deacons, then, who are reading these pages, I want to state clearly: *all of the above material is a needed interrelational context, helping you to understand your own interrelational life within the church's institutional ministry and leadership today. Without the larger context, deacon issues cannot be understood in their fullness.*

Basing ourselves on all the official documents just mentioned, let us begin our study of the current situation regarding the permanent diaconate. Methodologically, we can do this in a more successful way if we consider the conflictual issues in the three major dimensions of diaconal life, namely, the theological, the pastoral, and the personal. These issues tend to revolve around a single over-

---

89. See, e.g., John Bligh, "Deacons in the Latin West Since the Fourth Century," *Theology* 58 (1955): 421–29; Norbert Brockman, *Ordained to Service: A Theology of the Permanent Diaconate* (Hicksville, NY: Exposition Press, 1976); John N. Collins, *Diakonia: Re-interpreting the Ancient Sources* (New York: Oxford University Press, 1990); Edward Echlin, *The Deacon in the Church: Past and Future* (Staten Island, NY: Alba House, 1971); Donald Thomas, *The Deacons in a Changing Church* (Valley Forge, PA: Judson Press, 1969); Ormonde Plater, *The Deacon in the Liturgy* (Boston: National Center for the Diaconate, 1981); idem, *Many Servants: An Introduction to Deacons* (Cambridge, MA: Cowley Publications, 1962); William Ditewig, *Deacons: 101 Questions & Answers* (Mahwah, NJ: Paulist Press, 2004); Owen Cummings, *Deacons and the Church* (Mahwah, NJ: Paulist Press, 2004) and *Saintly Deacons* (Mahwah, NJ: Paulist Press, 2005); Owen Cummings, William Ditewig, and Richard Gaillardetz, *Theology of the Diaconate: The State of the Question* (Mahwah, NJ: Paulist Press, 2005); Michael Bulson, *Preach What You Believe* (Mahwah, NJ: Paulist Press, 2005); Ruth Wallace, *They Call Him Pastor* (Mahwah, NJ: Paulist Press, 2003).

arching problem. **What is the precise role of a permanent deacon in the clerical leadership of the Roman Catholic Church today?**

In the past forty years, the actual presence of permanent deacons within a diocesan and parish structure has been a grace and a gift for the people of God, but the actual presence of deacons in parishes and dioceses has also engendered a number of difficult boundary issues. These issues have affected, sometimes positively and sometimes negatively, the pastor or parish priest vis-à-vis the permanent deacon. Similarly, boundary issues have arisen regarding the role of the deacon and his relationship to the local bishop, since in the context of today's Roman Catholic juridical organization, it is the diocesan bishop, *not the pastor,* who is directly in charge of the permanent deacons. A third area of tension is the relationship between a permanent deacon, on the one hand, and an officially appointed lay minister, on the other hand. The individual deacon himself has experienced boundary issues that have affected positively and negatively his own personal identity as a deacon.

Although the permanent deacons together with the bishop and the priests constitute the clerical leadership in a diocese,[90] deacons are excluded from the diocesan presbyterate, which means that they are excluded from many leadership and decision-making bodies, for example, the priests' senate. In other words, although deacons are sacramentally and juridically part of the clericate, deacons within a parochial or diocesan structure are often excluded from key decision-making bodies. As clerics, the deacons are rightfully part of the major leadership groups in the Roman Catholic Church, namely, the clerical state. However, their belonging to the clerical state does *not always* include a membership in the major

---

90. An enlightening task is to search for the "deacon's office," as listed by the various dioceses in *The Official Catholic Directory* (New Providence, NJ: P. J. Kenedy and Sons, 1913–). Sometimes the office for the permanent diaconate is listed under "Departments of Ministry Formation," or at times under "Departments of Parish Life." It is *not* listed in the central areas of diocesan church leadership, which is always found in the first listings under chancery office, vicar general, council of priests, etc. From the placement of these listings, one would never guess that the diaconate is a sacred order or that deacons are part of the diocesan clergy.

clerical decision-making entities in either a diocese or a parish. This situation raises the question: Is the deacon really an integral part of church leadership, or is the deacon only a peripheral member of the diocesan church leadership?

Even the role of the deacon in the liturgy of the church has come under question. Since the close of Vatican II and the official reinstatement of the permanent diaconate by Paul VI, the liturgical role of the deacon has been changed on several occasions. The instruction *Redemptionis sacramentum* (2004) by the Congregation for Divine Worship and the Discipline of the Sacraments is the most recent official document that indicates changes in major areas regarding duties that a deacon had previously done frequently but juridically should not do today or do only occasionally. The deacon's call to prayer after the consecration at Mass, "Let us proclaim the mystery of our faith," is now restricted to the priest or bishop, since the total Eucharistic Prayer is to be said by the priest alone (52). In the same instruction, deacons are now able to preach the homily only "occasionally, according to circumstances" (64). Care of the sick, baptism of children, assistance at weddings and the celebration of Christian funerals are all "matters which pertain in the first place to Priests assisted by Deacons. It must therefore never be the case that in parishes Priests alternate indiscriminately in shifts of pastoral service with Deacons" (152). All of these statements indicate a peripheral role of the deacon—not an integral role.

The recently published *National Directory for the Formation, Ministry, and Life of Permanent Deacons in the United States* (2005) presents a picture of the liturgical ministry of a permanent deacon in a much more open way. This is noticeable in nos. 33–35 on the permanent deacon's liturgical functions, but it is also evident in this document's portrayal of pastoral functions (31–32; 36–38; 50–53; 56–61).

The development of official lay ministries, which is also part of the legacy of Vatican II, has clouded the role of the deacon. Many tasks that the deacon does can also be done by lay ministers. In principle, the deacon can baptize, but so can lay ministers in extreme circumstances. The deacon can witness Christian marriages, but so can lay ministers. The deacon can conduct eucharistic services in the absence of a priest, but, under certain circumstances, so can lay ministers. The deacon can preside at funerals and burial services, but, under certain circumstances, so can lay ministers. The presence of lay ministers in these various functions of church life may be more prominent in the so-called missionary countries, but church legislation that allows these religious tasks to be done by laymen and laywomen raises the issue of the value of the diaconal ministry. These issues have created serious problems at three different levels in the structures of the church.

At the theological level, the problematic issues just enumerated are basically *relational* problems on the very meaning of the sacrament of sacred orders: that is, the theological relationship of bishop–priest–deacon. In today's Roman Catholic theology, these three orders constitute one Sacred Order. Within the one sacrament of orders, there are three orders. With the reintroduction of the permanent diaconate, the question regarding its theological interrelationship needs to be more clearly studied. The Vatican Council not only reestablished the permanent diaconate, but it also reestablished episcopacy as the major order in the sacrament of orders. It also redefined the theological meaning of priest. The point that I wish to make at this moment is the following: Vatican II and the aftermath of Vatican II have presented a theological situation on the issue of the sacrament of Sacred Order that is different from the theological situation prior to Vatican II. One can say that the definition of bishop has changed with the official reestablishment of the bishop into the sacrament of holy orders. One can say that the definition of presbyter has changed with its focus on the *tria munera*. One can say that the definition of deacon has changed with the reestablishment of the permanent deacon. My contention is, therefore, that we, as theologians, need to rethink not just episcopacy, presbyterate, and diaconate individually; we need to rethink the very meaning of the sacrament of orders. The three orders are interrelated within one sacramental order. Interrelationship is first; only then is there a division of orders. What is this foundational, basic, and primordial interrelationship that provides the unity of the sacrament of orders? Until this is clarified, the secondary divisions of order into orders will not make theological sense. It is the foundational interrelationship of bishop, priest, and deacon in the one sacrament of order that is to date theologically unclear.

At the pastoral level, there are also serious problems, which are basically boundary problems. Boundary problems at this level generally involve the issue of who does what? This includes the specific roles and tasks of deacons vis-à-vis the pastor or parish priest. It involves the specific roles and tasks of deacons vis-à-vis his primary superior, the diocesan bishop. It involves the inclusion-exclusion factor of deacons as regards the clerical leadership within a diocese. It involves the specific roles and tasks of deacons vis-à-vis lay men and women. Without a solid theology, the pastoral institutional ministry and leadership of the church tend to flounder. However, the setting of boundaries even in the pastoral area of church life rests on a more primary understanding of pastoral ministry itself: namely, on its foundational interrelationship. The pastoral ministry is the sharing in Jesus' own ministry and mission *in action*. It is the *actual doing* of this Jesus mission and ministry in the parish, in the diocese, in the regional church, and in the total church. All pastoral ministry leads back to a communal sharing in the one mission and ministry that is Jesus' own mission and ministry. No pope, no bishop, no presbyter, no deacon, and no lay minister has his or her own mission and ministry. Each *shares* in the one ministry and mission of Jesus himself. Again the term *share*, which the documents of Vatican II reiterate time and time again, indicates that there is an underlying unity in which all ministers share. This underlying unity, as the conciliar documents and the texts of the *Catechism* indicate, is the mission and ministry of Jesus. It is fundamentally a "we" who share, not an "I" who shares. Before boundaries, then, there is an area of no boundaries. Before distinction there is interrelationality. Pastorally, all of this needs to be sorted out in a clearer way. Otherwise there remains a quibbling about pastoral boundaries that causes serious pastoral problems.

At the personal level, the serious problems for the deacons that have arisen since Vatican II include problems of a diaconal self-identity. These identity problems are closely aligned with the theological and pastoral levels just mentioned. How does a permanent deacon truly envision himself as cleric, as church leader, as liturgical minister, and as a pastoral minister? The lack of a clear self-identity as a deacon has created, in many dioceses, a morale problem for the diaconal ministers. Part of self-identity includes the factor: Am I *appreciated* for what I have been asked to do? Or, am I not appreciated for all the time and energy I expend on my diaconal ministry? Most often, this diaconal expending of energy and time has no or very little financial remuneration, while the priests and the bishops are paid. The financial situation has implications for a diaconal self-identity that go beyond mere finances and move into the dimensions of theological and pastoral worth.

Moreover, there is the issue of the deacon's marital status. On many occasions, the marriage or family requires the full attention of the deacon, but the celibate clerical leadership, both bishop and priest, is not always sensitive to or appreciative of the factors in this pull between family and ministry. The married permanent deacon lives day by day in a dual sacramental situation: his married life and his diaconal life. Bishops, pastors, and priests may verbally extol the value and beauty of marriage, but—in ways similar to situations found in the economic and corporate worlds—the deacon is not always provided the latitude that the commitment of marriage requires.

These three dimensional forms of difficulty are sharply present in today's permanent diaconate. They are also a part of the contextual framework that any study of today's diaconal life must include in its agenda. It is hoped that the reader of this volume sees the validity of this emphasis on the issue of context: namely, the current historical context in both its ecclesiastical and its theological-pastoral framework, as well as the current theological, pastoral, and personal context of contemporary diaconal life. Whenever the issue of context is removed from theology and pastoral practice, an ideological and nonreal conversation begins to take over. One cannot speak of the diaconal ministry today in a contextual vacuum. Such a noncontextual conversation may sound erudite and even spiritual, but it lacks historical credibility and contemporary, existential actuality. It is ideological. It is not real.

Since this volume is focused on the diaconate, it seems better, if, at this point of time, I simply state that the reestablishment of the permanent diaconate was and is one of the five major changes regarding ecclesial ministry and leadership that the bishops at Vatican II authorized. In the material in part 2, I will deal specifically and abundantly with the diaconate's current status.

Chapter Eight

AN OFFICIAL AND MORE INCLUSIVE RECOGNITION OF SPECIFIC CHURCH MINISTRIES BY LAY MEN AND WOMEN: THE FIFTH MAJOR CONCILIAR CHANGE IN MINISTRY

On November 30, 1962, during the first session of Vatican II, the bishops began their discussion on a draft entitled *De Ecclesia* [On the Church]. This draft had been prepared by Roman theologians prior to the convocation of the council and was 122 pages in length divided into eleven chapters. In the discussion of this draft, many bishops complained that there was no chapter on the laity. At first, Cardinal Spellman was one of the major proponents for a greater focus on lay ministry. Spellman (with others) argued that Catholic Action—the usual name given to lay activity in the church prior to Vatican II—should be given more specific attention by the conciliar bishops. Antoine Wenger describes this insistence as follows:

> It is indispensable that Catholic Action be included in the constitution of the Church. Several interventions [of the bishops] also requested that the specific role of Catholic Action in the Church should now be fully recognized. The laity, organized and commissioned by the

hierarchy, must hereafter have its full place in any treatise on the Church.[91]

At that moment in time, the majority of the conciliar bishops viewed the laity primarily from the standpoint of the Catholic Action movements that were so numerous in the late nineteenth and the first half of the twentieth century. *That* the bishops wanted to make a major change of some sort is clear. *What* that major change might actually be was, however, not clear at the beginning of the council, nor did the exact meaning of the major change become crystal clear at the end of the conciliar deliberations. Even in the postconciliar period, a clearly articulated expression of this major change regarding the laity remains unclear. *That* a major change regarding the laity took place is agreed on by almost everyone; *what* that major change is remains a debated issue. Let us move carefully, step by step, through this issue of a major change.

The focus of the intent at the beginning of the council can be negatively stated: there was no urgency to change anything regarding the basic understanding of Catholic Action. Positively stated, however, there was a strong desire to produce a major conciliar acknowledgment regarding the activities of laypeople, particularly in such activities as Catholic Action. The bishops wanted to elevate lay activity—if that is the correct term—as follows.

- The bishops wanted to recognize fully in an official and conciliar way the status of lay ministerial activity within the Roman Catholic Church.
- They wanted, thereby, to indicate that lay ministerial activity must be considered a constitutive part of any and every theology of church.

Such a major integration of lay activity into a theology of church can be considered the first step of the conciliar bishops. In the course of the council, other conciliar issues enlarged and deepened this first

---

91. Antoine Wenger, *Vatican II: Première Session* (Paris: Éditions Centurion, Bonne Presse, 1963), Eng. trans. by Robert Olsen, *Vatican II*, vol. 1, *The First Session* (Westminster, Md: Newman Press, 1966), 114.

step, so that a dimension of major change on the status of laypeople in the Roman Catholic Church became more comprehensive.

Our next step places us at the end of the council in 1965. When we review all of the texts produced by the bishops at Vatican II, we find three major sources on specific lay ecclesial ministry in the documents of Vatican II.

- First, chapter 4 of *Lumen gentium*
- Second, the Decree on the Apostolate of the Laity, *Apostolicam actuositatem*
- Third, the Pastoral Constitution on the Church in the Modern World, *Gaudium et spes*

In the course of the conciliar deliberations, the leading voice for an expanded view of lay ministry and leadership in the Roman Catholic Church was that of Bishop Leon-Joseph Suenens of Malines, Belgium.[92] His interventions helped guide the bishops toward a deeper understanding of lay ministerial activity, on the one hand, and, on the other hand, its profound and constitutive relationship to any and every theology of church.

During the entire conciliar debate and discussion on the layperson's activity in ecclesial activity, the theme of the laity was, in general, not controversial. The vast majority of the bishops were unified on the issue of integrating lay activity more constitutively into a theology of church. As Paul Lakeland notes:

> The teaching on the laity [at Vatican II] seemed to be breaking new ground. As a matter of fact, the curious thing about the council's teaching on the laity is that it is at one and the same time new and relatively uncontroversial. There was near unanimity on the need for a document on the laity. Of course there were differences about detail and whether the chapter on the laity should be part of *Lumen gentium*, but there was remarkably little controversy about the content.[93]

---

92. See Paul Lakeland, *The Liberation of the Laity: In Search of an Accountable Church* (New York: Continuum, 2004), 82–87.

93. Ibid., 87–88.

To understand the final conciliar position on the laity, it is vitally important to make a careful but basic distinction, found in the most important conciliar document on laity, *Lumen gentium*. Chapter 2 of *LG* focuses on the "People of God," that is, on all baptized and confirmed Christians. In this focus, the distinction of hierarchy/laity is irrelevant. As people of God, all Christians are equal. Chapter 2 stresses what each and every Christian truly is, and in doing so the emphasis is on the dignity, equality, and importance of every baptized-confirmed Christian. The foundational source for this equality and dignity lies in the *tria munera:* all baptized Christians share equally in the *tria munera* mission and ministry of Jesus himself. Because of this equal sharing in Jesus' own mission and ministry, divisions such as hierarchical and lay are meaningless.

The same is not true, however, for chapter 4 of *Lumen gentium*. This chapter has a related but separate focus, namely, on those people of God who are *not* in sacred orders but who *are* called and commissioned by God to specific ecclesial ministries and leadership roles. This distinction between the people of God in chapter 2 and the lay ministers in chapter 4 is crucial for an understanding of the Vatican II text *Lumen gentium*, and for the subsequent material on lay ministry found in *Apostolicam actuositatem* and *Gaudium et spes*.[94] No equation should ever be made between the "priesthood of the all believers"—the conciliar phrase—and the laity as a sort of "priesthood of the laity"—a phrase that in the postconciliar period has no theological meaning.[95] Perhaps a diagram is helpful on this matter.

---

94. In the documents of Vatican II, the bishops never referred to lay activity as "ministry" nor were lay men and women called "ministers." The bishops scrupulously avoided this ministerial language and used only the language of lay apostolate. In this volume, I do use *minister* and *ministry* in reference to the Vatican II texts, and I do this only because from an English-language standpoint it is both easier and clearer.

95. Lakeland (*Liberation of the Laity*, 90ff.) is not totally clear on the distinction between the "laity" in general and the "priesthood of the all believers" as presented in chapter 2 of *LG*.

PEOPLE OF GOD
FAITHFUL OF CHRIST
PRIESTHOOD OF ALL BELIEVERS
All of whom share in the one and same priesthood of all believers

Some of whom are:	Some of whom are:	Some of whom are:
Hierarchy—bishop, priest, deacon	Lay men and women in specific ministry	Charismatic leaders

Chapter 4 of *Lumen gentium* focuses primarily on the middle group in the diagram above. This is clear from the opening paragraphs of the chapter. In these opening paragraphs the bishops describe what they mean by the term *laity*, that is, laypeople involved in specific ecclesial ministries and leadership roles. The bishops move carefully in stating their description. The initial section of this description reads as follows:

> The term laity is here understood to mean all the faithful *except* those in holy Orders and those who belong to a religious state approved by the church. (*LG* 31; emphasis added)

The word *except* is a negating word. The negative description presented in this paragraph follows the usual Roman Catholic, pre–Vatican II description of the term *laity*. In this pre–Vatican II description, the laity was described most often in a negative way, that is, laity included people who were *not* in religious life and who were *not* ordained. In making this negative statement, the conciliar bishops bracket those in religious life, since there is an entire chapter in *Lumen gentium* devoted to the religious, and they also bracket the ordained, since in many other sections of the Vatican II documents the bishops focus directly and at great length on the ordained.

The description, however, in its negative aspects cannot help but be seen as ambiguous. Whenever one says that the laity is not this and not that, a question immediately arises: If not this or that, then what is the laity? Fortunately or unfortunately, every positive answer to this question depends on the *context in which the term "laity" is used*. In chapter 4 the bishops describe their context, first negatively: *not* ordained and *not* in religious life. Then, they do so positively. To see this negative-positive balance we need to consider the entire paragraph.

> The term laity is here understood to mean all the faithful except those in holy Orders and those who belong to a religious state approved by the church: all the faithful, that is, who by Baptism are incorporated into Christ, are constituted the people of God, who have been made sharers in their own way in the priestly, prophetic and kingly office of Christ and play their part in carrying out the mission of the whole Christian people in the church and in the world. (31)

One can see that the bishops are compiling a number of items in this description of the laity.[96] Positively, all lay men and women who are engaged in ecclesial ministry have to be connected foundationally to the people of God, a foundation that comes from the sacraments of baptism and confirmation. Out of this large foundational group of baptized Christians called the people of God, some of them are considered laity, constituting a specific group, numerically distinct from people of God. Thus, the laity are joined to the people of God in a foundational way, but they are not coterminous with the people of God. The bishops are clear on this matter: basically or foundationally there is an interrelational link between the people of God, on the one hand, and, on the other hand, the specific lay men and women who are active in various ecclesial ministries. The bishops even indicate in a strong way that the foundational link is the actual sharing in the *tria munera* mission and ministry of Jesus himself.

Although the bishops at this juncture make no mention of the fundamental basis for all mission and ministry in the church, namely, God's sending of Jesus, the trinitarian sending of Jesus remains throughout all the documentation of Vatican II as the primordial relationship for each and every ministerial aspect within

---

96. The bishops at Vatican II were well aware that they were only describing the laity; they were not defining what the term *laity* might mean.

the church. Nor do the bishops, at this juncture, give any focused attention to Jesus' own mission and ministry in itself. Rather, the bishops simply indicate that both the people of God and the specific lay ecclesial ministers share in Jesus' own mission and ministry. The emphasis is on *their sharing, not* on what constitutes Jesus' own mission and ministry. It is *their sharing* in the *tria munera*, not an analysis of Jesus' own *tria munera* mission and ministry that is center stage.

Presupposed Issues

- The sending of Jesus by the Triune God
- Jesus' own *tria munera* mission and ministry

Stated Issues

The primary foundation:

- All baptized-confirmed Christians share in the *tria munera* mission and ministry of Jesus in virtue of their baptism and confirmation.

Therefore:

- *All lay men and women* who are in a special ecclesial ministry share in the *tria munera* mission and ministry of Jesus in virtue of their call and commission to a special ministry.
- *All ordained* also share in the *tria munera* mission and ministry of Jesus in virtue of ordination.
- *All religious* also share in the *tria munera* mission and ministry of Jesus in virtue of their religious profession.

One must first be a baptized-confirmed Christian before one can be an ordained minister, a minister in religious life, or a lay minister in a specific role. However, for all these groups, the divine sending of Jesus and Jesus' own mission and ministry are the most fundamental interrelational aspects. Jesus' *tria munera* ministry and mission is his alone, given to him by God. All others—including the clergy—simply share in Jesus' ministry and mission. This is clearly the position of Vatican II in all its documentation, and we have treated this theme many times in the above material.

The sharing in Jesus' own mission and ministry is the common thread that gives the basic interrelational unity to all baptized Christians, the ordained minister, the religious minister, and the lay minister. In this listing, however, the Vatican II documents are also clear that no ordained, no religious, no lay minister is acceptable unless they are first of all baptized-confirmed Christians. They come to ordination, to religious life, and to lay ministry already sharing in the *tria munera* ministry and mission of Jesus. This already sharing is a *prerequisite for* ordination, *for* religious life, and *for* lay ministry. Jesus' own ministry and mission are primordial, and being part of the people of God is foundational. Only on these two foundational dimensions can we begin to distinguish ordained, religious, and lay ministers in any specific way. The issue of a foundational interrelation prior to a distinctive ministry was seen above when we considered the hierarchy (pope, bishop, priest, and deacon), and the same issue now reappears in the discussion of special lay ecclesial ministers. The thorny issue of acceptance or nonacceptance of the conciliar position reappears as well. What I have presented above is indeed the lens through which the material on lay ministry as found in *Apostolicam actuositatem* and *Gaudium et spes* must be seen.

Let us now consider the postconciliar period of today's church with its discussions and arguments over text and interpretation and over acceptance and nonacceptance. In the postconciliar period, the effort to define lay ministry has continued with great fervor. In 1987 there was a Roman synod on the role of the layperson in the church. A preparatory document, a *Lineamenta*, had been circulated in 1985 to all the bishops. Lakeland makes a reference to the problems to which the *Lineamenta* referred.

> Arising out of misreading of Vatican II, these problems are summarized in the words of the present pope as the "clericalization of the laity" and the "laicization of the clergy" (*Lineamenta* 9). They include issues such as confusion about which ecclesial ministries are open to the laity, and also the tendency to assume that only ecclesial ministry

(often construed on a clerical model) qualifies as apostolic activity. The document also mentions the tendency of lay people involved in public life to make divisions between their faith and their professional responsibilities (one thinks of inevitably here of John F. Kennedy, Mario Cuomo, and Geraldine Ferraro). Further, it adds the opposite problem of that negative flight from the world that constitutes a derogation of the lay duty to enliven the temporal order with the grace of Christ.[97]

The bishops were encouraged to disseminate the *Lineamenta* to a variety of people in their respective dioceses and so obtain a large spectrum of feedback. The American bishops did this and those who went to Rome for the synod took with them a large amount of data. The synod, however, was tightly controlled and highly influenced by members of Opus Dei and Communione e Liberazione.[98]

After such synods, the pope then produces a postsynodal document. This was published in February 1989, with the Latin title *Christifideles laici (CL)*, which is most often entitled in English "The Vocation and the Mission of the Lay Faithful in the Church and in the World." The synod itself had called for a clearer definition of a layperson's vocation and mission. John Paul II answered this request by stating unambiguously that the specificity of the layperson is his/her secular character. Lay men and women are called to the secular world (*CL* 15).[99] However, the pope, in later chapters of

---

97. Lakeland, *Liberation of the Laity*, 121.

98. Ibid., 123–24.

99. In chapter 4 of *LG*, after the lengthy and fairly convoluted description of the laity presented above, the next paragraph begins as follows. "To be secular is the special characteristic of the laity" (31). This sentence has been taken up by some theologians as the radical difference of lay ecclesial ministry. Lay ministry, in their view, is secular-oriented in distinction to ordained ministry as church-oriented. Fortunately, in the report of the USCCB subcommittee, *Lay Ecclesial Ministry*, conclusion 6 reads: "One element of the unique character of the laity, within the one mission of the Church, is its secular character. Because of this secular character, the laity are the Church in the heart of the world and bring the world into the heart of the Church." In this same document, the laity's missionary activity in the world is sometimes referred to as an apostolate (conclusion 9). In this document, the secular orientation is presented as only one element of the uniqueness of lay ministry.

Christifideles laici, acknowledged that laypeople have a role not only in the secular world but also within the inner institutional church. John Paul II frequently repeated the position of Vatican II that laypeople share in the mission of Jesus. However, he avoided adding the words "and in the ministry of Jesus." It is well known that at the time of the synod, the term *ministry* was used with abundance in church life. The older term and the one which the Vatican II documents continuously used was *lay apostolate*. This term had been virtually abandoned by 1987. Since *Christifideles laici*, however, the use of the terms *ministry* and *mission* for lay activity have continued to be used with great abundance.

In the postsynodal document, the question of boundaries between cleric and lay are emphasized with noticeable frequency. This frequently noted concern about boundaries is reechoed in the 1997 *Instruction on Certain Questions Regarding the Collaboration of the Non-Ordained Faithful in the Sacred Ministry of Priests*. The impact of *Christifideles laici* on the American church has been neither overly intensive nor overly extensive. Lay ministry has simply continued to grow. In 2004, it is estimated that there were in the United States more than thirty thousand lay men and women involved in lay ministry. Permanent deacons, in the same year, were estimated at roughly half that number.

In 1980, the American bishops published a small report entitled *Called and Gifted: The American Catholic Laity*. This brief volume was presented as a pastoral statement. Fifteen years later, in 1995, the United States Catholic Bishops published an updated version entitled *Called and Gifted for the Third Millennium*. In 1986, the NCCB through the Bishops' Committee on the Laity published a small statement entitled *Consulting the American Catholic Laity: A Decade of Dialogue*. In 1990, the same committee published a small paper entitled *Gifts Unfolding: The Lay Vocation today with Questions for Tomorrow*. In 1987, the same committee published a booklet entitled *One Body, Different Gifts—Many Roles: Reflection on the American Catholic Laity*. In 1999, the same committee published a brief report entitled *Lay Ecclesial Ministry: The State of the Questions*. In this report, we once again see a concerted effort to describe what lay ecclesial ministry is (7–14). The very fact that the 1999 report begins with an effort to define lay ministry indicates that thirty-some years after the council the definition of lay ministry remains unclear. We are, therefore, still trying to enunciate clearly what the major change regarding lay ministry truly is but with no clear-cut description of the term *lay*. The 1999 committee report in its own description of lay ministry makes mention of the secular character of lay ministry, but it describes the secular focus as only one element in its descriptive definition of lay ministry:

> **Conclusion 7:** All of the laity are called to work toward the transformation of the secular world. Some do this by working in the secular realm; others do this by working in the Church and focusing on the building of ecclesial communion, which has as its ultimate purpose the transformation of the world. Lay ecclesial ministry should not be seen as a retreat by the laity from their role in the secular realm. Rather lay ecclesial ministry is an affirmation that the Spirit can call the lay faithful to participation in the building of the Church in various ways. (cf. *LG* 12)

In this conclusion, the members of the subcommittee say clearly that there is both a secular orientation and an inner ecclesial orientation, and this position on church involvement is continued in **Conclusions 9** to **12**. This kind of language was deftly employed with some deliberate intention. At the end of the second millennium and the beginning of the third millennium some highly influential members of Roman Catholic leadership, both ecclesiastical and theological, were trying to claim that lay ministry was basically secular.[100] There was a clear intent by these influential leaders to minimize lay ministry within the liturgical and administrative dimensions of church life.

The very fact that so much discussion on what *lay* means has continued from the end of Vatican II down to the present indicates that the council *did* indeed bring about a major change in

---

100. This secular focus is the view of A. Sarmiento, T. Rincon, J.-M. Yangua, and A. Quiros, eds., *La Misión del Laico en la Iglesia y en el Mundo* (Pamplona: Ediciones Universidad de Navarra, 1987).

the Roman Catholic Church regarding the role of the laity. If this issue was not a major issue, discussion of the matter would have fizzled out shortly after Vatican II ended. The continuing presence regarding a description of lay ministry attests to its major status in today's church. Even though this major change may not be readily defined or described, the large amount of theological and official material on the question of lay ministry from 1965 to the present indicates that something major regarding the layperson has been established. This ongoing discussion of the very meaning of *lay* affects not only the theology, the pastoral ministry, and the personal identity of lay ministers themselves, but the discussion also affects the theology, pastoral ministry, and personal identity of all institutional ministers in the Roman Catholic Church. The discussion on lay ministry is interrelated to all other forms of institutional ministry. An ambiguity in one form of lay institutional ministry brings ambiguity to all other forms of institutional ministry. In our postconciliar period of church history, this ambiguous situation is where we are today. Interpretation of many texts in Vatican II remains divisive; there is acceptance or nonacceptance of certain conciliar positions, an acceptance or nonacceptance often based on particular interpretations. All of this renders the issue of the major change by the Vatican II bishops regarding lay ministry as yet unclarified.

In my view, one of the most serious reasons why the efforts to describe lay ministry have been (at least to date) woefully unsatisfactory is as follows. However, I present this simply as my view, *not* as an interpretation of the conciliar documents *nor* as a theological position that has an abundance of followers. My view is this: from the documents of Vatican II to the present one of the most extensive areas of lay ministerial activity of the church has simply been removed from the defining table. This extensive area of lay activity is the activity of nonordained religious men and women. In *Lumen gentium*, the discussion of religious was united intimately to the chapter on holiness (chapter 5). Without any doubt, there were solid reasons for doing this. However, the conciliar connection, which focuses religious life uniquely on the holiness of the church and not on the ministry of the church, has removed from the field of discourse something like 90 percent of lay ecclesial ministry. In the church's two thousand years of existence, the ministry of lay religious men and women has been enormous. To remove this vast amount of data from the discussion on lay ministry left the bishops and subsequently those in the postconciliar period struggling to define 10 percent of what lay ministry is all about. I use 90 percent and 10 percent more rhetorically than mathematically. In my judgment, lay ministry in the church includes the long history of lay ministry performed by many lay men and women who were also religious while they were ministering. The richness of their experience has helped, in actuality, to define what lay ministry in the church is all about. How can this material be summarily dismissed? Permit me to indicate the richness of this data by a quick overview of church history.

First, in the New Testament itself, we read about men and women involved in ministry. There is absolutely no way to determine with any certainty whether these people were ordained or not.[101] We see only that followers of Jesus from a variety of backgrounds served as ministers to the community, and even to people outside the Jesus communities.[102]

Second, there are the data from early monasticism (AD 200–600) that involve lay ministry.[103] In the first two centuries of Christian history, religious life cannot be pinpointed with any accuracy. The importance of religious life may not have begun with Anthony of Egypt (ca. 251–356); but the movement he invigorated developed rapidly, and the increase in numbers rose in geometric

---

101. B. D. Dupuy ("Theologie der kirchlichen Ämpter," *Mysterium Salutis* 4/2 [Einsiedeln: Benziger, 1973], 505) states the issue clearly: "Wie man in der Urkirche zum kirchlichen Dienst berufen wurde, wird im Neuen Testament nicht beschrieben, so dass jede dies bezügliche Theorie zum Teil hypothetischen Charakter hat." ("How someone in the early church is called to ecclesial ministry is not described in the New Testament, so that theories relative to ordination have in part a hypothetical quality about them.") Only with the *Apostolic Tradition*, sometime around the beginning of third century, do we have the first extant ritual of ordination; prior to this date the conjectural nature of all ordination theories cannot be denied.

102. See Osborne, *Priesthood*, 3–85.

103. See Osborne, *Ministry*, 233–72.

proportions.[104] Other leaders of this early movement can be enumerated: Pachomius, Horsiesios, and Theodore come to mind.
Two issues in this early movement are important for our concern:

a. Monastic life was *experienced* as a nonclerical movement.

b. Monastic life was *thought through* within nonclerical
categories.

Monastic or religious life in this early period of time was overwhelmingly *lay*. Men and women entered these communities of
laypeople and for the remainder of their lives everything around
them and about them was interpreted by lay leaders (e.g., abbots,
abbesses, priors, sub-priors, spiritual directors, and so on). For
them, Christian life was experienced in a profoundly lay fashion.
For a majority of these groups of people, only the celebration of
Eucharist was a clerical moment. History also indicates that many
men and women in these religious groups were engaged in ministry: namely, ministry to the sick and dying (early hospital ministry); ministries of education (monastic schools, which were highly
respected); ministries to the poor and needy (ministries of social
justice); missionary activities in areas where as yet there were no
bishops and priests (a phenomenon that continues to the present).

The importance of this historical datum is this: lay ministry
was a major part of life for many of these early religious communities. Lay ministry was also part of later religious communities such
as the Benedictines, the Cistercians, the Dominicans, and the
Franciscans, to cite but a few examples. Lay ministry was part of the
religious communities that arose at the time of the Protestant
Reformation. Lay ministry was a major part of the many religious
communities of both men and women that were established in the
nineteenth and twentieth centuries. In other words, religious life
and church ministry have always been deeply interrelated. This fact

---

104. There are some historical data on monastic life prior to Anthony, but it is
very thin and not easily interpreted with any clarity. Still, history indicates that a
monastic type of movement began sometime in the early part of the third century.
See Osborne, *Ministry*, 237ff.

alone indicates that there is a wealth of information on the meaning of lay ministry in this enormous amount of historical data.

Third, these religious movements, from 300 onward, were for the most part not under the control of local bishops, although some bishops even in the early centuries attempted to gain control over the monks.[105] Such episcopal efforts to control monks and religious have never been totally successful. In the last eighteen hundred years, religious life, by and large, has never been under the control of the episcopal hierarchy. In other words, not only their spiritual life but their ministries as well were under their own tutelage. Any study of the history of canon law indicates an ongoing struggle on the issue of independence or interdependence between religious communities and episcopal oversight. Such a struggle continues to this present day. Because of this relative independence, the lay religious ministerial experience brings to the table a rich history of lay ministries that were often not hierarchically controlled. The church is more than an episcopally determined institution, and episcopally determined institutional structures do not and cannot define the church. Chapter 1 of *Lumen gentium* was deliberately constructed as an ongoing development of Pius XII's *Mystici corporis*.[106] This deliberate stance, both in *Mystici corporis* and in chapter 1 of *Lumen gentium* entitled "The Mystery of the Church," indicates that episcopally determined institutionality is only one aspect of the mystery of church. Nor is such an institutionality presented as the defining element of the church. Thus, mission and ministry—or the sharing in the *tria munera* mission and ministry of Jesus—cannot be enclosed within episcopally determined institutional boundaries. The experience of lay religious, with its collegial or relational independence, provides contemporary discussion of lay ecclesial ministry with a necessary characteristic. Lay ecclesial ministry has its own legitimacy. Legitimacy does not come foundationally from episcopal endorsement. This issue is extremely touchy and divisive, and I realize this. We see the nervousness in

---

105. For early struggles between monks and bishops, see ibid, 263–69.

106. See Kloppenburg, *The Ecclesiology of Vatican II*, 37ff., for the connection of the encyclical *Mystici corporis* and *Lumen gentium*.

the many caveats that appear in today's literature on lay ministry, namely: "with the proper ecclesiastical authorization," or "in offices open to the lay people by canon law" or "in communion with the hierarchical pastors of the church," or "with proper delegation by church authorities." The collegial independence of religious life in the church gives an affirmation of the mystery of the church itself, a church that is larger and deeper, wider and broader than episcopally determined institutionality. The largeness of this religious-based ministry and its own relatively independent and intrinsic validity are a major part of any and every theology of lay ecclesial ministry. In such a theology of church, the very term *ecclesial*, expressed by the phrase "ecclesial lay ministry," is not centered on episcopally determined institutionality.

Fourth, lay religious ministry cannot be boxed into a form of charismatic ministry. One might be tempted to say that these lay religious ministries are simply examples of charismatic ministries, but this is not quite accurate. The institutional framework of ministries performed by lay religious men and women has been very much a part of the Roman Catholic Church structure itself. Few dioceses could have existed in the past and still cannot exist today unless there is a major presence of religious in their dioceses. Episcopal jurisdiction over these religious is not at all uniform. What religious have done and continue to do institutionally and ministerially in a given diocese is indeed a major part of church life. Institutionality and episcopal oversight, however, are not coterminous.

Fifth, it would be shortsighted to say that these activities are ministries of a special group: namely, lay religious men and women under vows. In religious hospitals and care centers, in religious educational institutions, in religious outreach to the works of social justice (e.g., homelessness, housing for the poor, hunger and therefore dining rooms for the needy)—in all of these there exist numerically more lay men and women who are *not* religious in *vows* but who are working as lay ministers in these various ministries. My emphasis here is this: the experience that the religious and their ministerial activities bring to the table is not simply that of lay religious or vowed men and women. A great part of the experience belongs to the numerous, nonreligious lay men and women who share in these same ministries of the vowed religious.

Sixth, the experience of lay ministry brought to the table by the religious and their nonreligious co-workers also brings an over-powering amount of feminine experience of both church and ministry. From 1950 onward many religious women have joined other groups of women to further today's presence of feminist theology, feminist action, and feminist self-identity. These vowed religious women have often been key personages in this feminist phenomenon, since they have brought to these movements a depth of spirituality and a depth of already formulated ministerial action. The leadership of these women deserves to have a place at the table.

All of this is a richness in lay activity that cannot be set aside by some negating brackets: not this and not that. Such bracketing of this enormous historical data of lay involvement in ministry leaves a residue that defies adequate definition. The presence of this almost two thousand years of experience in lay ministry brings to the table a historical rootage and strength for all lay ecclesial ministry. It brings a dual comprehensive grasp—a grasp of the rich possibilities of lay ministry and a grasp of personal spiritual life of men and women. In both instances, the data come from thousands of people, some of whom are vowed religious and many of whom are not vowed religious.

Religious life in the Roman Catholic Church has a long history. Some of it is, unfortunately, not that helpful. Most of it is, however, profoundly enriching. Religious life, more often than not, is a response to the working of the Holy Spirit. This working of the Holy Spirit has been associated again and again with a specific charism. Nonetheless, the charismatic life and the charismatic ministry of these religious groups differ from a single person who has been and is today a marvelous exemplar of a charismatic church leader. The religious groups—this is the community, not the individual—are central in religious life. The very term *group* indicates an institution, and the ministry of this religious institution is institutional, even though episcopal jurisdiction over it is minimal. There is more to church institutionality than hierarchical institutionality. Religious institutional life, which includes both religious members and nonreligious members, involves the cooperative work of vowed and nonvowed in a given religious institutional ministry. It is this vast experience that is needed today if we are to understand the major role that laypeople bring to the mystery called "church." The current ignoring of this wealth of lay ministerial experience in the church has made the search for the meaning of lay ecclesial ministry myopic.

In this sense, Vatican II did not make a major change, since it left this group to one side. The aftereffects of Vatican II on the issue of lay ecclesial ministry remain in a struggling-to-be-understood status. We need to look at a *larger context of lay ecclesial ministry*. It is this context—as mentioned above, not just the religious men and women but the many co-workers with them—that will help us see today what is the depth and height, length and breadth of lay ecclesial ministry in the church. Without this context, we are describing an abstract group of people who exist only on paper but not in reality.

The expansion of lay ministry and leadership in the Roman Catholic Church includes a sense of coresponsibility. In the post-conciliar Roman Catholic Church, the 1984 revised *Code of Canon Law* has juridically endorsed lay leadership and ministry in many significant areas. The presence of lay men or women is at times a mandated juridical presence; at times it is an optional but approved presence. In virtue of this mandated or approved expansion of lay presence in the ministry and leadership of the church, boundaries once again appear as the most difficult source of friction. Laypeople, so it is argued, have taken over tasks that the priest alone formerly did. Others note that it is not simply a matter of taking over a task, but a consequent owning of the task. There have been questions about the source of these ministerial duties: Are they only delegated and therefore contingently dependent? Or is there a stability to some of these tasks, so that a new bishop or pastor cannot simply "clean house"? The presence of officially appointed women ministers has raised the issue of gender. Many priests are still not comfortable with women at the boundaries of their own positions.

The postconciliar ambiguity on the expansion of lay ministry has a clear root in the Decree on the Apostolate of Lay People, *Apostolicam actuositatem*. In this decree, the reasons for an expanded presence of lay activity in the church are discussed. The following reasons are given:

1. The world is today more populous and complex, and trained lay men and women are needed to meet this complexity.

2. There is a legitimate autonomy for many sectors of human life, and a lay presence is far more effective than an ordained presence.

3. There is a current lack of vocations to the ordained ministry, with the exception of the growing numbers of permanent deacons.[107]

Two issues from this decree have colored the response of many postconciliar church officials and theologians to the presence and activity of an enhanced laity. First of all, some Roman Catholics emphasize that lay ministers are needed today since there is a crisis of priestly vocations. This means that if there were more priests available, the lay ministers would disappear. This is a view that has often been deliberately voiced by bishops and priests, but it is also a view that several bishops and priests themselves quietly maintain. On the other hand, there is a major theological position in the church today that sees lay ministry, of both men and women, as a major breakthrough in the very understanding of ministry.[108] The presence of lay ministers is not seen as provisional or temporary. Lay ministers have become an integral and constitutive part of church structure.

Second, the presence of lay influence has become clearer in recent years, for many lay men and women have attended accredited schools of theology and have received official degrees in theology and ministry. This accreditation gives them not only credibility but also a level of theological knowledge that rivals that of the clergy. The number of these accredited ministers in the church

---

107. Lakeland, *Liberation of the Laity*, 95–98.

108. There are many books on lay ministry today. Some have been very thought-provoking, such as Edward Schillebeeckx, *Ministry: Leadership in the Community of Jesus Christ* (New York: Crossroad, 1981); Leonardo Boff, *Church, Charism and Power: Liberation Theology and the Institutional Church* (New York: Crossroad, 1985); Rosemary Radford Ruether, *Women-Church: Theology and Practice of Feminist Liturgical Communities* (San Francisco: Harper & Row, 1985).

continues to grow today. On the other hand, from the beginning of the new millennium onward, several American bishops have set up their own diocesan ministerial formation programs for lay ministry. These programs are not accredited, and they do not provide the lay ministers with a theological competence on a par with the clergy. The current trend in these dioceses is to hire such locally generated ministers, who are clearly of lesser theological integrity, with the consequence that bishops do not hire people who have received accredited theological degrees. In this way, the intellectual and theological quality of the lay minister in a diocese moves downward, and the theological influence of accredited lay ministers has been somewhat neutered, since there is no employment for such people. Diocesan control, not theological or professional control, has taken over. In many ways, such locally trained and formed ministers do not and cannot present a strong theological and professional challenge to the bishop, to the local priests, and to the people of God generally.

These diocesan-based formation programs for lay ministers also allow the local bishop to control the kind of theology that the lay ministers receive. It is more than evident today that some bishops want only the theology as found in the *Catechism of the Catholic Church* to be operative in their diocese. Generally, bishops do not control the theological faculties of the seminaries to which they have sent their own students, and so in many seminaries the professors are not constrained by one source: namely, the theology of the *Catechism*. In these institutions, students read primary sources of theology, such as Augustine, Thomas Aquinas, and Bonaventure. However, the theology in the diocesan formation programs for lay men and women—and this also holds for the formation programs for permanent deacons—is under the supervision of the local bishop. The issue of accepting the *Catechism*'s views as the only view to be tolerated makes an eventual major confrontation inevitable. The *Catechism* presents a Thomistic view of theology. Other theological views remain integral to the church's own tradition.

For all Catholic Christians, the New Testament is the primary lens through which our faith is understood and interpreted. Without the New Testament, there would be no church at all, since we would know practically nothing about Jesus. There is also the teaching of the magisterium, but this magisterial teaching is also judged by the New Testament. Magisterial teaching is not above and beyond the Word of God. We read in *Dei Verbum (DV):* "This magisterium is not superior to the word of God, but is rather its servant" (7). Even the *documents* of Vatican II are servants to the Word of God: "Following, then, in the steps of the council of Trent and Vatican I, this synod wishes to set forth the authentic teaching on divine revelation and its transmission" (*DV* 1). Any and every catechism, including the present *Catechism* is likewise a servant to the Word of God. The Word of God remains the lens through which a *Catechism* is to be understood. However, it is becoming evident in the United States that for many powerful groups the *Catechism* is at least indirectly considered the only lens through which one interprets the documents of Vatican II and, indeed, through which one judges all theology. All of this points to a not-too-distant major confrontation over theological and faith criteria. This is, unfortunately, part of the context for today's institutional ecclesial ministry and leadership, and this disturbing current contextual situation affects lay ministry more decisively than other institutional church ministries.

A different approach can be seen in such movements as The Voice of the Faithful and Call to Action. In several dioceses, the views of these groups have been judged unacceptable. In theology, however, the phrase *sensus fidelium*—sense of the faithful—has usually been interpreted precisely as the voice of the laypeople. Although the term *sensus fidelium* has had many differing interpretations, it has consistently been an honored theological principle. In a general way, *sensus fidelium* indicates that the laypeople have a sort of intuitive understanding of God's presence in a given situation. Its existence is even described in *Lumen gentium:* "The body of the faithful as a whole anointed as they are by the Holy One, cannot err in matters of belief" (*LG* 12). Such a sense manifests itself when there is "universal agreement in matters of faith and morals" (ibid.). The *sensus fidelium* historically has often been most apparent in the reception and acceptance of official statements, including conciliar statements. Yet another issue in which *sensus fidelium* might be applied is the reaction of the Roman Catholic community to *Humanae vitae* by Paul VI. On July 29, 1968, Msgr.

Ferdinando Lambruschini, who officially promulgated this encyclical, did so by stating clearly that it was not intended to be an infallible document.[109] Since then, Catholic lay men and women in large
numbers have rejected the decision of Paul VI, since it was not an
issue of infallibility.

In 1988, Giovanni Magnani, wrote a lengthy essay entitled
"Does the So-Called Theology of the Laity Possess a Theological
Status?"[110] In this essay, Magnani assembles all the major issues on
the enhancement of lay ministry by Vatican II that have had a major
impact on the postconciliar church. There are several key conciliar
texts whose exact meaning is hotly disputed. There is a variety of
interpretations given to particular conciliar texts after Vatican II.
This variety of interpretations of a given text offers another example of present-day, highly sensitive dispute. Then there are the
struggles either to accept certain conciliar positions or in one way
or another not to accept a conciliar position at all. This acceptance
or nonacceptance ranges from a fairly radical rejection of some
interpretations to a minimizing rejection as regards other interpretations. One of the key issues in all the official writings and theological discussions of the issue of lay ministry in a postconciliar
church is the search for a definition of lay ministry. The general
goal for many of the writers Magnani cites is this: if we can define

---

109. Msgr. Ferdinando Lambruschini officially presented the encyclical *Humanae
vitae* at a press conference at the Vatican Press hall, July 29, 1968. In his presentation, Lambruschini officially stated: "The pronouncement has come. It is not
infallible but does not leave the questions concerning birth regulation in a condition of vague problematics....The assent of theological faith is due only to the definitions properly called infallible, but there is owed also loyal and full assent,
interior and not only exterior, to an authentic pronouncement of the magisterium,
in proportion to the level of the authority from which it emanates—which in this
case is the supreme authority of the Supreme Pontiff—and its object, which is
most weighty since it is a mater of a tormented question of the regulation of
births." See *The Tidings* (Archdiocese of Los Angeles), August 2, 1968, 1. Paul VI
did not issue this as an infallible statement, and since 1968 the issue has never been
settled infallibly.
110. Giovanni Magnani, "Does the So-Called Theology of the Laity Possess a
Theological Status?" in *Vatican II: Assessment and Perspectives: Twenty-five Years
After (1962–1987)*, ed. René Latourelle, 3 vols. (New York: Paulist Press, 1988),
1:568–633.

lay ministry, the problem issues will go away. Not all agree with this goal-definition position. Theologians, in particular, have argued pro and con. Among the theologians whom Magnani cites as leading figures in these debates are I. de la Potterie, J. B. Bauer, M. Jourjon, L. Pizzolato, Yves M.-J. Congar, P. G. Bruno, E. Schillebeeckx, P. Guilmot, J. Daniélou, F. Klostermann, G. Philips, A. Oberti, G. Lazzati, to mention only the more frequently cited. We would not have this theological material by eminent theologians if there was not some sort of major change involved over the issue of lay ecclesial ministry.

As mentioned above, definitions of various individualized church ministries will not settle all the problematic issues, since definitions tend to isolate and nonrelate a given reality. Since there is such a profound interrelational quality about ministry, which is evident throughout the documents of Vatican II, definitional theology ends up in nonrelational dimensions. As a result, the contextualized interrelationality of ministry found in the documents of Vatican II is omitted. Such is the situation with lay ecclesial ministry today. Too many official texts and theological positions move in the direction of definitional theology. The very presence of this theological literature is one of the major reasons why this particular change in ecclesial ministry, which Vatican II clearly established, remains in a morass of ambiguity and uncertainty.

There is, however, a second reason for the uncertainty and ambiguity: the arena in which lay ministry is discussed takes place with either an acknowledged or a nonacknowledged presupposition, namely, that Jesus established the church in a clearly definable way. There is today a dominant and normative theology of the church that needs to be reconsidered in a radical way, since major scholarly research from the twentieth century has seriously questioned the way in which Jesus established the church. This material on the institution of the church has not been faced by church authorities and some theologians. Not facing these issues gives to this dominant and normative theology of the church a resounding incredibility.

Chapter Nine

THE POSITIVE AND NEGATIVE REALITIES OF THE FIVE MAJOR CONCILIAR CHANGES IN CHURCH MINISTRY

Each of the five major changes in ecclesial ministry that took place during the sessions of Vatican II has had positive and negative reactions. The changes in ecclesial ministry, which are highly contextual in nature, have also engendered major implications for the theological, pastoral, and personal understanding of the permanent diaconate. This chapter, then, is divided as follows: first, we will consider the positive and negative realities that each of the five major changes has brought about. Second, we will consider the more important implications that the contextualization of ministry has had on the permanent diaconate.

The Positive and Negative Realities That the Five Changes Have Engendered

In this section we will consider each of the five major changes, indicating the key positive gains that these changes have actually made, as well as the still unsettled issues that each of the changes has brought about.

1. The Establishment of the Mission and Ministry of All Baptized-Confirmed Christians as a Foundation of Institutional Church Ministry

POSITIVE RESULTS

The first change concerning the institutional and sacramental sharing in the mission and ministry of Jesus himself by all baptized and confirmed Christians is, in many ways, the most important and significant of all the five changes. This change enhanced in a far-reaching way the role of the baptized within the church itself. It reestablished the sacraments of baptism and confirmation as the true door into the church, whereas from AD 1000 onward the door into the church was, practically speaking, the sacrament of ordination. The dignity of Christian life has been profoundly enhanced, and the spirituality of a Christian woman or man has been powerfully endorsed.

NEGATIVE RESULTS

Only a few Roman Catholics have rejected outright this change. Daniele Menozzi cites some of these people: the followers of Abbé George de Nantes and their journal *Contreréforme catholique au XXe siècle*, the Dominicans of the Cahiers de Cassiciacum; E. Gerstner's Liga katholischer Traditionalisten; the followers of the periodical *Fortes in fide*, edited by N. Barbara; and the readers of *The Remnant*. All of these simply accuse the pope of heresy and therefore declare a state of *sede vacante*. Other groups are less radical, such as the associations of Una voce, Opus sacerdotale, Credo, Silenziosi dell Chiesa. These groups accept the decisions of Vatican II, but only as pastoral; therefore, in their view they have no dogmatic value at all.[111]

Among those in the mainstream of catholic life, there are only a few who reject the positions presented in chapter 2 of *Lumen gentium*. Publicly, the changes presented in chapter 2 of *Lumen Gentium* are accepted and acknowledged. The implications of these changes

---

111. Daniele Menozzi, "Opposition to the Council (1966–1984)," in *The Reception of Vatican II*, 325–26.

are, however, minimized or to a degree neglected. In the *Catechism of the Catholic Church*, there is a section on the people of God (781–86). This section begins with a long citation from the opening chapter of *LG* (9). "The people of God participates in these three offices of Christ and bear the responsibilities for mission and service that flow from them" (783).[112] This is followed by three paragraphs, repeating the material from *Lumen gentium* on the people of God as priestly, prophetic, and royal. When the *Catechism*, in this same section, moves to a full explanation of the ministry of the church (857–945), there is a section on the lay faithful that corresponds to *Lumen gentium*, chapter 4. However, in chapter 4 of *Lumen gentium* the focus is on certain Christians who are engaged in ecclesial ministry, which is totally different from the focus of chapter 2. Today we would speak of such ministerial Christians as the lectors, the communion ministers, the ushers, and so on. In the *Catechism*, a reference to the ministry and mission of all the baptized and confirmed Christians is simply omitted in this lengthy section, which is entitled "Why the ecclesial ministry?" In other words, in the section on "Christ's Faithful—Hierarchy, Laity, Consecrated Life" (871–945), there is no effort to integrate the mission and ministry of all baptized Christians into the answer of the question: Why the ecclesial ministry? The mission and ministry of all baptized and confirmed Christians are not presented as a foundational ecclesial ministry. This form of subtle minimizing of the implications of chapter 2 indicates that there is a certain discomfort with the sharing in Jesus' mission and ministry by all baptized and confirmed Christians. The sharing is acknowledged when church ministry itself is the center of attention, but it is kept at a low profile. *Why the ecclesial ministry?* The focus is on pope, bishop, priest, deacon, and only to some degree *certain* lay men and women. The *Catechism* answers its own question but without any mention of the people of God and their ecclesial ministry.

---

112. This is really a citation from the encyclical by John Paul II, *Redemptor hominis*, 18–21.

2. The Reestablishment of the Episcopacy as an Official Part of the Sacrament of Orders

POSITIVE RESULTS

The second change was more a matter of recognition than of content. Most theologians in the two centuries prior to Vatican II were urging that episcopacy was an integral part of the sacrament of holy orders. From 1150 to Vatican II, the theological position that priesthood was the highest order in the sacrament of orders, thus eliminating episcopacy, was the official position of the church. The Council of Trent had not rejected this common theological view. What theologians after Trent were asking for was an official or magisterial approbation of the theological view that bishops were indeed an intrinsic part of the sacrament of holy orders. When the bishops stated the following: "This sacred synod teaches that by episcopal consecration is conferred the fullness of the sacrament of orders" (*LG* 21), a magisterial approbation occurred. This was the major impact of the change. The standard theology of the Roman Catholic Church was changed for the better. There is no doubt about this positive step, and there is really no nonacceptance of this position.

NEGATIVE RESULTS

The position itself is accepted, but the implications of this major change have, as yet, not been accepted. Many bishops in the United States and elsewhere continue to see themselves as vicars of the pope rather than as bishops who are called and commissioned by God *vi sacramenti*. These bishops, as well as some episcopal leaders of the United States Conference of Catholic Bishops, tend to foster a dependence on Rome, rather than see themselves as bishops by the grace of God for their dioceses. Even the *Code of Canon Law* fosters this dependence, since there is in the canons an ongoing mention that episcopal conferences must present their major conclusions to Rome for some sort of "recommendation." In all honesty there is a political dimension to episcopal life, as far as promotions to better dioceses are concerned. Good relationships with Rome are a benefit to a bishop who wants to move to a better diocese. Rome, for its part, has fostered this vicarious dependence. Bishops who express views that are considered outside the accepted pale are at times given an early retirement or are promoted in order to be removed. Some dioceses have been literally divided in half, so that an outspoken bishop or even a cardinal is deprived of a strong official base. Letting bishops truly be bishops has often not been the major effect of this particular change.

Collegiality was stressed at Vatican II, and bishops are meant to be *collegial*. Their collegiality involves the papacy, and the papacy as well must be collegial. In practice, however, the collegiality or interrelationality of bishops is not a major part of episcopal and papal life. Nor are bishops keen on their interrelational role with the presbyterium. Some bishops see themselves more as a CEO than a collegial-presbyterial-interrelational minister and leader. This is simply a fact of our time, which leaves the theology of episcopacy with its collegial and interrelational aspects in an abstract life of its own, while the pastoral life of bishops and the personal identity of bishops remains far more individualized.

3. The Redefinition of Priesthood on the Basis of the Tria Munera

POSITIVE RESULTS

This conciliar change has provided priests with a much more Jesus-centered view of their priesthood. The use of the *tria munera* to describe priestly theology, pastoral practice, and personal identity has enriched the meaning of priestly life. There are no open voices of major dissent on this change made by Vatican II, except for those persons and groups who were mentioned above. Not all priests have reached an understanding of what this change implies, but priests generally find this approach to priesthood far more nourishing than the scholastic view, which dominated the Roman Catholic Church from 1150 to Vatican II. The change was sudden and dramatic, but nonetheless one that has been encouraging and nourishing.

NEGATIVE RESULTS

In many ways, this change was dropped on the church without much preliminary catechesis. The *tria munera* open wide vistas, but in the pastoral life of many priests the time and effort in a typical workweek devoted to the primary *munus*—**teaching** and **preaching**—involve only a small portion of the priest's time. The second *munus*, the priest as **sanctifier,** receives more time and attention. The third *munus*, the **administrator-leader,** takes up most of his time and effort in any given workweek. In other words, the theology is fine with teacher-preacher as top priority, sanctifier as second priority, and leadership as the third priority. Pastoral practice, however, is just the opposite with most of the priest's time caught up in administration. This situation is complicated by the presence of permanent deacons and various lay men and women in ministerial positions. Boundaries are not honored, especially in the area of administration and leadership. Yet, if this area is only a *third* priority, then there is much that a priest might cease doing and concentrate more on the teaching and sanctifying aspects of priestly life. When this happens, however, the priest's personal identity often becomes ambiguous. "What am I doing," he may ask, "if I am not running the parish?"

Finally, the bishop is presented in Vatican II as the highest priest. Where does this leave a lower priest and what does this mean? What does this mean for permanent deacons as well? This issue was simply mentioned in the documents of Vatican II. Nowhere in the documents was it explained. The bishops left the task of explanation to theologians. To date, we theologians have not adequately clarified the meaning of this phrase—*the highest priesthood.* Similar to the collegial nature of bishops, the notion of presbyterium has not been adequately dealt with theologically, pastorally, or for one's personal identity. The emphasis on presbyterium is an emphasis on interrelationality. Priests are meant to act not as *individuals* but as a *group.* Here, too, this has not been fully articulated from the standpoint of theology, pastoral practice, and personal identity. The ordinary priest as well as the permanent deacon should be interrelational with the bishop and his fellow priests and permanent deacons, but busy schedules disallow time for interrelational contact. The crisis today regarding clerical sexual abuse and the episcopal efforts of cover-up have also affected this isolationist situation. The Dallas declaration by the bishops of the United States accepted a zero-tolerance stance. Priests are seeing fellow priests removed from all diocesan ministries and placed in a limbo of total ineffectiveness. To relate to these priests might be seen as improper, so they are left alone by their fellow priests. To complain to the bishop might be seen as improper, so priests move more strongly into an individualistic lifestyle. Bishops, for their part, are trying to maintain their own reputation so their contacts with priests of their diocese are minimized. The relationship of many bishops to the permanent deacons in their dioceses is no different. Some make only cameo appearances at deacon retreats and deacon gatherings. Some make no appearance at all. In all of this, what do presbyterium, permanent deacon, collegiality, and interrelationality mean? John Paul II even called the presbyterium—and interrelational group— necessary, but current circumstances move against interpersonal priest–bishop and deacon–bishop contact. Even between permanent deacon and pastor there is a similar nonrelationship.

4. The Reestablishment of the Permanent Diaconate

POSITIVE RESULTS

The reestablishment of the permanent diaconate has brought blessing to church ministry itself and to those who are permanent deacons. The willingness of so many Catholic men to be permanent deacons is an indication that there is something very meaningful in this conciliar change. The permanent deacons, in strong ways, have been spiritually nourished by their sacramental activity, whether this be the Eucharist, baptism, or marriage. They have become better followers of Jesus. To this one must add that these men have been of great help pastorally to many men and women. By and large, they are available and compassionate. Some deacons have moved into ministries in which today's priests do not enter in any large number. In Canada, for example, a Roman Catholic permanent deacon can be a chaplain for the military. Some deacons have been exceptional in their work in prison ministry. Others have reached out to the social needs of the parishioners or have moved strongly into hospital ministry and ministry to the sick and shut-ins. All of this has been a very positive enrichment of Roman Catholic life.

NEGATIVE RESULTS

Permanent deacons are still very much at sea regarding their personal identity as a full and equal order in the clerical world of the Roman Catholic Church. On the one hand, parish priests often consider the permanent deacon to be a person who is crossing their priestly boundaries. Yet on the other hand, qualified lay men and women are doing many things that deacons are doing, thus raising the question: Why be a deacon? Where are the boundaries of the diaconate? Again there is a mixing of theology, pastoral practice, and personal identity. If the theology is not clear, can the pastoral practice and the personal identity be clear? If the pastoral practice seems to run the show, then where is the theology, which often remains abstract and unrealistic? If personal identity is unclear, then there is an antagonism when pastoral practice and theology move in directions that clash with one's identity. Finally, there is the balancing, for most permanent deacons, between the responsibilities and legitimate joys of married life, on the one hand, and the responsibilities and delights of being a deacon, on the other. Permanent deacons who are married live two lives, and either the wife and the family are, at times, not content, or the pastor, other parish priests, or even the bishop are, at other times, not content. Clerical life has been monogamous for centuries; the intrusion of married people into the clerical world has yet to find its happy way.

5. The Official Expansion of Lay Ministry into the Ecclesial Dimensions of the Tria munera

POSITIVE RESULTS

Since Vatican II, Roman Catholic lay men and women have entered the ministerial life of the church with abundance and enthusiasm. Many have prepared themselves for such ministry by years of study at schools of theology. In many ways, the Rite of Christian Initiation of Adults (RCIA) (1972), religious education programs, confirmation programs, along with parish societies and sodalities, would never take place at all without these dedicated and trained men and women. In many dioceses, the chancery office works well because of an abundance of lay ministers. The enrichment of the American church by these dedicated men and women cannot be overestimated. For many of these men and women the work is voluntary; for others there is a salary, but a salary that in no way reflects their talents and expertise.

When one considers the world of Roman Catholic life, the presence of lay men and women in ministerial roles throughout South America, Central America, and Mexico is astounding. In many areas, priestless Catholic life is simply a given; these lay men and women become, for all practical purposes, the "priests" of these areas. The same is true in Africa. The statement of the Vietnamese bishops on the role of the laity in Vietnam was a major statement for a church that is limited in activity by governmental restrictions.

NEGATIVE RESULTS

No one openly contradicts the change that the conciliar bishops mandated for lay ministry. The presence of lay ministers has become a fairly accepted part of Roman Catholic life. Nonetheless, in some chanceries all main roles have been entrusted to priests, with the laypeople moved out of any high-ranking diocesan roles. In this way, some bishops indicate their opposition to lay leadership in their dioceses. Where lay men or women have been placed in charge of a parish, a new bishop sweeps them out and finds a replacement, often a priest from another country. Lay groups such as Voice of the Faithful are publicly disparaged not only by some bishops but also by some pastors. Call for Action is suspect. Although we read in the documents of Vatican II that the lay men and women have been given a voice by the Holy Spirit (*LG* 12) and have a right and duty to be apostles (*AA* 3), there are many clerical leaders who do not want to hear this voice. Even some diocesan seminaries are training a new generation of priests who prefer not to work with laypeople.

The bishops of the United States are not all that helpful. Lay men and women have been highly critical of the bishops' conduct regarding clerical sexual abuse. Lay men and women have openly questioned the validity of the bishops' moral authority because of their conduct in these instances. To say that the bishops have lost their moral authority in the American church is, in many ways, a given. The bishops have focused more on themselves and their prestige than on the pain and abuse caused by some clergy. We will feel the effects of this entire situation for the next two to three generations, and the lay men and women who have generously given time and effort to the church will need to see major changes in episcopal leadership and style. They do not see Jesus in these bishops; they see hierarchs, and this must change. Only the bishops themselves can do this.

6. Concluding Observations

In all of the material discussed in part 1 of this book, the phrase *tria munera* has been used over and over again. I am well aware that this phrase is new for Roman Catholic theology. In the early fathers of the church, one reads a binary connection, such as, priest-prophet or prophet-king, but none of the early fathers of the church used the triadic form: prophet-priest-king. Protestant theologians in the sixteenth century (Calvin and Bucer) began to use the triadic form, *tria munera*, in church ministry. In reaction, Catholic theologians in those centuries tended to avoid using this phrase. In the nineteenth century, a few spiritual writers for priestly religious life began to use the phrase *tria munera*. Thomas O'Meara, in his volume *Theology of Ministry*, states:

> The ecclesiology of "priest, prophet, and king" is a transitional theology. It has some rich biblical and patristic sources, and permitted Roman Catholic thinking to move away from an isolation of all activity in the ordained. But it remains a theology that has considerable limitations and is not adequate for today's local church.[113]

---

113. O'Meara, *Theology of Ministry*, 265. A postconciliar emphasis on Spirit Christology and even on Spirit ecclesiology indicates that the *tria munera* approach, which is dominantly christological, needs to be broadened into a pneumatological dimension as well. This development is moving, although slowly, within the thinking of Roman Catholic leaders since Vatican II.

O'Meara is correct in his assessment. In part 1 of this present work, I have used *tria munera* again and again, simply because it is the phrase used by the conciliar bishops in their many documents. The phrase is used for the mission and ministry of Jesus himself, and then for all those who share in the mission and ministry of Jesus. This includes *all* baptized-confirmed Christians, the pope, the bishop, the priest, the deacon, and the layperson. The documents of Vatican II speak of all ministries, but there is no specific connection of the papacy to the *tria munera* nor of the permanent diaconate to the *tria munera*. The bishops avoided a section on the papacy,[114] and they left the description of the permanent diaconate up to the pope and the conferences of bishops. Paul VI, as we noted above, did use the phrase tria munera when he reinstated the permanent diaconate.

A *tria munera* theology, however, is not the basic issue. The bishops deliberately used a *tria munera* theology to indicate a foundational and interrelational base for all who share in the mission and ministry of Jesus. O'Meara's word, *isolation*, indicates that the major change is from an isolated theology of ministry to an interrelated theology of ministry. This is the most important issue; not the use or nonuse of the phrase *tria munera*. God sent Jesus with a mission and a ministry. Jesus spent his life with a mission and a ministry. In the church, Christians do *not* have their own mission and ministry; they *share* in the mission and ministry of Jesus himself. This sharing in Jesus' own mission and ministry is the foundational, interrelational base for all institutional ministry in the church. This sharing begins with baptism and confirmation and therefore is itself institutional and sacramental. Any baptized-confirmed Christian *must* be part of the people of God if he/she wishes to take on a particular ministry, such as papacy, episcopacy, priesthood, permanent diaconate, or a specific lay ministry. It is this interrelational context of all institutional ecclesial ministry that is the focus of part 1 of this book. I am not defending the use of a *tria munera* theology. I am,

---

114. The hesitation of the bishops at Vatican II vis-à-vis the papacy has been discussed at length in Gérard Philips, *La Chiesa e il suo Mistero* (Milan: Jaca Books, 1975), 247ff.; and in Lukas Vischer's "The Reception of the Debate on Collegiality," in *The Reception of Vatican II*, 233–48.

however, stating that an interrelational theology of ministry is today the teaching of the Roman Catholic Church. The documents of Vatican II leave no doubt on this issue. Consequently, the acceptance or nonacceptance of this interrelational context for all institutional ecclesial ministries today is of immense concern. The acceptance and nonacceptance situation is, in my view, the most overwhelming reason why we have today's problematic areas on the issue of institutional ministry in all its forms. Unless this struggle over acceptance or nonacceptance is ameliorated, the problems of ministry today, whether theological, pastoral, or of one's personal identity, cannot and will not be resolved.

The reluctance to accept a relational form of ministry is perhaps more philosophical than theological. In the Roman Catholic Church some form of scholastic theology has dominated the Western church from roughly 1300 onward. Gradually, a neo-Thomistic theology became the dominant form of theological thinking. In scholastic theology, the philosophy of Aristotle was pervasive, although some medieval scholastic theologians were more accepting of Aristotelian philosophy than some of their counterparts. Still, in all of the scholastic writers a basic philosophical stance is evident. In the dominant Roman Catholic theological thinking of the past century a basic philosophical stance is also evident. Perhaps it is not immediately evident, but philosophical thinking does pervade theological thinking. In the Aristotelian form of philosophy, substance, quantity, quality, and relationship are the four predicamental categories. All reality is either substance or quantity or quality or relation. This was the genius of Aristotle. He presented a comprehensive philosophy that took into account all of reality.

Primary substance for Aristotle dominates these four predicamental categories, and primary substance is presented as that which can be defined with no relationship to anything else. At its depth, Aristotelian philosophy is nonrelational. Thomas Aquinas cites this description of substance several times in his works, and he accepts it as his own working definition of substance. Substance can also be considered the basic nature of some reality, as the essence of some reality, and so on. In other words, essential reality is nonrelational. This nonrelational aspect allows us to see what things truly are.

Truth, therefore, in this view depends on a nonrelational understanding of what something ultimately is. Something is true when
we can clearly understand it in itself, not in a relational way. I mention this because the reluctance to accept an interrelational theology of ministry might be indicative of a basic philosophical stance
rather than a basic theological stance. If this is true, then the problem is refocused to a philosophical field of discourse and there is no
such thing as a defined philosophy. I mention this only to make
note of it.[115]

The Major Implications of the Contextualization of Contemporary Ecclesial Ministry for a Theological, a Pastoral, and a Personal Understanding of the Permanent Diaconate

The diaconate of itself is a part of an *institutional leadership*
within the Christian community. So, too, the episcopacy, the presbyterate, and the papacy are parts of the *institutional leadership*
within the Christian community. All of these ministries are basically and constitutively institutional. That some deacons, bishops,
priests, and even popes have been, over the centuries, not only
revered institutional ministers but also highly honored charismatic
leaders does not mean that magnetic charismatic leadership is part
of the job description for the diaconate, episcopacy, presbyterate,
and papacy. Each of these ministries is fundamentally an institutional form of church leadership. Since they are all institutional and
existing within one and the same institution, they are also tightly
interrelated and mutually interfacing. What seriously affects any
one of these institutional forms of church leadership also affects, in
a fairly strong way, all the other institutional forms of church lead-

---

115. A relational position dominates the Franciscan approach to theology and
philosophy, and this is evident in the thirteenth-century authors such as Alexander
of Hales, Bonaventure, and John Duns Scotus. There are clear differences
between the Franciscan intellectual tradition and the Dominican intellectual tradition, and the issue of relationship remains key to this differentiation.

ership. None of these institutional forms of leadership is an island unto itself.

Since there is this basic interrelationship, numerous official and unofficial descriptions of their interfacing boundaries have been issued over the course of time. Protocols that set limits and mark out areas of authority between these institutional ministries have been drawn up repeatedly over the centuries of church life. In each of these descriptive and even proscriptive documents, one finds some clearly stated tasks reserved to each form of leadership, and at the same time one discovers areas of unresolved task-assignment. Each new publication of regulations and guidelines seems to engender another new series of questions about the unresolved areas. As a result, still more regulations and guidelines are needed, and therefore a new set of publications is required. There seems to be an endless cycle of these kinds of protocols. The recent publication of the *National Directory for the Formation, Ministry, and Life of the Permanent Deacons in the United States* (2005) is a high point for this kind of publication. There is a maturity of perspective throughout this document, indicating that the experience of the permanent diaconate in the United States has been deeply evaluated and honored. The two secondary documents in this volume, *Basic Standards for Readiness* and *Visit of Consultation Teams to Diocesan Permanent Diaconate Formation Programs*, provide keen insights into the ways in which an interrelated understanding of diaconal ministry might take place.

This line of thought leads us to the issue of *historical context*. When one takes a long and wide-angled glance over the centuries of the history of church leadership, one can easily say that there are no water-tight bulkheads when it comes to institutional church leadership. This should not be startling, for there is a porosity not only in various specific forms of church leadership but also in all institutional forms of societal leadership. Porosity is present, whether one likes it or not, because institutions are radically historical. Institutional leadership is continually changing, since people are changing, societies are changing, institutions are changing, and cultures are changing. Changes rearrange boundaries. For human and societal leadership of any and every nature, there is no single, cookie-cutter format. Between a given group of leaders and a given group of the led, there is always a process of give and take, of offering leadership and accepting the offer of leadership. Only when one considers this human-historical context of societal leadership will a historical-theological study of the diaconate be meaningful.

From the material in this first part, we can draw some helpful guidelines for the ministry of today's permanent deacon. These all have to do in one way or another with the self-identity of the contemporary permanent deacon, for at this moment of time the self-identity of what a permanent deacon should be is still a matter of discussion and investigation. It is hoped that the following points, based on the material from the initial part of this volume, will be of assistance to the many deacons who are working for the people of God in the Christian communities throughout North America.

   a. The self-identity of a permanent deacon today involves a self-identity as an institutional leader in the Roman Catholic Church. This means that the diaconal self-identity is communal and participatory in its very nature, since the leadership of the church is basically institutional rather than charismatic.

   b. The self-identity of a permanent deacon today involves not only institutional leadership but a leadership that the Christian tradition calls Sacred Order. The self-identity is, therefore, sacramental, which involves an interrelationship of episcopacy, priesthood, and diaconate as one single leadership order. Neither a bishop, nor a priest, nor a deacon can act in an individualistic, autocratic, or "Lone-Ranger" way. The ministries involved in the sacrament of orders are interwoven with one another and must be seen as one sacrament. This involves the sacramental bishop, priest, and deacon in an ever-present and existential struggle for clearer boundaries, on the one hand, and more cooperative services, on the other.

   c. Because we are living in the immediate postconciliar situation of Vatican II, a council that deliberately repositioned bishop, priest, and permanent deacon, there is bound to be an atmosphere in which the very self-identity of bishop, priest, and deacon is as yet not clarified. This is particularly noticeable in the current struggle over the interrelationship of the three orders within the sacrament of orders. Pastors and priests have felt threatened by the presence of permanent deacons in their parishes. Bishops have felt threatened by their role as a major person within the communal presbyterium. Permanent deacons have felt threatened by the defensive attitude of many priests and by the exclusion from a clear role in diocesan leadership. Permanent deacons are welcome in some parishes, where the shortage of priests is keenly evident. Nonetheless, in such parishes, the permanent deacon seems to be present only until a priest is available to replace him. In this postconciliar period, when there is still a major and worldwide struggle within the Roman Catholic Church to understand and accept the conciliar changes, two words need to be etched in the hearts of every bishop, priest, and deacon. These two words are *patience* and *tolerance*.

d. The self-identity of a permanent deacon today involves an identity with the contextual history not only of the diaconate itself but of all institutional leadership within the church. Within this historical context, the self-identity of a contemporary deacon recognizes that history has occasioned limitations and boundaries on what diaconal leadership can and cannot do. A deacon who acts as though the historical diaconate means nothing is not a healthy member of the contemporary permanent diaconate. This same position applies to bishops and priests who may act as though the historical episcopacy and presbyterate mean nothing. Such bishops and priests are, likewise, unhealthy members of the church's current leadership.

e. Charismatic qualities of a permanent deacon are neither secondary to nor dominated by institutional demands. As Vatican II indicates, the church is both institutional and charismatic, and consequently the permanent deacon is likewise both institutional and charismatic. A bishop and a priest are likewise both institutional and charismatic. The guiding issue is not either one or the other; the guiding issue is what at a given existential moment of time best serves the people of God. The needs of the believing community can at times be met in a better way by institutional leadership, and yet at other times such needs can be met more effectively by strong magnetic charismatic leadership. Canon law and juridical directives cannot be seen as the answer to the institutional–charismatic tension. Canon law and juridical directives are, by their very nature, institutional, and the tension between charismatic and institutional leadership is not settled by a dominance of the institutional. The needs of a Christian community ultimately form the normative resolution.

f. The self-identity of a permanent deacon today can only grow in a strongly spiritual way if the central image of his ministry remains the icon of Jesus washing the feet of his disciples, and the central call is that of Jesus who came to serve and not be served. Service is the foundation of Christian ministry. The icon of the foot washing and the New Testament word of the Lord on service remain the foundational source for the spiritual and theological growth of all Christian ministries. Even the very term *ministry* is the English translation of a widely used New Testament term: *diakonia*. The very name *deacon* reminds the permanent deacon today to be a servant-minister.

The above considerations are meant to help today's permanent deacons come to an understanding of the reasons why there are problematic issues regarding the diaconate. These contextual considerations do *not* provide solutions. They *do*, however, clarify the current context in which a rethinking of the diaconate is taking place. In the second part of this volume, we will consider in a specific way the possibilities of diaconal service in a third-millennium church.

Part Two

Diaconal Ministry in a Post–Vatican II Church

In the second part of this book, I will consider the permanent diaconate as it exists today within a distinctive post–Vatican II church. As mentioned previously, a postconciliar church is a very distinctive time for church life. It involves an extended time of elation and of struggle. Conflicting interpretations of conciliar texts are defended by their respective protagonists. Both the acceptance of conciliar positions and the nonacceptance of conciliar positions compete openly. Ecumenical councils, by and large, offer new insights and new visions, and therefore there is a period of elation. On the other hand, ecumenical councils also offer issues that are provocative and require change, and therefore there are periods of tense struggle. Vatican II offers no exception to this pattern of postconciliar existence. Each and every contemporary, third-millennium permanent deacon finds himself within this postconciliar context. What contemporary, third-millennium permanent deacons are able to do and even to *be* is deeply shaped by this postconciliar context. Particular aspects of postconciliar elation and struggle cannot help but influence diaconal life today. This is a given.

On the other hand, the fact that for almost twelve hundred years, the permanent diaconate in the Western Roman Catholic Church has been nonexistent as a clerical order in its own right also plays a major role for any rethinking of the permanent diaconate. Because of this long historical hiatus, the revival of the diaconate, in many ways, is not tied to ongoing, long-standing, and untouchable traditions. Even the earlier history of the permanent diaconate, interesting as it may be, does not offer a large number of constraints of any overwhelming nature, since throughout the earlier history of the permanent diaconate the precise meaning of the diaconate ministry was in constant change and development. In the first eight hundred years of Christian life, the permanent diaconate was not always of one piece. From region to region, there were noticeable differences. For the early deacons, adaptation was part of diaconal existence. What the early deacons could do or could not do depended heavily on where they were at a given moment of time.

Given the variability of early diaconal history and the hiatus of twelve hundred years, we today in our dreams and planning for a third-millennial permanent diaconate need to think creatively or, as the contemporary phrase expresses it, we need to think "outside the box." We must dream, imagine, dare, and test. Even though this dreaming and daring, testing and imagining should be done to some degree outside the box, third-millennial permanent deacons remain within a contextual box, and the constraints of the current context cannot help but shape one's dreams and tests. As a result, even our dreaming and testing remains contextualized, but dreams and hopes move us to the edges of our context and even point beyond these edges.

Some readers might wonder why this volume does not contain a detailed section on the New Testament passages regarding the diaconate as well as an analysis of the deacon in the first eight centuries.[1] Certainly, the New Testament is fundamental for an understanding of the diaconate, as I mentioned in the introduction. Likewise, the early history of the diaconate offers basic insights into its meaning as a church ministry. A focus on the New Testament's presentation of the deacon would involve a volume in its own right, which is beyond the intent of this current work. However, there is a remarkable presence of deacon-words in the entire New Testament. One finds deacon-words eighty-five times in the New Testament. In many ways, these are key words for an understanding of the New Testament's entire presentation on ministry. Service is the one characteristic of Jesus' own ministry that the authors and communities who were involved in the writing of the New Testament remembered in the strongest of ways. Jesus was one who came to serve, not to be served (Mark 10:45; Matt 20:28; Luke 22:27). This form of service, *diakonia*, characterizes every mention of ministry in the entire New Testament. A specific focus on a particular ministry (deacon) is a rarity, compared to the many, many times the deacon-words are used for any and every kind of

---

1. For an overview of the history of the diaconate, see Cummings, *Deacons and the Church*, 30–52. In this essay, Cummings also focuses on four historical figures, Lawrence of Rome, Ephrem of Nisibis, Francis of Assisi, and Nicholas Ferrar (54–69). Cummings also has published a small volume, *Saintly Deacons*.

ministerial service by the Jesus community. Thus, when one reads the New Testament, one should pay far more attention to the widespread use of deacon-words for all ministerial services, since words for a specific diaconal ministry are few. Moreover, the New Testament, in these few instances of a specific deacon ministry, presents very little specific data as to what these particular ministers did, how they were selected, and how they related to other ministries of the early Jesus community.

The same caveats apply to the data from early church writers who mention the specific ministry of the diaconate. If one finds mention of a deacon, as for instance in the letters of Ignatius of Antioch, one can only conclude that in the churches of Asia Minor to which these letters were written a deacon ministry took place. To generalize the Ignatian letters and conclude that deacons were a part of all or the majority of the churches in the earliest decades of the first century cannot be done. In other words, the early church documents indicate clearly that in *some* areas of church life there were indeed deacon ministries. Documents also indicate that in one of the areas of early church life at the end of the second century, there was even an ordination ritual for a deacon.[2] But this ordination ritual cannot be generalized in a way that maintains an ordination in other churches either at the end of the second century or throughout the third century as well. What a deacon's specific ministry was in one particular area of the early church—and for this one area there is specific data—does not allow any generalization that this same type of ministry was done by deacons throughout the church of that time. In fact, diaconal ministry, as we see from the historical data, was very diverse and not at all universal.

The deacon's ministry in the first eight hundred years of church history requires a carefully constructed volume. Because of this I limit my observations to the paragraphs above. This is not to

---

2. The first extant ordination ritual we know of is found in the *Apostolic Tradition*, which has been ascribed to Hippolytus of Rome (ca. 170–236). In this volume one finds the ordination prayers for an *episkopos* (bishop), a *presbyteros* (priest) and a *diakonos* (deacon). For information on this first extant ordination ritual, see Paul Bradshaw, *Ordination Rites of the Ancient Churches of East and West* (New York: Pueblo, 1990); and James Puglisi, *The Process of Admission to Ordained Ministy: A Comparative Study*, 3 vols. (Collegeville, MN: Liturgical Press, 1996), vol. 1.

say that New Testament data and early church history data are not important. Indeed, this material is vitally important. However, an adequate discussion of this material goes beyond the goals of this present volume.

Part 2 of this volume is divided into six chapters. Five of these chapters focus on positive areas of diaconal life. The sixth chapter is cautionary and focuses on three issues that are of major concern. From 1966 to 2005, many documents regarding the current permanent diaconate have been published, and in them the richness of the permanent diaconate is clearly stated and developed. I do not want to restate all the positive issues one finds in these documents. Rather, in looking forward to the immediate future of the permanent diaconate, I have selected issues that in my judgment are particularly vital for the life and ministry of permanent deacons today. My goal is threefold, namely, to enrich (a) the *theology* of today's deacons, (b) the *pastoral ministry* of today's deacons, and (c) the *personal identity* of today's deacons. The chapters of part 2 of this volume are as follows:

1. **Current Pastoral Needs and the Role of the Permanent Deacons**

2. **Deacon Formation**

3. **Deaconesses**

4. **Anointing of the Sick**

5. **Church Leadership**

6. **Three Contextual Aspects for the Future**

Chapter One

CURRENT PASTORAL NEEDS AND THE ROLE OF THE PERMANENT DIACONATE

Ecclesial ministry, mission, and leadership are ultimately judged by a twofold standard. The first standard is *Jesus*. Since ecclesial ministry, mission, and leadership are, in Vatican II terms, a sharing in the ministry, mission, and leadership of Jesus himself, the foundational gauge can therefore be clearly stated: Does a particular ecclesial ministry, mission, or leadership reflect Jesus or not? For the permanent diaconate in the American church, the basic criterion is the same: Does the contemporary permanent diaconate in the United States reflect the ministry, mission, and leadership of Jesus or not?

The second standard is *existential*. When one studies the contemporary ecclesial ministry, mission, and leadership in the Roman Catholic Church, can one honestly say that this ministry, mission, and leadership provide for the glaring pastoral needs of the people of God? In other words, the most pressing pastoral needs in today's church are themselves major criteria for evaluating all ministry, mission, and leadership in the current church. These glaring pastoral needs as major criteria help judge the value of today's papacy, episcopacy, priesthood, diaconate, and lay ministry. If the glaring pastoral needs of the people of God are overlooked, placed to one side, or given only token attention, then the ministry, mission, and leadership of the church are keenly negligent.

When we, therefore, ask about the future of the permanent diaconate, we cannot avoid a realistic assessment of the glaring pastoral needs in today's church. However, even more pointedly we need to consider the concrete and glaring pastoral needs *existentially*, that is, in a given diocese and at a given moment of time, namely, here and now. The permanent diaconate does not exist in a temporal-spatial vacuum. It exists in a given diocese—in fact, only in *some* dioceses, not all—and at a given moment of history. What, then, are the glaring pastoral needs of a given diocese at a given moment of history? Second, does the permanent diaconate in that diocese face up to the glaring pastoral needs of the diocese in question? If one talks about the future of the permanent diaconate and remains oblivious to the glaring pastoral needs of the existential permanent diaconate—its actual existence in a given diocese—such talk is not only out of the box but also out of line. Such a discussion on the permanent diaconate becomes unreal and totally ideological. It is for this reason that I begin with the issue of pastoral need.

Some years ago, the bishops in the church in Holland raised the issue of whether or not the Netherlands should establish the permanent diaconate.[3] In order to decide on the establishment of a permanent diaconate, the Conference of Bishops in the Netherlands issued in 1988 "The Platform Diaconal Ecclesiology." After a small theological introduction on the mission of the church, the document presents an analysis of the Dutch society and the Dutch church in seventeen pages, which amounts to almost one-half of the entire document. Only after this fairly lengthy analysis did the document address the main question: *Should the Dutch church establish a permanent diaconate?* What is important today is the process that the Dutch Church used in order to formulate this document. The method indicated that prior to any determination of a permanent diaconate there should be a pastoral-needs analysis of the Dutch society and church. This analysis was set in motion, and when the results were drawn up and made public, then—and only then—did the leaders of the Dutch church face the question: Will the establishment of the permanent diaconate help or hinder the resolution of these pastoral needs? This procedure was very insightful and helpful, since it established pastoral needs as a major (if not a top) priority when they pursued the question: Should the

---

3. J. Wissink, ed., *Towards a Diaconal Ecclesiology for a Servant Church* (Rotterdam: Committee of the Platform Diaconal Ecclesiology, 1988).

Dutch church establish the permanent diaconate? In other words, the permanent diaconate as an institutional ministry could be considered necessary only if the pastoral needs of the church throughout Holland would benefit.

In the United States, the permanent diaconate began to be established in 1968, and it is continuing to thrive.[4] However, as a major ecclesial ministry within a given diocese, the permanent diaconate, like the ministries of priesthood and episcopacy, needs to be reconsidered from time to time. How do these institutional ministries correlate to the most important pastoral needs of a diocese? In every diocese there are glaring pastoral needs, and the institutional ministries in a diocese are called on to meet these glaring pastoral needs as best as they can. However, since pastoral needs change from time to time, there is also a need to reevaluate the specific, existential needs of a diocese. Such a reevaluation helps to keep the focus of institutional ministries up-to-date. What are the most glaring and demanding pastoral needs for a particular diocese at this particular time? In a given diocese, answers to this question can vary considerably. What is regarded as glaring within the chancery building may not be considered equally glaring in the majority of parishes. What one parish experiences as glaring may not be equally glaring in other diocesan parishes. Who, then, determines which glaring pastoral need deserves the primary focus?

In today's Roman Catholic American Church, a particular bishop might be the last person who should make this choice, since too often the local bishop is mired in the adjudication of sexual-abuse issues. For such a bishop, the most glaring problem is the resolution of these problems by the courts. A given bishop might also be too involved in the major foci of the USCCB, and the major foci of the more generalized episcopal conference might not be the major foci of his own diocese. Consequently, a larger group or a committee needs to be established in the diocese. This group is

---

4. In the spring of 1968 the U.S. bishops voted to petition the Holy See for authorization to establish the permanent diaconate. On August 30, 1968, the apostolic delegate informed the U.S. bishops that Paul VI had agreed to their request. In 1971, the Conference of Bishops approved and authorized the publication of the committee's document, *Permanent Deacons in the United States: Guidelines on their Formation and Ministry.*

not a deacon-focused group, so that the deacons themselves would determine the major pastoral needs. The focus of an all-deacon group is too biased. The makeup of such a pastoral needs committee should be diverse and widely representative. There is clearly an advantage to having an outside resource conduct the survey regarding the most important societal and ecclesial needs of a given diocese.

Once the pastoral needs of a diocese are established, three or four major or pressing needs have to be selected, and this is probably the most painful part of the process. Realistically, not all diocesan needs can be met at one time. If all needs are given the same priority, too often no needs at all are met. A choice is needed, painful as the choosing might be. A time limit also is helpful in this difficult matter. For instance, in the next three years four major and distinct pastoral needs of a diocese will have priority. At the end of three years a rethinking of the situation would take place.

What has this to do with the deacon? The role of the deacon vis-à-vis these selected urgent pastoral needs is key. Ecclesial ministry in a diocese is meant to provide for the spiritual and at times temporal needs of the people of God. Pastoral need in large measure determines ministry. As a consequence, it is essential to the diocesan ministers to ask what particular roles each ministerial group, including the permanent diaconate, should play in order that the glaring pastoral needs of the people of God can be met to some degree.

In the discussions on the formation programs for the Diocese of Oakland, which is my own diocese, the issue arose regarding the number of deacons needed for the Oakland diocese. In the committee meetings, questions arose such as: Are there currently enough deacons? Does the diocese need more deacons? The answers to these questions were of great interest, since there was no one answer. One committee member mentioned that when he asked various pastors about the number of deacons needed in the diocese, the answer was generally: *We need a lot.* The priest-pastors then explained their view. "I need someone for baptisms and marriages and visiting the sick. I haven't time for all of these pastoral needs." In other words, the shortage of priests meant that a pastor had too much to do. Permanent deacons provided the help needed.

One might immediately argue that the shortage of priests should not determine either the establishment of the permanent diaconate or the number of deacons within an already established permanent diocesan diaconate. Permanent deacons are not meant to be seen as the Band-Aid for the shortage of priests. On the other hand, glaring pastoral needs did indeed arise because the priest-pastor was overworked. Major pastoral needs of the people in his parish were at an almost emergency level, and some resolution was needed.[5]

Another answer at the committee meetings was this: *The deacon formation program of the diocese should not become over-extended; otherwise the diocese will end up with too many deacons and too few opportunities for their ministry.* Still another answer tended to be more personal. Some pastors were not very excited about having a permanent deacon assigned to their parishes, since they had experienced the permanent deacon as a threat to their own priestly ministry. In their experience with permanent deacons, these pastors felt that ministerial boundaries had not always been honored. Still other pastors noted that permanent deacons had been financial burdens on an already financially overburdened parish budget. In their mind, an overabundance of deacons was not helpful for genuine ministry. In all of this, the important pastoral needs of a diocese were not always the guiding principles. Some of the priorities were primarily personal.

From the standpoint of current deacons another set of priorities becomes evident. Laypeople *can* do most of the ministries that deacons do, so the diocesan diaconal formation program should not be overpopulated. Many permanent deacons today realize that they are actually performing ministerial tasks that lay men and women are also performing. In today's church discipline, lay ministers can visit the sick and bring holy communion to those who are shut-ins or who are too ill to leave their homes. Lay missionaries can baptize and even witness marriages although often under fairly restricted conditions. If lay men and women are eligible for such ministerial services, why become a deacon? Why encourage the permanent diaconate?

---

5. On these practical questions, see the intriguing book of Ditewig, *101 Questions & Answers on Deacons.*

The foci at these meetings were clearly too narrow. The main focus was the permanent diaconate alone. Perhaps, a larger contextual view of the situation was needed. When a diocese engages in a pastoral needs assessment, there is an advantage of bringing to the table *all* the major pastoral needs that a diocese at a given point in time must face. Such an assessment should involve an outside agency, at least to some extent. An outside agency is not a controlled agency, and thus the results will not be overly controlled results.

Once a committee with the involvement of an outside agency has presented its findings, then—and only then—should the entire ministerial leadership of a diocese ask the question: How can we meet the major pastoral needs of the diocese? Each ministerial sector needs to express honestly how it brings something to these most serious needs. The bishop should explain publicly what *he* can bring. The priests should explain publicly what *they* can bring. The permanent deacons should explain publicly what *they* can bring. Lay ministers should explain publicly what *they* can bring. Each area of institutional ministry should be open to hearing a public response to its public presentation. The publicness of these issues does not require a large townhall-type of meeting by the entire diocese. Such a meeting can be done in a smaller way. The goal is *feedback* so that each institutional ministry presents its value and its limitations vis-à-vis the immediate needs of the diocese. In all of this, glaring pastoral needs of the entire diocese remain major criteria for what is best, what is better, and what is harmful or inadequate. Pastoral needs remain a major benchmark for determining the value and direction of institutional, ecclesial ministry and leadership.[6]

In this process of mutual discussion, the interrelationality of ministry becomes very evident. It is no longer simply a question,

---

6. In chapter 2 of the *National Directory for the Formation, Ministry, and Life of Permanent Deacons in the United States*, paragraphs 41–61 reinforce the interrelationality of ministry: the permanent deacon and the bishop (41–47); with the diocese (48–49); with priests (50–53); with one another and with those in formation (54); with women and men religious (55); with the laity (56–57); and with society in general (58–61). All of these interrelationships mentioned in the directory reflect the major thesis of part of this volume: in Vatican II, all ministry is seen as interrelated.

for example, of what the permanent *deacons* can do, but what the permanent deacons *together with* the bishop, the priests, and the lay ministers can do. The pastoral needs of a given diocese cannot be met by simply one area of ecclesial ministry. Moreover, the pastoral needs, presented by a committee, indicate the weak areas of a diocese as well as the areas of strength. In meeting pastoral needs A or B or C, which groups in the diocese will be left by the wayside? Which group of needs—that is, D or E or F—will be overlooked? Where are the diocesan ministerial priorities? Ministry is interrelational and the overwhelming pastoral needs of a given diocese can be met only in an interrelational ministerial way. We cannot dream in any realistic way unless the actual and glaring pastoral needs of a given diocese remain an integral contextual part of our dreams and hopes, our daring and our testing.

Chapter Two

DEACON FORMATION

A second key issue for the future of the permanent diaconate in the United States is the issue of deacon formation. The *Ratio Fundamentalis Institutionis Diaconalis* (Basic Norms for the Formation of Permanent Deacons), which was published in 1997 by the Congregation for Catholic Education (for Seminaries and Educational Institutions), presents the basic elements for a diaconal formation program. This document, although focused primarily on the formation of permanent deacons, includes in an official way what the Roman Catholic Church hopes to realize in post-formation ordained deacons. Thus, the document presents the goals of permanent diaconal ministry, which can only be realized in a deacon's life *after* formation. The document, though concentrating on the formative years for a deacon-to-be, looks beyond the ordination of a deacon to the time when he is a major leader in ecclesial ministry. The document indicates to us what a deacon is hoped to be.

I do not want to enter into a discussion on the fine points of the formation program, as outlined in the *Ratio*. Rather, I want to center my comments on a single, basic question. That question is: Formation for *what*? What kind of diaconal minister and what kinds of diaconal ministry are envisioned as the end product of a formation program? The *Ratio*, of course, presents its vision of post-ordination diaconal life from a universal or international perspective of diaconal ministry in the church today. What needs to be done is to use these universal and international perspectives but bring them into dialogue with the North American context. Universal and international perspectives tend to be highly abstract and even at times highly unrealistic. Our dreams and hopes need to have a realism about them. What does diaconal formation mean in the contemporary setting of the Roman Catholic Church in the United States?

Fortunately, the USCCB in 2005 published a *National Directory for the Formation, Ministry, and Life of Permanent Deacons in the United States*. This National Directory is a culmination of many realities. In his foreword, Bishop Frederick Campbell, the chair of the Bishops' Committee on the Diaconate writes of extensive consultation at many levels involving many diaconal groups. He also lists a number of people who were involved in the formation of this document. In other words, the diaconal experience of the last twenty-five years has been incorporated into this directory. Indeed, the directory indicates a solid maturity of experience regarding the permanent diaconate.

Two formational issues stand out in a stark way as regards the current permanent diaconate in the United States, first the issue of the age of deacons, and, second, the issue of the multiculturalism of the diaconate. Standardized formation programs do not monolithically "fit" all age groups. The age of the deacon candidates requires a formation program that responds to the age level of the various men involved. In the United States, a diaconal formational program should be clearly honed to meet the needs of men who are of mature age. By mature age I mean that a person is thirty-five and above. In priestly formation, candidates are still taken into a formation program at an earlier—and therefore less mature—age. Second, at a regional level, a given class of deacon candidates usually has in it members from a variety of cultures. In themselves, these cultural differences preclude a monolithic, all-encompassing vision of the permanent diaconate. Cultures require a large measure of variations both in formational approach and in ministerial activities. Culture betokens variation and adaptation.

The Issue of Age

Let us consider the age factor first and then move to the cultural factor. When the permanent diaconate was restored by Paul VI, it was clearly established as an ecclesial ministry for mature men. Youthful or teenage candidates were not envisioned. This already indicates that the diaconal formation program was seriously different from the then normal priestly formation program. Even in the late 1960s minor seminaries were still flourishing, which took in teenagers as seminarians. From the beginning, teenagers were *not seen* as part of the deacon formation program. Indeed, the revised *Code of Canon Law*, which was first promulgated on November 27, 1983, mentions the age level for deacon candidates in a clear-cut manner. Canon 1031 §2 states:

> A candidate for the permanent diaconate who is not married is not to be admitted to the diaconate unless he has completed at least twenty-five years of age; if the candidate is married, he is not to be admitted to the permanent diaconate unless he has completed at least thirty-five years of age.

Diaconal formation precedes the ordination of a deacon by at least four years. Thus, from the standpoint of canon law, entry into a diaconal formation program could be as young as twenty-one or thirty-one. In the United States, the vast majority of diaconal candidates are married. Few diaconal candidates enter at the canonically noted minimal age. Currently, the average age of a permanent deacon in the United States is sixty-one.[7]

The *National Directory* presents the issue of age for the church in the United States in a different way:

> In accord with Canon Law, the United States Conference of Catholic Bishops establishes the minimum age for ordination to the permanent diaconate at thirty-five for all candidates, married or celibate. The establishment of a maximum age for ordination is at the discretion of the diocesan bishop, keeping in mind the particular needs

---

7. The *Ratio Fundamentalis Institutionis Diaconalis* presents a very unrealistic approach to the formation of a permanent deacon. It envisions young men who would go to a seminary-type of formation; see *Sacrum diaconatus ordinem*, which the *Ratio* cites in its opening statement. In the *Ratio* (chapter 3) even older men are envisioned as attending a "special institution." There is an unrealism about this *Ratio*.

and expectations of the diocese regarding diaconal ministry and life. (87)

In the United States, the formation programs for permanent
deacons are *programs* that the candidates attend at regular but
somewhat widespread intervals. Moreover, the teaching in these
programs for older men is modular, which generally takes place on
weekends at some retreat center or college center in the diocese.
Modular teaching means that on a given weekend, the theme might
be Christology; on another weekend the theme might be New
Testament; on another, moral theology, and so on. There is no special institution for diaconal training. At best, there is a monthly
weekend experience of being together, usually in a retreat house.[8]
Why is age important? For the permanent diaconate, the vast
majority of whose members in the United States and the vast number of whose candidates are older, a *Ratio formationis* that mirrors
the *Ratio formationis* for priests is unrealistic. One should start realistically with the premise that the diaconal formation program in
the United States today is basically for older men. Such a premise
places the diaconal formation programs squarely within a distinct
focus. Often, becoming a deacon is a second, third, or even fourth
career for some men. These men have lived through many experiences, have trained for many jobs, and have developed skills in
many fields. They bring a wealth of human potentiality to the permanent diaconate. They also bring a long history with the church,
which means that over the years of church life they have been given
many graces, suffered through many church issues that are negative, and yet have remained faithful to the gospel. They bring a
wealth of faith in Jesus and in God to the permanent diaconate.
These are all issues and qualities that are treasures which they
intend to offer to the local church. Faced with such maturity and
experience, the issue of formation takes on a much different role.
Older men bring to the ministerial table treasured gifts, and these

---

8. The *Ratio Fundamentalis* also mentions different types of diaconate (i.e., for
celibates, married people, those destined for mission countries, those in developing nations, and so on). In the *Ratio* the age issue is relegated to footnotes. See also
Gaillardetz, "On the Theological Integrity of the Diaconate," in *Theology of the
Diaconate: The State of the Question*, 67–97.

must be acknowledged. The formation program in many ways is shaped by the very men who are going to be formed; not vice versa. Perhaps the very first question a person inquiring about the diaconate should be asked is this: **What major gifts do you, as a mature and experienced person, bring to the diaconal world?**

In the times when young teenagers went to seminaries, formation in their lives was still in progress, and this yet-to-be-attained formation included years of intellectual formation, spiritual formation, emotional formation, and social formation. It included learning skills and learning about oneself. At age forty-five or fifty-five or sixty-five, however, *formation* is a strange word. In many ways these men are already "formed." Therefore, other phrases such as "what you see is what you get" and "as is" come to mind. These phrases are certainly not meant to be negative: what you see of a mature person's talents and experiences, of his abilities and educational background is indeed a great treasure. What appears "as is" is *not* second-rate; it means that a person is already mature, developed, formed, and well put together.

This is the starting point: an acknowledgment by the candidate himself and by others of the gifts and talents that the respective candidate brings. The candidate has knocked on the diaconal door and asks for entry. Our first question should be: What treasures do you personally bring? Before any and every word about formation is said, there should be respect and honor for an adult and experienced candidate. In doing this, we are not only honoring and welcoming a candidate; we are honoring and welcoming the Holy Spirit, who is at this moment at least calling this individual to consider a diaconal vocation. Treat the *adult* individual as a mature *individual* might be the foundational axiom.

The initial conversation is, of course, not *formation*; it is, rather, a time of *discernment*. Is the man who claims personal maturity and talent truly being called by the Spirit to be a deacon in a given local church? A negative answer in no way deprives the person of his mature and experiential treasures. It is simply a discernment that at this given moment it does not seem that the diaconal ministry and this individual person should be related to each other.

If there is a sense of discernment that this person does offer a good prospect as a deacon, then a second question should follow at once. **How can your gifts and personal talents advance the diaconal ministry in a particular local or regional church?**

Once again, we are honoring the candidate's gifts and person. We are asking how the local or regional church can benefit from this person's maturity and individuality. In this second step, the diocesan leaders are explaining what the diocese brings to the table. This does not mean simply: "Here is our diaconal formation program and our diaconal diocesan ministry. Take it or leave it." Rather, the goal is to find a way in which there is an interconnection of the candidate's specific gifts not only with the formation program but with the *entire* diaconal ministry of a *particular* diocese. It is a *quid-pro-quo* relationship. The diaconal formation program cannot be a prepackaged, take-it-or-leave-it program. There is a definite need for flexibility.

Once again, we see how an analysis of diocesan pastoral needs truly assists in the way diocesan leaders will assess an inquirer, and how the inquirer assesses his contribution to these pastoral needs. If the primary pastoral needs of a diocese at a given time desperately require x, y, or z, then one can ask: Is there some correlation between the talents and gifts of the inquirer and the major needs of the diocese? And the inquirer is able to correlate his own personal attributes with such pastoral needs. In this instance, the candidate perceives that he, as a mature individual, can contribute in a special way to the diocese.

From the standpoint of the diocesan directors of the diaconate ministry, a third question might summarize this interrelational aspect. **Can we, the leaders of the local or regional church, help you, the candidate-to-be, enrich your life by accepting your gift of your own experience and maturity and at the same time enrich the community called church, if and when you are accepted as a diaconal minister?** Such a question acknowledges that the candidate, because of his age, comes with experience, maturity, insight, education, and talents.

In this question, one is focused on both the *candidate* and his experience and talents and on the local church with its needs as discussed above. Can the local church leaders offer a reciprocal service to this very existential, personal, and individualized mature and talented man. Does the formation program fit the candidate and not simply the candidate fit into the formation program? The candidate has a treasure to offer, and the ministerial leaders of the local and regional diocesan church have treasures to offer, which, one hopes, will help a future diaconal minister use his own treasures in a way that is enriching to the local and regional church. There is once more a *quid-pro-quo* situation.

Once this scenario has taken place, the local diocesan leaders of diaconal formation need to ask themselves very honestly: Is our formation program one that will honor the talents and treasures of the person under consideration? In other words, when one is dealing with people who are already mature, there cannot be a formation program that is like a cookie-cutter. Adaptability is needed. Even Paul VI's letter *Sacrum diaconatus ordinem* realized this, since it dedicates an entire chapter (3) to adult candidates. A formation program for the dioceses of the United States needs to take into account all that the phrase "adult or older candidates" implies. The formation program needs to be developed with this mature candidate in mind. The usual priestly seminary formation pattern cannot apply and should not apply to mature deacon candidates. Moreover, since there is no institution or formation house in which these older candidates live, the formation program is much more a mentoring program. Deacon formation, especially on a monthly basis, is not similar to the formation programs in priestly seminaries, even those that have been established precisely for the older priestly "seminarian." In other words, the modular program for deacons, which most dioceses have, must find a different model than the seminaries for priests, whether these seminaries are meant for younger or for older men.

The Issue of Culture

Besides age, culture is certainly a distinguishing mark of the American church's diaconal structure. By and large, the diaconal formation programs make strong attempts to be multicultural. In some dioceses there are distinct programs for the English-speaking and other programs for the Spanish-speaking. Some analysis of these two kinds of programs needs to be done. English-speaking programs more than likely include Filipinos and Vietnamese. They might even include Pacific Islanders, Haitians, Jamaicans, and other ethnic members. Even in the Spanish-speaking group, one must realize that there are major differences between Mexicans and Cubans, between El Salvadorans and Guatemalans, between Puerto Ricans and Colombians. Naturally, there cannot be diaconal formation programs for each cultural group, but there needs to be some understanding of the cultures represented.[9]

Modular education often defeats the very goals of such multicultural endeavors, since the presenter comes for only a weekend or two. He or she is followed by a totally different instructor, who is then succeeded by a third, quite different instructor. All the instructors have an expertise, but not all are sensitive to cultural differences.

The cultural issue also affects the post-formation and post-ordination ministerial work of deacons. One might have an Indonesian or a Korean in the diocesan diaconal formation program, but are there enough Indonesian Catholics or Korean Catholics in the diocese who will benefit from an Indonesian or Korean deacon? If not, then such a deacon is placed, most often, in an English-speaking American-oriented parish. In some cases this may work out well; in other cases it may not. Placement and multicultural issues need to be thought through in a respectful and sensitive way. The cultural issue and the formation of permanent deacons are also stressed in the *National Directory for the Formation, Ministry and Life of Permanent Deacons in the United States* (144). All of the above is simply saying that a cookie-cutter model of diaconal formation and placement does not meet the needs of either age or of culture.

In every discussion of culture, however, there is often an unspoken element. This unspoken element is bluntly named "racism." Naturally, this word sounds harsh, but there exists, too, often, in every intercultural relationship a form a racism: namely, an attitude that one culture is better, is normative, and is superior to the other. The current church in the United States is not devoid of its own racist tendencies. In the United States, which includes

9. Paulist Press Pastoral Spirituality Series, ed. Peter Phan.

the political, social, and economic areas of life, a clearer phrase might be "white supremacy." By this, I do not mean an outspoken Aryan white supremacy. Rather, it is a phrase that indicates that among the racisms in the United States, a sense of white (that is, Euro-American) supremacy exists in a large majority of the U.S. citizenry. People from other races might be American citizens, but too often there is a sense of white supremacy even vis-à-vis a so-called equal citizenship.

Most immigrants to the United States and many first-, second-, and even third-generation Americans have experienced some sort of racial put-down. When we look at diocesan structures and their *modus operandi*, we also see a subtle but clear normative approach, which means that the Euro-American structures are both normative and definitive. What occurs in white parishes is often presented as normative for all non-white parishes.

In some forms of multicultural church celebrations, hymns in languages other than English are used. Pictures of statues of another culture are given a place of honor, for instance, a picture of Our Lady of Guadalupe or a statue of the Santo Niño. In many ways, this is simply a form of tokenism. *Tokenism* is not a foreign word to our American church behavior, and the liturgy too often exhibits a form of tokenism that, while trying to honor some other culture, at the same time indicates a second-level status for the other culture. The theme of racial supremacy is not one that we Catholics like to make center stage. Even in dual diocesan formation programs for deacons, one in English and one in Spanish, there are subtle but clearly evident indications that the English program is better and the Spanish program is merely tolerated. The difficulties go even further. In the Spanish-speaking programs, little attention is paid to the cultural differences between Mexicans and Cubans, between Guatemalans, El Salvadorans, and European Spaniards. All Spanish-speaking diaconal candidates are Hispanic. Asians, too, are blended into a common denominator, and this blending is a subtle discrediting of their many individualized cultures.

When one moves to the diaconal ministry in a given diocese, the cultural issue remains. Non–Euro-American deacons are often seen as not equal to their Euro-American counterparts. In every diocese in the United States we need a much more concerted effort not simply at multiculturalism but at *equi-culturalism*. Diocesan leadership needs to ask itself: Is its leadership racist? Is there a subtle but constant atmosphere of racial discrimination within the leadership of a diocese? If the third-millennial diaconate wants to help revitalize the church, the permanent diaconate in the United States should take a major stand and raise the issue of racism from its usual hidden presence to an issue of center stage. In this way, the diaconate would be deaconing the church itself.

Clearly, age and culture affect the permanent deacons in the United States in a major way, and therefore some intercommunication on these issues would assist the diocesan diaconal leadership. Without a better formation program that incorporates a different approach to both age and culture, the future of permanent deacons in the United States will remain at a stagnant level. Since the two issues are vitally important for the deacons, some major steps to improve the situation are also vitally important and pressing.

Chapter Three

DEACONESSES

The role of women in diaconal ministry remains a major issue for the early decades of the third millennium and will continue to be an issue for a long time after these early decades are completed. The "deaconess" issue has intricate relationships to the question of the presbyteral ordination of women. Women's priestly ordination is also a theme that will remain prominent in the Roman Catholic Church for many generations to come. Efforts to silence discussion and debate on the issues of women in ministry are ineffective. Attempts to ignore the issues are equally feckless. Moreover, the ongoing conversations about women in ecclesial ministry cannot help but include the issue of ordination, since the foundational issue is not ordination. The foundational issue is twofold: (a) the very understanding of God; and (b) the dignity of every human person. Let us first consider some of the official statements made by Roman Catholic leaders on the issue of the dignity of every human being, and then, second, we will consider the issue of God.

In the past fifty years, serious statements on the issue of human freedom, dignity, and equality have been made by official Roman Catholic Church leaders. These official statements are profoundly important, since they deliberately address all forms of discrimination as offensive to the personal dignity of the individual. Moreover, these official statements on the dignity and equality of all human beings are theologically based on God's creation of human life. However, it is also clear that the official statements on human dignity, on the one hand, and the official statements on the role of women in church ministry, on the other hand, do not coincide in a way that honors both the dignity of every human person and the dignity of women.

The bishops at Vatican II, in *Lumen gentium*, expressed the equality of every human being in a detailed and forceful way:

> Therefore, the chosen people of God is one: "one Lord, one faith, one baptism" (Eph 4:5). As members, they share a common dignity from their rebirth in Christ. They have the same filial grace and the vocation to perfection. They possess in common one salvation, one hope and undivided charity. Hence, there is in Christ and in the church no inequality on the basis of race or nationality, social condition or sex, because "there is neither Jew nor Greek; there is neither slave nor freeman; there is neither male nor female. For you are all 'one' in Christ Jesus" (Gal 3:28, Greek text; cf. Col 3:11). (32)

The statement "'in the church' there is 'no inequality on the basis' of 'sex'" cannot be interpreted in one way while the interpretation based on race, nationality, and social condition is held in a different way. The meaning of this paragraph is clear: discrimination based on *any* of these areas of human life is morally wrong. If the phrase "in the church" means anything at all, it should indicate that "in the church" such discrimination should be eminently lacking.

In the *Instrumentum Laboris: De Vocatione et Missione laicorum in ecclesia et in mundo viginti annis a concilio Vaticano II elapsis* (a presynodal document for the synod on the laity) we hear, twenty years later, a similar official church voice. This is a singularly important document. For the many synods of bishops, a preliminary document, called an *Instrumentum laboris*, is prepared in Rome and sent to the various bishops stamped with the words: for your information only, or *sub secreto*. However, for the synod on the laity, the preliminary draft was sent with two official letters, advising the world's bishops to disseminate this *Instrumentum laboris* in a wide way throughout their dioceses and to come to Rome with the reactions of the Christians in their diocese. The uniqueness of the *modus operandi* for this synod on the laity should be noted. In the preliminary document we find the following:

> The affirmation of the dignity and freedom of each person, the basis for the dynamic of participation, characterizes the life of a great many people in our day. However, in spite of this, many different forms of oppression against the dignity of the human person and whole peoples are increasing, demonstrating the urgent need for total liberation of all people. (8)

The words "urgent need for total liberation of all people" include women. *Total* is a word with wide implication. If inequalities are creating oppression to the dignity of a human person, and this oppressive inequality urgently calls for total liberation, then the leaders of society—in this document these leaders are the bishops attending the synod—should look at their own house first. In the Roman Catholic Church itself, one might ask, is there an inequality of the human person evident in the ways in which men and women are treated differently. "Physician, heal yourself" is an axiom that comes readily to mind whenever church officials make public statements such as the one just cited. In the *Instrumentum laboris*, the next paragraph focuses directly on the issue of inequality vis-à-vis women, and it is treated at great length.

> The movement for the advancement and liberation of women is certainly one of the more significant manifestations of the general tendency toward participation. The just struggle in favor of recognizing the equality of rights between women and men at all levels, founded upon the assertion of their equal dignity, has not failed to bear fruit. (9)

Once again, these words can be applied not only to the social and economic areas of the present world situation but to the ecclesial area as well. When high-ranking church leaders draw up this kind of statement, which was deliberately meant to be circulated throughout the dioceses, one cannot be surprised if a question such as this begins to appear: What about the inequality of women in your own diocesan house? It would be strange if church leaders, who claim to walk the higher road on social and economic matters, blamed other sectors for inequality and failed to admit to the inequality in their own intraecclesial sector.

John Paul II, in his encyclical *Dignitatem mulieris*, raises the identical issue of equality for all women. We read:

> Every individual is made in the image of God, insofar as he or she is a rational and free creature capable of knowing God and loving him. The foundation of the whole human "ethos" is rooted in the image and likeness of God which the human being bears within himself from the beginning. (7)

The equality of women and men is foundational, rooted in the human person's image and likeness of God. To argue that Jesus only chose men implies that Jesus himself set to one side this foundational moral equality regarding a human person's imaging of God. Such an argument makes Jesus the scapegoat for an exception that "every individual is made in the image of God insofar as he or she is a rational and free creature capable of knowing God and loving him." The interfacing of these official statements on the equality of all human beings and the argument for a male-only clergy has not been handled well. One cannot simply say that "Jesus did it." Jesus, in the Gospels, never advocates his privilege of abrogating a foundational aspect of God's creation. To hide behind Jesus disrespects Jesus himself.

In the *Instruction on Certain Aspects of the "Theology of Liberation"* (1984), another official church document, we hear the following:

> The yearning [for liberation] shows the authentic, if obscure, perception of the dignity of the human person, created "in the image and likeness of God" (Gen. 1:26–27)....The yearning for justice and for the effective recognition of the dignity of every human being needs, like every deep aspiration, to be clarified and guided. (I/1; II/1)

In a subsequent document, *Instruction on Christian Freedom and Liberation* (1986), we hear a similar injunction.

> Awareness of man's freedom and dignity, together with the affirmation of the inalienable rights of individuals and peoples is one of the major characteristics of our time....The church of Christ makes these aspirations her own. (1)

In the matter of ecclesial ministry, one might ask whether officially the church of Christ, in the actions of her major leadership, has indeed made these aspirations her own.

Other Roman Catholic official statements on the matter of the dignity, freedom, and equality of all human beings, based on the image and likeness of God, could easily be included in this listing. All of these citations state the same thing: because all human persons are made in the image and likeness of God, all human persons are equal.

Some detailed explanation of this human equality based on God needs to accompany the statement found in the *Declaration on the Question of the Admission of Women to the Ministerial Priesthood* (1976), namely: "Jesus Christ did not call any woman to become part of the twelve." Even if one passes over in silence the document's selective interpretation of the Twelve,[10] the implied exclusion of women from ministerial priesthood in this statement and in the explicit statements of the church just cited above needs a better and more careful and more credible explanation. The mixed signals in these two clashing views cannot be overlooked or ignored.

The second issue, the issue of God, is also central, since in all of the above statements the basis for human equality, dignity, and

---

10. For an understanding of the Twelve as found in the New Testament, see John P. Meier, "Jesus," in *The New Jerome Biblical Commentary*, ed. Raymond E. Brown, Joseph A. Fitzmyer and Roland E. Murphy (Englewood Cliffs, NJ: Prentice Hall, 1990), 1322, who writes: "Jesus' choice of precisely twelve men symbolized his mission to gather and reconstitute the twelve tribes of Israel in the end-time, thus fulfilling the hopes of OT prophets and apocalypticists." See also Raymond E. Brown, "The Twelve and the Apostolate," ibid., 1377–81, for a lengthier discussion of the Twelve and their relation to the role of apostle.

freedom is that God created each individual in God's own image and likeness. Any disrespect to the image and likeness of God is a disrespect of God's own self.

Rosemary Radford Ruether, some years ago, stated the critical principle of all feminist theology in the following way:

> The critical principle of feminist theology is the promotion of the full humanity of women. Whatever denies, diminishes, or distorts the full humanity of women is, therefore, appraised as not redemptive. Theologically speaking, whatever diminishes or denies the full humanity of women must be presumed not to reflect the divine or an authentic relation to the divine, or to reflect the authentic nature of things, or to be the message or work of an authentic redeemer or a community of redemption.[11]

Feminist theologians and other writers have often focused on the issue of language when speaking of God. Clearly, noninclusive language denies, diminishes, and distorts the full humanity of women. Other feminist theologians and writers have complained about the paternalism and androgynous mentality of Christian liturgy, theology, and catechesis. Clearly, paternalism and androgynous exclusivity deny, diminish, and distort the full humanity of women. These two issues, the issue of language and that of paternalistic-androgynous exclusivity, need to be faced.

However, the critical principle of feminist theology that Ruether enunciates goes to a more radical area: namely, to the very understanding of God. The critical principle is heard in its depth, height, length, and breadth in the following terms:

1. *not to reflect the divine or an authentic relation to the divine;*

2. *[not] to reflect the authentic nature of things;*

3. *[not] to be the message or work of an authentic redeemer or a community of redemption.*

---

11. Rosemary Radford Ruether, *Sexism and God-Talk: Toward a Feminist Theology* (Boston: Beacon Press, 1993), 18. Ruether explains this principle in the entire section (18–20).

The primary issue or critical principle in all of these words from Ruether is a "God issue." Did God create only men in the image and likeness of God? Or did God create both men and women equally in the image and likeness of God? Did God create men as a "more complete" image and likeness of God's self? Did God, therefore, create women with an "incomplete" image and likeness of God's self? Does a diminishment of the full humanity of women truly reflect the very nature of God's creation? Is not the diminishment of the full humanity of women a blatant distortion of the authentic nature of all things? Is a diminished humanity of women a contradiction to the very message or work of the redemptive Christ? These kinds of questions indicate in an intensive way that the critical principle of feminist theology is a wake-up call about God.

Too often feminist theology is officially set to one side because it is viewed as simply a matter of language or of a so-called paternalism. These issues, though serious, are not at the heart of the matter. The critical principle of feminist theology centers on God and God's mission and ministry of redemptive love. It is precisely at this foundational level of faith and theology, that is, the God level, that the issues of women in ministry must be discussed. Until now, the issues of women in ministry—including the issue of ordination—have been relegated to language or a "Jesus did it" response. There is, however, a far deeper base. The way in which the *leadership* of the Roman Catholic Church officially considers the role of women in the church itself indicates that this same high leadership offers to the rank and file of Catholic Christians a distorted view of God. Such an accusation cannot be set aside in the same way that the issues of language and paternalism have been set aside.[12]

Deaconesses in the History of the Christian Church

As regards deaconesses, historical data are certainly available, and the historical data clearly indicate that deaconesses were part of

---

12. I have had the opportunity to discuss my interpretation of the feminist principle with my colleague here in Berkeley, Rosemary Radford Ruether. She has read the text and states that it clearly expresses her view.

the ministerial leadership at least in certain sectors of the early church community. Let us review the current standing as regards this data.

Paul E. Bradshaw writes that between 396 and 553 "[d]eaconesses appear to have been virtually unknown both in the ancient churches of the West and also in Egypt. Only in Gaul are any traces found of the existence of female deacons, and this institution was condemned by successive councils (396–553)."[13] The Western and Egyptian church communities evidently took a fairly negative approach to deaconesses. Still, the fact that councils of the church had the issue of deaconesses on their agenda indicates that there were, though not in overwhelming numbers, deaconesses in certain parts of the Western church. This is borne out by statements in the *Apostolic Tradition,* which speaks of an Order of Widows, but not of deaconesses.[14] The *Canons of Hippolytus* go even further by stating rather bluntly that "ordination is for men" (canon 9).

In the Eastern areas of church life, things were different. In Syria, the *Didascalia Apostolorum* offers us the first clear indication of deaconesses.[15] This document speaks of deaconesses and their role in the baptismal liturgy, but it provides no indication of how these women were designated for liturgical ministry. The *Apostolic Constitution,*[16] the *Testamentum Domini* (using the term "widow" rather than "deaconess"),[17] and the Byzantine Rite[18] all mention the

---

13. Bradshaw, *Ordination Rites of the Ancient Churches of East and West,* 83; see also Herbert Krimm, *Quellen zur Geschichte der Diakonie* (Stuttgart: Evangelisches Verlagswerk, 1960), vol. 1. In this book, Krimm cites verbatim passage after passage from the first to the sixteenth century in which deaconess is mentioned (19–141). From p. 152 to p. 160 Krimm draws up a chronological listing of all these passages, giving date, author, and content. Another volume of considerable value is the study written by Sévérien Salaville and G. Nowack, *Le Rôle du diacre dans la liturgie orientale* (Paris/Athens: Institut Français d'Études Byzantines, 1962). This volume traces the early history of the deacon in the Syriac and Byzantine churches (1–44), and it presents differences in the western Syriac rites, the Syro-Chaldean rites, and the Coptic rites (87–120).

14. Bradshaw, *Ordination Rites,* 83.

15. Ibid., 84. The *Didascalia Apostolorum* makes a clear distinction between the recognized group of widows and deaconesses. In the text, deaconesses have certain specific institutional ministries.

16. Ibid., 84–87.

17. Ibid., 83.

18. Ibid., 88–89.

ministry of deaconess. In the *Didascalia Apostolorum* the deaconess is not only assigned baptismal duties, but she was also the person who visited Christian women in their homes and anointed those who were ill. In the *Byzantine Rite*, not only is the institution of deaconess described as a liturgical ritual, but the ritual itself is more closely assimilated to that for a deacon, even to the extent that the deaconess, like the male deacon, is given a chalice during the ordination ritual. In the *Code of Justinian*,[19] deaconesses are officially called members of the clergy, and the ritual of ordination is parallel to the ordination ritual of a male deacon. Nonetheless, as Bradshaw mentions on many occasions, we cannot impose the understanding of a cleric/lay church, which dominates later centuries of Christian life on the early patristic church.[20] In its canons, the Council of Chalcedon, another voice of the Eastern Church, speaks openly of an ordination of women as deaconesses.[21] Nonetheless, this clear statement on ordination of women is con-

---

19. Aimé G. Martimort cites the *Code of Justinian (Novella)* nos. 3, 6, 123, which speak of deaconesses as clerics and name them in the listings of those who are ordained (see Martimort, *Deaconesses: An Historical Study*, trans. K. D. Whitehead [San Francisco: Ignatius Press, 1986], 109–12). Nonetheless, Martimort argues against an ordination of deaconesses. John Wijngaards cites the *Novella* as well: 3, prol; 3, I, I; 3, 2, I; 6 tit; etc. *(No Women in Holy Orders? The Women Deacons of the Early Church* [Norwich, England: Canterbury Press, 2002]). He cites the Greek: Ανδρες και γυναικες διακονοι. Wijngaards comes to the opposite conclusion: "The laws of Justinian more than once mention the men and women under one heading: 'men and women deacons'. What further proof de we require?" (102).

20. Bradshaw, *Ordination Rites*, 83, 84, 85. See Roger Gryson, *The Ministry of Women in the Early Church* (Collegeville, MN: Liturgical Press, 1976), 62–66; and Martimort, *Deaconesses*, 75. The First International Congress on the Diaconate and Women took place in Stuttgart, April 1–4, 1997. Peter Hünermann, Albert Biesinger, Marianne Heimbach-Steins, and Anne Jensen, published the acts of this International Congress in the volume *Diakonat: Ein Amt für Frauen in der Kirche— Ein frauengerechtes Amt?* (Ostfildern: Schwabenverlag, 1997). Even more recently, Phyllis Zagano has published a volume entitled *Holy Saturday: An Argument for the Restoration of the Female Diaconate in the Catholic Church* (New York: Crossroad, 2000). Zagano argues convincingly that in the Eastern churches not in communion with Rome the ordination of women has been a constant if not a totally universal factor. Since the Roman Catholic Church acknowledges the Non-Uniate churches as true churches, there is an implicit acknowledgment of the ordination of women to the diaconate.

21. See Gryson, *Ministry of Women*, 51.

textualized differently from the clergy/lay context that developed after Gratian's influence from the twelfth century onward.

A. G. Martimort's volume *Deaconesses: An Historical Study* argues that a woman was indeed ordained for the diaconate, but the male diaconate and the female diaconate involved a differing set of ministries.[22] In other words, there was not a diaconate in which some members were male and other members were female. Roger Gryson in his volume *The Ministry of Women in the Early Church* takes an opposing stand: namely, that the diaconate in this early period was indeed open to male and female members, at least in some areas of the church.[23]

Agnes Cunningham, in an article entitled "Deaconess," notes that "it is possible to understand the word 'deaconess,' in at least three different senses, although scholars remain divided in their opinion on this matter."[24] The first meaning of the word *deaconess* indicates indeed a female deacon.

> Admission to the diaconate for a woman was the same as for a man, with the manner differing only (for both) according to the custom of the church to which they belonged.…The female deacon was as truly the assistant to a bishop as a male deacon. In the East, there are indications that she was invested with the stole.[25]

In the second place, deaconess was simply a title given to any woman who fulfilled an assigned function in the church.

> This interpretation respects the complexity of the subject, as scholars have sought to study it, the ambiguity which results from the vocabulary associated with the

---

22. Bradshaw, *Ordination Rites*, 84.

23. Gryson, *Ministry of Women*, 66.

24. Agnes Cunningham, "Deaconess," *The New Dictionary of Theology*, ed. Joseph Komonchak, Mary Collins, and Dermot Lane (Wilmington, DE: Michael Glazier, 1987), 270. See also, Gary Macy, *A History of Women and Ordination* (Lanham, MD: Scarecrow Press, 2002); C. R. Meyer, "Ordained Women in the Early Church," *Chicago Studies* 4 (1965): 285–308.

25. Cunningham, "Deaconess," 270.

question and the confusion, noted above, between widows and deaconesses in their roles of ecclesial service. This understanding of the term recognizes more extensive limitations to the woman's role and a greater difference between her ministry and that of a male deacon.[26]

The third interpretation of the term *deaconess* is that of a wife of a deacon. One finds a similarity in this interpretation to the appearance of the terms, *presbyterissa* (wife of a *presbyteros*) and *episcopissa* (wife of an *episkopos*). Cunningham notes that recent studies have brought to light evidence of the importance of the role of these "wives" within a Christian community. She also notes: "In the East, the office of the female deacon perdured from the fifth to the eleventh century. In 1736, the Maronite Synod of Mount Lebanon empowered their bishops to ordain deaconesses in selected monasteries."[27]

Historical data state clearly that deaconesses were official church ministers in some areas of the early Christian church, while in other areas deaconesses were condemned. These conciliar condemnations were made, so it appears, because of Monophysite or Nestorian influences in the churches that maintained the service of deaconess. Thus, the issue for condemnation was not the role of deaconess because she was a woman. Rather, the condemnation rested on "heretical issues" in the Christian communities, some of which had women as deaconesses. There is, consequently, a tradition in the church of the presence of women ministers who had the rightful title of deaconess. This tradition may be limited geographically, but the Eastern Church world remains a very large environment. If the permanent male diaconate can be reestablished after eleven hundred years of inactivity, then in a similar way there can be a reestablishing of the ministry of deaconess after a similar length of inactivity. Moreover, just as the permanent male diaconate today does not replicate the male diaconate of the patristic period of church life, so too a permanent female diaconate would not need to replicate the female diaconate of former centuries.

---

26. Ibid., 271
27. Ibid.

Restoration of the Deaconesses Today

What would be the motivating force for such a reestablishment? As I have mentioned on several occasions, pastoral need has been the primary cause for the establishment of official church ministries or for the reconstruction of existing church ministries. The church does not operate out of a pre-set theology. Nor has it operated over long centuries out of a mandate from a central office. Rather, time and again, the pastoral needs of a given community or region have given rise to new ministerial roles or have changed the very meaning of the ministerial roles already in place. So too today, serious pastoral needs should be the catalyst for ministerial change. Do we have, today, serious pastoral needs within the Roman Catholic Church for which there is no provision? The answer is a resounding yes. Sunday celebration without Eucharist is rife throughout the Catholic world, and yet only secondary solutions are officially recommended. On an issue as important as Sunday Eucharist, change must take place, and the rigidity of contemporary ministerial roles needs to be removed. If major church leadership cannot meet major pastoral needs, then there is something deeply amiss about the leadership itself.

The leadership of Catholic women in the United States is vital for any restoration of the role of deaconess. Some of this leadership will consider the restoration to be tokenism, and this is a legitimate concern. Diaconal women are not women who are ordained priests, and as a result the restoration of the deaconess could easily be seen as a token gesture. Some of the women's leadership might be in favor of such restoration, since a door is opened for further leadership by women within the ministerial structures of the Roman Catholic Church. A small step forward might be taken, therefore, by such a restoration. My own suggestion would be to reconsider the glaring pastoral needs, since pastoral need has been and remains a major driving force for ministerial change. Is there an obvious pastoral need in the Roman Catholic Church in the United States that would be met by such a diaconal restoration? The issue cannot be simply an insertion of women in a stronger way into church ministry. The issue must be more comprehensive—namely, pastoral need. What would the restoration of the order of deaconess bring to the urgent pastoral needs that the Roman Catholic Church experiences today? This question moves beyond the male/female issue and goes to the center of what church ministry is all about. The voice of Roman Catholic women on this issue of pastoral need is central. Without that voice, a restoration of the deaconess would be superficial. With that voice, the possibility of restoring an order of deaconesses would be justifiable. Data, however, need to be gathered on this pastoral need, and such data, as of this writing, are not adequately organized. This does not mean that the data are not available; it means, rather, that some additional studies need to be made, organizing the data on pastoral need into a convincing presentation.

Chapter Four

ANOINTING OF THE SICK

A major pastoral need today focuses on the spiritual and pastoral care of the sick. The Roman Catholic Church considers the sacrament of the anointing of the sick to be an integral part of its pastoral care for those who are ill. However, the church's care for the sick today remains a pastoral problem of no small dimension. If one views the sacrament of anointing from an international perspective, then the extreme shortage of priests in many countries automatically precludes the anointing of the sick for a vast majority of Catholic Christians who are ill or near death. The number of Catholic Christian communities throughout the world that do not have a resident priest is staggering. Even more, many of these Catholic Christian communities do not have the services of a priest except once or twice a year. If the lack of Sunday Eucharist is a major pastoral problem for the international world of Roman Catholics, then the lack of a minister for the anointing of the sick is of at least equal proportion.

In the United States, too, the number of priestless communities is growing and there are Catholic communities in almost every diocese of the United States that do not have a resident priest. However, when compared to the global situation, the problem in the United States cannot yet be called "critical." The same non-critical verdict, however, cannot be applied to the pastoral care of the sick. In 1994, a national survey on the sacrament of the anointing of the sick was taken by the NACC (National Association of Catholic Chaplains).[28] In this survey, the first set of questions was

---

28. I was privileged to be a part of the National Association of Catholic Chaplains committee. My task was, however, not the computerization service but providing a theological background.

the following, and the person answering the poll was to give in the blank space the realistic appraisal of his or her situation. The survey provided a numerical key to grade the situation.

- ____ a. A priest *always* arrived to meet with the patient or their family.
- ____ b. A priest arrived *more than half* the times requested.
- ____ c. A priest arrived *less than half* the times requested.
- ____ d. A priest *never* arrived to meet with the patient or their family.
- ____ e. Not applicable.

The second set of questions read as follows:

- ____ a. A priest was notified but did not come at the time requested.
- ____ b. A priest was notified but was unavailable.
- ____ c. A priest could not be notified.
- ____ d. Too few priests were located in the immediate area.
- ____ e. No priests in the area were willing to come.
- ____ f. The priests asked not to be called.
- ____ g. Not applicable.

The questionnaire went on to ask: "When a priest was unable to respond to the needs of a seriously ill patient, what was typically done?" "If there is not a priest on staff, what arrangements have been made for contacting a priest to anoint a seriously ill patient?" "What is the predominate type of community that you serve (central, suburb, small town)?" "In which care facility do you work (hospital, long-term care facility, hospice, etc.)?" The survey was sent to 6,299 members of the NACC and also to the College of Chaplains. Ninety-five percent of all respondents completed the entire survey; 68 percent submitted additional comments. The response to this survey was 47 percent, totaling 2,971 responses. These responses were then transcribed into a computerized form, through which each diocese in the United States could be identified. Within each diocese the number of answers to a, b, c, d, and so on above also was identified. In other words, in a given diocese the number of times that a priest never arrived to meet with the patient or his/her family could be specified. The number of times that a priest was notified but did not come could also be determined. Needless to say, the results from this survey indicated that a large number of Catholic Christians in the United States who were seriously ill did not have the pastoral care of the sacrament of anointing.

The results of this survey, together with other documents, were sent to the NCCB. No action was ever taken by the American bishops. A similar endeavor was initiated almost at the same time by the National Association of Diaconate Directors, requesting the NCCB to consider the matter of asking Rome for permission to allow deacons to be the extraordinary ministers of the sacrament of the anointing of the sick. There was no action taken by the NCCB to the request of the NADD. In other words, the status quo was simply allowed to continue. The status quo, however, indicates that there is a serious pastoral need on this matter. Serious pastoral need, as has been mentioned often in this volume, has tended to be the catalyst for major changes in the history of the church. In the last ten years, the issue has not gone away; indeed, it remains even more compelling.

One of the primary reasons for the episcopal hesitancy is the view that *only* priests are eligible to administer this sacrament. In the twentieth century, substantial research on the history of this sacrament was done by biblical scholars, patrologists, and early church historians. For the first time in the entire life of the Christian church, we today have a fairly clear historical understanding of this sacrament of the anointing of the sick. We are in a privileged position. Some of these well-respected scholarly studies include the following: A. Boudinhon, "La théologie de l'extrême onction," *Revue catholique des Eglise;*[29] J. B. Bord, *L'extrême onction, d'après l'Epître de Saint Jacques, Examinée dans la tradition;*[30] A. Chavasse, *Etude sur l'onction*

---

29. A. Boudinhon, "La théologie de l'extrême onction," *Revue catholique des Eglise* 2 (1905): 385–411.

30. J. B. Bord, *L'extrême onction, d'après l'Epître de Saint Jacques, Examinée dan la tradition* (Brussels: Beyaert, 1923).

des infirmes dans l'Eglise latine du IIIe au XIe siècle;[31] A. Chavasse, "L'onction des infirmes dans l'Eglise latine du IIIe siècle à la réforme carolingienne: Les textes," *Revue des sciences religieuses;*[32] and J. Dauvillier, "Extrême onction dans les Eglises orientales," *Dictionnaire de droit canonique.*[33]

The history of this sacrament of anointing of the sick can be divided into five periods of time. The dates for these periods are very general and correspond more to other issues that occurred in the Christian church, rather than specific times that affected the history of this sacrament. The five periods of time are as follows:

1. From the time immediately after the apostles down to 313, when Christianity was legitimized within the Roman Empire.

2. From 313 to 751, when Pepin was elected king by the Franks and the foundations for the Carolingian reform were put into place.

3. From 751 to 1100, the period when early scholasticism began to develop.

4. From 1100 to 1563, the year in which the Council of Trent came to a close.

5. From 1563 down to the Second Vatican Council, 1963–1965.

Let us consider some salient points regarding the sacrament of anointing of the sick that took place in each of these five historical periods.

---

31. A. Chavasse, *Étude sur l'onction des infirmes dans l'Eglise latine du IIIe au XIe siècle* (Lyons: Librairie du Sacré-Coeur, 1942).

32. A. Chavasse, "L'onction des infirmes dans l'Eglise latine du *IIIe* siècle à la réforme carolingienne: Les textes," *Revue des sciences religieuses* 20 (1940): 290–364.

33. J. Dauvillier, "Extrême onction dans les Eglises orientales," *Dictionnaire de droit canonique* (Paris: Librairie Letouzey et Ané, 1953), 5:725–89. See also Bernhard Poschmann, *Busse und Letzte Ölung* (Freiburg: Herder, 1951).

From the Time Immediately after the Apostles down to 313, When Christianity Was Legitimized within the Roman Empire

During this period there is only one solid historical datum relating to the sacrament of anointing, namely, the section from the *Apostolic Tradition*.

> If anyone offers oil, he [the bishop] shall make eucharist [or, render thanks] as at the oblation of the bread and wine. But he shall not say word for word [the same prayer] but with similar effect, saying: "O God who sanctifies this oil, as Thou doest grant unto all who are anointed and receive of it the hallowing wherewith Thou didst anoint kings, priests and prophets, so [grant that] it may give strength to all that taste of it and health to all that use it.[34]

Certain key issues should be noted. First, the formula or prayer is not prescribed. At this time of church history, liturgical prayers could be expressed freely and creatively by the liturgical minister. This freedom of expression applied to the Eucharistic Prayer as well. Second, the *episkopos* blesses the oil, but the lay Christian uses the oil.[35] Third, the effect is bodily health; there is no mention that one can use this oil only if there is danger of death. Fourth, the oil is not "secular," for with the blessing it is now "holy oil." Naturally, no general or universal conclusions can be drawn from this single indication of blessed oil during the first two hundred years of church life. Whatever might have taken place beyond the church in Rome remains unknown.

---

34. *Apostolic Tradition* V. 1 and 2; text is taken from Paul Palmer, *Sacraments and Forgiveness: History and Doctrinal Development of Penance, Extreme Unction and Indulgences* (Westminster, MD: Newman Press, 1959), 277. See also John Ziegler, *Let Them Anoint the Sick* (Collegeville, MN: Liturgical Press, 1987), 36–38.

35. A. Chavasse (*Étude sur l'onction des infirmes dans l'Eglise latine du IIIe siècle à la réforme carolingienne* [Lyon: Librairie du Sacré-Coeur, 1942]) has made a thorough study of the Greek version and the Ethiopian version.

This sole non–New Testament reference from AD 30 to 313 leaves us in a very conjectural position. Mark 6:13, "They [the Twelve] drove out many devils, and they anointed many sick people with oil and cured them," indicates that oil clearly had a medicinal use at the time of Jesus. James 5:14, "Is one of you ill? He should send for the elders of the congregation to pray over him and anoint him with oil in the name of the Lord," also affirms that in the first centuries oil was used as medicine. The elders (*presbyteroi*) in this letter cannot be equated to the order of priests that developed in a later period of Christian life. Statements made from a dogmatic standpoint, that is, using the medieval understanding of the sacrament of the anointing of the sick as a benchmark, is eisegesis, not exegesis. The earliest data are, therefore, slim, and one must simply acknowledge the lack of data and avoid generalized and universal statements on the anointing of the sick by Christian communities during this early period.

From 313 to 751, When Pepin Was Elected King by the Franks and the Foundations for the Carolingian Reform Were Put into Place

During these four hundred years, there are a number of historical sources describing the church's anointing of the sick. In these citations, laypeople clearly anoint the sick. The following list gives the most valuable references.

- Innocent I (d. 471), *Letter to Bishop Decentius of Gubbio*,[36] chapter 8: "Ut oleum sanctum non solum sacerdotibus, sed et omnibus Christianis, in sua suorumque necessitate ungere liceat" (so that holy oil is licitly anointed not only by priests but by all christians for their own need and for the needs of others).
- Serapion (d. ca. 362), *Euchologion*. This work contains three blessings for oil nos. 18, 25, 29: (1) for oil and water that have been offered by the faithful; (2) for

---

36. *Epistula Innocentii Papae I ad Decentium Episcopum Eugubinum* (Turin: Tiposervizio), 7.

chrism with which the baptized are anointed; (3) for oil of the sick. The last blessing indicates only that the oil is blessed by the *episkopos*. Nothing indicates which Christians actually anointed the sick.[37]

- Athanasius (ca. 295–373), *Encyclical letter to the Bishops.* Athanasius complains that the sick people under the Arian *episkopos*, Gregory, are not visited and no one lays hands on them.[38]

- Victor of Antioch (d. ca. 450), *Commentary on Mark* (6:13): "Now oil is both a remedy against fatigue and a source of light and gladness, and so the anointing with oil signifies the mercy of God, a remedy for sickness, and enlightenment of the heart. For it is clear to all that the prayer effects all this, but, in my opinion the oil is a symbol of these things."[39]

- Caesar of Arles (470–542), *Sermon 279, 5.* Paul Palmer states that Caesar of Arles encourages the practice of lay anointing.[40]

- Eligius of Noyon (641–660), *Tractatus de rectitudine catholicae conversationis* (5). Palmer notes that presbyteral anointing had yielded at this period of time almost wholly to anointing by the laity.[41]

- Various lives of the saints should also be mentioned, since in these lives we find account of lay men and women anointing the sick:

1. Sulpicius Severus, *Dialogue III* (ca. 404)

2. *Vita Caesari ep. Arelatenensis* (542–549)

3. Gregory of Tours (538–593), *De virtutibus Sancti Martini*

4. *Vita Germani ep. Autissiodorensis* (ca. 480)

---

37. Palmer, *Sacraments and Forgiveness*, 279–80.
38. Ibid., 279.
39. Ibid., 282.
40. Ibid., 284–85. The text of *Sermon 279* states "with oil that is blessed to anoint in all faith themselves and their dear ones."
41. Palmer, *Sacraments and Forgiveness*, 285–86.

5. *Vita beatae Genovesae virginis Parisiensis* (520–550)

6. *Vita Patrum iurensium Romani, Lupicini, Eugendi* (500–550)

7. *Vita S. Radegundi* (ca. 600)

8. *Vita S. Austrebertae* (ca. 700–730)

It is remarkable that during these years there are so many references to the blessing of holy oil and the anointing of the sick and the dying with holy oil that include anointings by lay men and women. Generalizations on this data must be kept in check, but certain issues remain constant:

- Lay anointing was considered normal.
- Presbyteral anointing coexisted with lay anointing.
- Anointing with holy oil centered on *sickness*, not a deathbed situation. Any illness seems to be envisioned, including demonic possession.
- Children and mentally ill people were anointed.
- The blessing of the oil was performed by either a bishop or a priest.
- As the liturgy developed, the ritual for the blessing and anointing with holy oil also became more formalized, but even the *Gelasian Sacramentary* gives evidence of anointing by lay people.[42]

From 751 to 1100, the Period When Early Scholasticism Began to Develop

A diagram might be helpful to understand why the Carolingian reform set the stage for the twelfth-century theology of the sacrament of the anointing of the sick.

---

42. As regards the *Gelasian Sacramentary*, Palmer notes that the text indicates how extensively anointing with oil took place, especially in Spain and in southern Gaul (*Sacraments and Forgiveness*, 287–88).

From apostolic times to AD 751	Scholastic theology from AD 1100 to 1300
• Lay and priestly anointing	• Only priest can anoint
• All baptized could be anointed except those in the penitential rite	• Small children and Christians who are mentally handicapped from birth cannot be anointed
• Any illness is the focus of the holy anointing.	• Dying is the focus of the sacrament.
• Major effect: health of body	• Major effect: forgiveness of sin

If one studies this dramatic change in the theology of the anointing of the sick, one sees immediately that the root cause for the change occurs in the major effect, namely, the change from health to forgiveness of sin. As soon as *sin* becomes the major issue, clerical power begins to assert itself. At least, this is the way that the theologians from the Carolingian Reformation onward began to think of the situation. Once the major effect was seen as the forgiveness of sin, then all the other changes logically follow. Only a priest can forgive sin; lay people are excluded. Only those who can commit serious sin can receive this sacrament; infants and those mentally disturbed from birth are excluded. The sacrament of penance takes care of sin during the normal life of a Christian adult, but when the time of death has arrived, the Christian may not be able to make a complete confession or even if he/she has made a complete confession the remnants of sin remain. These remnants of sin are taken away by the sacrament of extreme unction. During the Carolingian Reformation, it took several centuries for this revision of the anointing of the sick to take place. One can say that only in the latter part of the twelfth century and the first part of the thirteenth century did a uniform and revised theological understanding of the anointing of the sick begin to dominate the Western church.

From 1100 to 1563, the Year in Which the Council of Trent Came to a Close

Peter Lombard in his *Four Books of Sentences* set the stage for scholastic sacramental theology.[43] Naturally, he had patristic and medieval sources from which he drew his comments, but the systematic way he arranged sacramental theology was new. Through the efforts of people such as Alexander of Hales and Albert the Great, Peter Lombard's volume became part and parcel of the university theological system. For all practical purposes his volume became the textbook for the next five hundred years, and those who wanted to receive the title of master of theology had to present a course in which their lectures offered a detailed commentary on Peter Lombard's *Four Books of Sentences*. Although the *Summa Theologiae* differs from his *Commentary on the Sentences*, Thomas Aquinas presented his views on the anointing of the sick in ways that follow the four points noted in the above diagram. The Franciscans, Bonaventure, and John Duns Scotus, in their *Commentaries on the Sentences*, discuss the sacrament of the anointing of the sick, following the same four points.[44] John Ziegler, however, indicates that the Dominicans and the Franciscans differed significantly on the origin of the sacrament of anointing the sick. The Dominican scholar Albert the Great disagreed with Peter Lombard and stated clearly that "Jesus instituted all the sacraments of the New Law, and this act of institution extended even to the essential aspects of the sacrament."[45] Ziegler also presents the position of Thomas Aquinas, who follows his teacher, Albert the Great.

---

43. Peter Lombard, *Libri IV Sententiarum*, L. IV, D. XXIII (Quaracchi: Typographia Collegii S. Bonaventurae, 1916), 2:889–92.

44. See Thomas Aquinas, *Summa Theologiae*, Pars III [Supplementum] QQ, XXIX–XXXIII; Bonaventure , *Commentaria in IV Libros Sententiarium*, L. IV, D. XXIII (Quaracchi: Typographia Collegii S. Bonaventurae, 1889), vol. 4; John Duns Scotus, *Quaestiones in IV Librum Sententiarum*, ed. Minges (Paris: Louis Vivés., 1884), 1–37. See also Palmer, *Sacraments and Forgiveness*, 299–303.

45. Ziegler, *Let Them Anoint the Sick*, 156. For Albert the Great, see *Commentarii in IV sententiarium*, lib. 4, d. 23, a. 13.

According to Thomas Aquinas, since the institution of the sacraments pertains to the fullness of power reserved only to the author of the New Law, all sacraments were instituted by Christ (*Scriptum super sententias,* t. 4, *Liber quartus sententiarum,* d. 2, q. 1, a. 4). Moreover, Christ's act of institution extended to all the essentials even though there may be no record of such determination in the New Testament (*Summa,* q. 3, m. 2, a. 3., par. 6).[46]

The Franciscans were sensitive to the silence of scripture and stressed the fact of historical development, even though they did not have access to any full historical presentation on the sacrament of the anointing of the sick. The Franciscan scholars such as Alexander of Hales, Bonaventure, and John Duns Scotus did not state that all sacraments were instituted directly by Christ. Ziegler describes their position as follows: "They used imprecise terms such as 'initiating' or 'insinuating' to describe the action of Christ."[47]

The Franciscan theologians recognized the special and unique role of the Holy Spirit, the Apostles, and the Church in the further determination of several sacraments, especially confirmation and extreme unction. While they held that whatever was determined later was always on the authority of Christ, these "further determinations" were understood to be more than the mere promulgation of what had already been fixed by the Lord, extending even to the assigning of the matter and form of the sacrament. The Franciscans did not indicate, however, whether they considered these determinations made by the Apostolic Church, and even by the post-Apostolic Church to be normative for all time.[48]

The theology of the sacraments that one finds in the various Franciscan theologians of the thirteenth and fourteenth centuries

---

46. Ziegler, *Let Them Anoint the Sick,* 156.
47. Ibid., 8.
48. Ibid., 8–9; see also 156–57.

differs from the theology of sacraments found in the Dominican theologians of that same time. Franciscan theology has been approved many times by church officials.

These differences between the Franciscan and Dominican theologians of the middle ages have a strong bearing on contemporary understanding of sacramental theology and, for our purposes, on the sacrament of the anointing of the sick. It is clear from the history of this sacrament that anointing of the sick for about one thousand years was *not* limited to priestly administration. Laymen and laywomen anointed, as did deacons. Even when the dramatic change in the interpretation of this sacrament slowly took place from the Carolingian reform to the beginning of the scholastic period, there was not unanimity of theological thought. The Franciscan scholars were far more sensitive to the historical situation than the Dominican scholars, who maintained that Jesus alone "instituted" all the sacraments in their essential details. In the three centuries following the Council of Trent, the Thomistic approach to theology slowly became dominant. In the twentieth century and even into the twenty-first century, the Thomistic view of the sacrament of anointing, in the minds of some key Roman Catholic leaders, has often been presented not as *theology* but as the *teaching* of the church. The detailed history of this sacrament, which today is readily available, calls into question the Thomistic view. The Franciscan approach, though tentatively expressed in its day and age, left many doors open regarding what is normative and what is not. The medieval Franciscans did this, in the case of the anointing of the sick, because of the silence of the New Testament and the early church.

By 1100, the praxis of the Western church followed the four points in the diagram above, which were centered on the anointing of the sick as a sacrament in which sin is forgiven. On this issue, there was no major divergence between the Dominicans and the Franciscans. Foundationally, the four points mentioned above indicate the common basis for every scholastic presentation on the sacrament of anointing for death: (1) only a priest can anoint; (2) small children and those who are mentally handicapped from birth cannot be anointed; (3) dying is the focus of the sacrament; (4) forgiveness of sin is the major effect of the sacrament. In this approach, *sin* dominates the entire theological understanding of the sacrament. Since forgiveness of sin is central, only the priest—so the medievalists argued—can administer this sacrament. Since forgiveness of sin dominates this development, and since the sacrament of reconciliation is available while one is alive, the sacrament of the anointing of the sick in the tenth, eleventh, and twelfth centuries became a sacrament for the dying. With the scholastic theology of the thirteenth century it became a sacrament called "extreme unction" and not simply anointing of the sick.[49]

It should be noted that the scholastic and medieval theology of sacraments was a theological interpretation of the praxis of that time. The major theologians, for the most part, did not disagree with the liturgical praxis of sacramental life which they experienced. These theologians simply accepted the praxis and theologized on this praxis. Today, we realize the historical relativity of that sacramental praxis and consequently the relativity of the theological explanation of that medieval praxis.

The Council of Trent, in its presentation of the sacrament of extreme unction, simply repeated the basic theological positions of the scholastic period.[50] The overriding focus of the tridentine bishops was to oppose the reformers who maintained that this sacrament (along with several others) was the creation of the church and not a true sacrament of Jesus Christ. Forgiveness of sin dominates the tridentine presentation of this sacrament, and therefore only a priest can forgive sin and only a priest can administer this sacrament. The bishops and theologians at Trent had no idea of the history behind this sacramental rite. Both the then-current praxis for administering the sacrament and the then-current theology that explained the sacrament were taken for granted. Tridentine theology, like the earlier scholastic theology, presents a theological position on the ongoing praxis of the church.

However, since this historically unreflected position on the anointing of the dying—*not* the sick—became part of the sacramental

---

49. Hubert Jedin (*A History of the Council of Trent*, trans. Ernest Graf [St. Louis: Herder, 1957], 2:372–74) offers a lengthy bibliography of the more important works on scholastic sacramental theology.

50. For an English translation of the 1551 *Decree on the Sacrament of Extreme Unction*, see Palmer, *Sacraments and Forgiveness*, 310–13; for the Latin, see Denzinger, 907–10; 926–29.

teaching of Trent, the positions of Trent came to be repeated again and again by later theologians, some of whom considered these tridentine positions as *De fide* statements. The phrase *Anathema sit* (Let the person be anathematized) is not, however, automatically meant to say that a person holding a particular view is a heretic. Rather, it is only a jurisdictional term; a heretical condemnation must be based on issues far more complex than simply the phrase *Anathema sit*.[51]

From 1563 down to the Second Vatican Council, 1963–1965

For the most part, the theology of the sacrament of the anointing of the sick in the Roman Catholic Church did not undergo any major changes throughout this lengthy period. Changes did begin when the monks of St. Maurus, Mabillon and Martène, began to uncover the history of this sacrament. As noted above, it was the scholars in the twentieth century who researched this history, which then brought about changes for the sacrament of the anointing of the sick.[52] At the same time that this historical research was being done, some key systematic theologians in the twentieth century began to speak of this sacrament as the "sacrament of the resurrection," since its connection with death was so central to scholastic theology. At death, if one was anointed by extreme unction, the person, if he or she died, would go straight to heaven, to risen life. This sacrament removed all traces of sin, even those of venial sin. Thus, in the twentieth century we have two different foci for this sacrament: the first focus was on the historical variations of the sacrament; the second was on the extremist posi-

---

51. I have summarized this discussion on the phrase *Anathema sit* and its jurisdicitional dimension in Kenan Osborne, *Reconciliation and Justification: The Sacrament and Its Theology* (New York: Paulist Press, 1990), 159–61, with references to the main theologians and historians who have researched this issue: H. Jedin, J. Umberg, H. Lennerz, A. Lang, P. Fransen and K. Peter.

52. Major scholars include J. B. Bord, A. Chavasse, A. Duval, P. Palmer, P. Fink, and C. Gusmer: see Osborne, *Reconciliation and Justification*, 159-61.

tion that the sacrament was truly meant to be a sacrament for those who are on the brink of death.

What do these historical data offer us today, particularly in reference to the ministry of a deacon? First of all, the evidence opens up a historically broader vision of the Christian use of this sacrament. Second, it indicates that the scholastic view of sacraments was basically a major example of praxis determining theology. Scholastic theologians were only giving a theological interpretation for the sacramental praxis of their day. Third, it indicates that over many centuries lay men and women administered this sacrament. These three issues speak to the tremendous pastoral need today. Care for the sick and the dying is a pastoral need that cannot be held captive by a theological opinion. The Council of Trent, in its decree and canons on extreme unction, presented only a theological view of this sacrament of anointing. The renewal of the sacrament of anointing mandated by Vatican II did *not* alter the basic theology of the sacrament. The current ritual for anointing the sick allows for an anointing *not* based on imminent death, but the ritual retains the centralizing issue of sin, not sickness. Today's leadership of the church is hard-pressed to meet the pastoral needs of Catholics who are sick and merit the administration of this sacrament. To demand that only priests can administer this sacrament is myopic, since the history of the sacrament indicates that there is a tradition of almost one thousand years allowing nonpriests to anoint. Which is more important: a major pastoral need or a theological interpretation? The answer is obvious: the pastoral need.

Chapter Five

CHURCH LEADERSHIP

Church institutional ministry and church institutional leadership are intimately connected. If institutional church ministry exhibits major difficulties, institutional church leadership also exhibits major difficulties. There are today in the American Roman Catholic Church major problems in both institutional ministry and institutional leadership. The negative aspects of today's ministry and leadership will be spelled out in chapter 6 of this work. In this section on church leadership, we continue our dreaming and our creative, out-of-the-box thinking. Our concern might be formulated as follows: *Can the permanent diaconate enrich the current leadership of the American Roman Catholic Church?*

Since a majority of permanent deacons are members of the North American Catholic Church, such a question has intensive and extensive value. That there are many permanent deacons in the contemporary church is a given; that these permanent deacons are limited in their role as church leaders is also a given. The glaring pastoral needs that were mentioned above require—one might even say *demand*—a better *form* of church leadership, since it is precisely under the current church leadership that these pastoral needs have become critical. An abundance of pressing pastoral needs indicates that ecclesial leadership has failed. Therefore, one can legitimately ask: Together with the bishops, the priests, and the lay ministers, can the permanent deacons in a leadership way help alleviate the urgent pastoral needs of today's church? I believe that the answer is *yes*, but a positive answer means that leadership in the church must be shared in more creative and decisive ways. For those in charge to share a leadership role is always a major difficulty, since sharing means that those in charge give up at least a part of their current control. To be blunt, sharing in leadership is a challenge to the current ecclesial power structures.

If current institutional leadership shies away from power sharing, one can legitimately ask: *Are such ministerial leaders truly servants to the church?* When the church presents glaring pastoral needs and the existent institutional leadership does little to alleviate these pastoral needs, then the foundation of all ministries, namely, service/*diakonia,* is compromised. Institutional ministerial leadership fails at its very foundation, which is service to the community, not power over the community.

The leadership in many American parishes is at present in major distress. The growing number of priestless parishes has been noted. Mega-parishes seem to be the leadership's response to the issue of priestless parishes, even though mega-parishes by their very nature diminish the *community* aspect of Eucharist. Liturgies in these mega-parishes become more and more theatrical in the sense that the majority of people are onlookers and not participants. Larger numbers of people become a crowd not an interpersonal community.

Are permanent deacons entrusted with the leadership of a parish? The overriding answer to this question is that deacons cannot be pastors—only priests can be. In fact, the number of deacons to whom a parish has been entrusted is minimal throughout the United States. More often than not, a layman or a laywoman—generally a religious—has been entrusted with the day-to-day leadership of such parishes, though they are not pastors. In the main, permanent deacons have not been invited to assume this task of church leadership. Why is this reluctance so prevalent throughout the dioceses of the American Catholic Church? Few answers have been given. Some speculation has been voiced. Deacons would be taking over priestly roles, and this is not healthy for the permanent diaconate. Nor is it healthy for the morale of the priests. Deacons would become more and more involved in sacramental life, and this is not in accord with canon law, nor in accord with the instruction *Sacramentum reconciliationis.*

Permanent deacons have been trained in lengthy formation programs. They have had theological and pastoral training. They have indicated by their diaconal experience a maturity of ministry and leadership. Why are they not at the top of the list when a parish no longer can be serviced by a live-in priest? Is there something theologically amiss regarding the prospects of a deacon taking over such leadership? Or is there only a canonical hurdle? Is service, *diakonia*, still the foundation of ministerial and leadership ecclesial activity, or are legality and canonicity the overriding foundation? Are the glaring pastoral needs of secondary importance to juridical structures? These are serious questions, and if we are to think of the future of the permanent diaconate, these questions need to be faced in an honest and truly spiritual way. What is best for the people of God is a top priority for all institutional ministry and leadership. Vatican II and the *Catechism of the Catholic Church*, as we saw above, placed service as the foundation of all institutional ministry and leadership. Are these statements on paper only? In practice, other priorities seem to be more telling.

Permanent deacons today do not rank high in diocesan church leadership. There is still a bishop-priest control, or at times simply a bishop control. John Paul II indicated clearly that ministry and leadership are necessarily communal. Again is this only a statement on paper? If there are glaring pastoral needs—and such pastoral needs clearly exist in the Roman Catholic Church of the United States—their presence may not be due to faulty leadership; but if they remain glaring and unattended to, then faulty leadership is the primary source of such inattention. We must think creatively in the face of glaring pastoral needs.

Chapter Six

THREE CONTEXTUAL ASPECTS FOR THE FUTURE

We have considered several positive ways in which the permanent diaconate in the United States might develop in a better and more efficacious way. There are, unfortunately, some negative issues that the leaders of the permanent diaconate must honestly face. Each of these negative issues currently influences in a very strong way (a) the *theology* of the permanent deacon; (b) the *pastoral life* of the permanent diaconate; and (c) the personal *identity* of the permanent deacon. To speak about the role of the deacon in the early years of the new millennium and not take these three issues into account would be similar to ignoring the proverbial clichéd elephant in the living room.

The First Major Issue: Conflicting Voices on a Theology of Church

We have already seen that there are specific texts in the documents of Vatican II that have engendered diverse interpretations, and the validity of these diverse interpretations continues to be hotly debated. There are also issues that individuals and groups in the Roman Catholic Church today do not wish to accept, and thus the postconciliar period is confronted with both acceptance and nonacceptance of some key conciliar positions. Since no theological position was defined by the bishops at Vatican II, the struggles that involve acceptance or nonacceptance of a particular conciliar position are not struggles over a defined teaching of the church. Rather, they are struggles over differing theological interpretations, which in the present situation are basically matters of ecclesiology. The emphasis on theology, not dogma, helps us pinpoint the locus of the first problematic issue. The locus is fundamentally *a theology of church*. The locus is not fundamentally a theology of God, a theology of Jesus, but it is ecclesiology. There is no disagreement today on any defined teaching regarding the church. The foundational faith expressions regarding church are honored by all involved. Rather, the discord eddies around theological issues, none of which constitutes a defined issue of our Christian faith.

In themselves, the texts of Vatican II do not offer a complete theology of the church. At best, the texts offer significant positions on certain ecclesiological issues. Only when these significant conciliar positions are incorporated into a more comprehensive theology of church do difficulties arise. This is most evident when one attempts to combine some of the major ecclesiological positions proposed by the council to the standard and normative theology of the church that has dominated Roman Catholic official thought from the post-Reformation times down to the middle of the twentieth century. Major members of the Roman Catholic Church today, both ecclesiastical and theological, wish to maintain intact the theology of the church that was normal and standard *prior* to Vatican II. There are also major ecclesiastical and theological members of the Roman Catholic Church today who strongly support the key issues in the texts of Vatican II. They also realize that these key issues cannot be in any facile way integrated into the standard, dominant theology of the church that has been in place for the past four hundred years. Consequently, there is major disagreement. That there exists a struggle over a theology of church is part and parcel of the post–Vatican II Roman Catholic world. Although this is a *theological* struggle, not a struggle over *defined issues*, the struggle is present and highly active, and it influences the theological understanding of ministry today including the ministry of the permanent diaconate.

A theology of ecclesial ministry flows from a theology of church, not vice versa.[53] Consequently, a theology of church impacts ecclesial ministry, including diaconal ministry, in a powerful way. I

---

53. See Osborne, *Ministry*, 518–95.

have already mentioned this in the first chapter, in which I presented the five major changes in ecclesial ministry that Vatican II espoused. The texts from Vatican II present a relational understanding of church ministry. In the course of the postconciliar debate over these five issues, there are strident voices disavowing such a relational approach and requiring a radical specificity for each grade of ministerial service. The foundational interrelationality of ecclesial institutional ministry and leadership as found in the conciliar texts is either ignored for the sake of radical specificity or it is minimized. The standard and dominant post-tridentine theology of church, which the proponents of radical difference want to maintain, centers on the unique, nonrelational positions of pope, bishop, and priest.

The permanent diaconate feels the effects of this postconciliar church discussion at three levels. The first level is *theological:* what is the theological understanding of the permanent diaconate? This question can be answered only on the basis of a theology of church. The second level is *pastoral:* what are the correct pastoral activities of a permanent deacon? This question, too, can be answered only on the basis of a theology of church. The third level is *personal:* what is the self-identity today of a permanent deacon? This question, likewise, can be answered only on the basis of a theology of church. The struggle to maintain the dominant and standard post-tridentine theology of church versus the struggle to implement a relational theology of church deeply affects at all three levels the efforts of permanent deacons in today's Roman Catholic Church. All the postconciliar agitation over texts, interpretation of texts, and the acceptance and nonacceptance of conciliar positions, as we have seen above, involves to some degree a theology of church and therefore the theology of ecclesial ministry. Since the permanent diaconate is a major part of today's ecclesial ministry, it shares in this factional argumentation. This too is a given for the context in which the deacon lives and ministers today.

The Second Major Issue: The Sexual Abuse by Clergy

In the United States today—although the situation can also be found in parts of Europe as well—the Roman Catholic Church continues to struggle with the scandals caused by the sexual abuse by the clergy. However, the sexual abuse is only part of the current scandal. Perhaps an even more difficult part of the scandal is the bishops' loss of their moral leadership. What the American bishops say today on moral issues is considered irrelevant by many Catholics, since the bishops themselves have not acted in accord with fundamental moral standards. From the publication of their Dallas Statement (2003) until today, the bishops of the United States have heard again and again and from many sources that they are no longer trusted as moral leaders of the church.

The bishops' response to this continual judgment has, however, not been overwhelming. Most of the American bishops have simply turned inward. They have publicly defended themselves and their reputations rather than face their own lack of moral integrity. In general, they have become inwardly focused, more concerned about their own prestige and position than about showing a genuine sense of *mea culpa*. Too often an individual bishop has prefaced his remarks on the scandal by saying: "If I have been wrong...." This "if" statement indicates that possibly the bishop has not been wrong. For many Catholics, the "if" statement is seen as a cover-up or a statement of noninvolvement; consequently, the "if" statement comes across as a nonadmission of moral wrong. The nonadmission is also seen as a lack of pastoral care and compassion for the victims and their families. It is perceived as another instance of *Prestigedenken*, thinking first about episcopal reputation and prestige. The negativity toward the moral authority of the American bishops will, in my view, remain part and parcel of today's Roman Catholic Church for at least the next two generations. Consequently, the leadership or nonleadership of the bishops will continue to play a contextual role in any and all visions and dreams for the permanent diaconate.

A typical example of this lack of public confidence in the American bishops is found in an essay by Hendrik Hertzberg. In his

"Comment" in a recent edition of the *New Yorker*, Hertzberg wrote: "The big shocker, for Catholic and non-Catholic alike, has been not so much the abuse itself—awful and heart-breaking though it is—as the coldly bureaucratic "handling" of it by hierarchs like Law and the current Archbishop of New York, Edward Cardinal Egan."[54]

One might consider this comment as typical media hype over a bad situation, and the tone is surely a hostile tone. However, remarks such as this occur again and again. Even the policy of zero tolerance espoused by the bishops in Dallas, has left many priests, for whom there has only been an informal allegation and no firm legal accusation, without any ministerial work in a diocese. These priests have been left by the wayside, and local bishops do little to help them. They are in a no-man's-land.

It should be mentioned that there are American bishops who have acknowledged their lack of strong supervision of recalcitrant clergy. Many of these men have shown profound care and compassion for the victims of abuse and their families. It is also true that every bishop has the opportunity to present his positions at the meetings of the National Conference of Catholic Bishops. They can even make proposals. However, unless the small core of bishops who control the agenda of the conference agree to what these bishops say, the issues they bring up go nowhere. There is clearly an episcopal political control of the conference itself, and this control at times prevents the views of individual bishops from being further discussed and reported on in a comprehensive and honest way. The voice of the episcopal conference, then, reflects the central leadership more than the common consensus of the American bishops. Because of this centralizing power in the conference itself, the conference of bishops also bears a responsibility for the decline in episcopal moral credibility.

This contextual ecclesial situation affects the permanent deacon, since the deacon must live with priests whose morale is low. Not just bishops but priests, too, have turned inward. They too struggle for a recognition of self-identity, and they find little support. The deacons in a parish situation must live with priests who are unsure of their own self-identity and their own acceptability.

---

54. Hendrik Herzberg, "Comment: Sins," *New Yorker*, April 1, 2002, 35–36.

However, throughout this sexual scandal in the church, the permanent deacons have remained the one clerical group that the laity can trust. In general, bishops and priests have been highly distrusted by the laity; permanent deacons have been highly trusted.

Whether today one is a bishop, a priest, a deacon, or an officially appointed lay minister, many Roman Catholic and many non-Roman Catholic people consider such leaders to be spokespersons for the church itself. What these church leaders say is the party line. The church leaders are expected to defend the reputation of the diocese, the parish, or even the church itself. Deacons fall under this classification. Deacons are public ministers in the church, and the public nature of what they do is seen as a public defense of church policy and activity. Every now and then, a bishop, a priest, or a deacon speaks out in a way that is considered a discredit to the public face of the church. Such leaders are censured in some way. An institutional minister is meant to uphold the church, not tear it down. An institutional minister is meant to speak correctly about the church, not malign it. Deacons, as official ministers and leaders of the church, cannot avoid this situation of public presence. With the scandals and the questioning of episcopal moral authority, deacons cannot help but be considered part of the defense of the church rather than part of the critics of the church. This situation will last for another two generations, and it, too, is part of the current context of institutional ecclesial ministry.

The Third Major Issue: The Bishops' Use of the *Catechism of the Catholic Church*

The normative role of the *Catechism of the Catholic Church* has been overstated by the Roman Catholic bishops, an overstatement that has even gained the approval of the National Conference of Catholic Bishops itself. Many American bishops, in an effort to find theological unity, have selected the *Catechism of the Catholic Church* as the lens through which all their major educational programs in a given diocese must be viewed. In their judgment, the selection of the *Catechism* as the *tessera fidei* (a token of faith) places the *Catechism* above the current discussions on the meaning of conciliar texts or the issues of acceptance or nonacceptance. The bishops' acceptance of the *Catechism* as normative for all religious teaching indicates that, for all practical purposes, the *Catechism* in their dioceses has become the lens through which one understands the New Testament and the documents of Vatican II. Other theological and catechetical writings are judged by their literal adherence to the *Catechism*.[55]

In reducing the view of all theological teaching to the *Catechism*, the bishops have overlooked the richness of the church's vast theological tradition. Theology, of course, is never the same as dogma or solemnly defined teachings of the church. Theology is a continual reflection on faith; it presupposes faith; it is not in competition with faith. However, beginning with the subapostolic period of church history, one finds a number of similar reflections on Catholic faith, each specifically differing either in philosophical approaches or in theological approaches.

In the history of the Western Catholic Church, the Augustinian intellectual tradition extended its own overarching popularity from AD 400 to 1300. Even after 1300, the Augustinian intellectual tradition has remained profoundly influential. In the sixteenth century, for example, both Martin Luther and John Calvin employed citations from the writings of St. Augustine second only in number to their citations from the scriptures. Catholic theologians at the Council of Trent were also very competent in their knowledge of the Augustinian intellectual tradition, and the Council of Trent was in many ways an Augustinian council. Tridentine bishops and theologians often argued against the Augustinian approach of the major

---

55. See the USCCB Ad Hoc Committee to Oversee the Use of the *Catechism*, www.usccb.org/catechism. This committee stresses conformity of all catechetical texts and series. Works that do not meet the standards of conformity to the *Catechism of the Catholic Church* are not considered acceptable. This ad hoc committee has prepared a *Protocol for Assessing the Conformity of Catechetical Materials with the Catechism of the Catholic Church*. In the notification entitled *Catechism Update* (Spring 1998), the authors indicate that there is a distinction between ecclesiastical approval, on the one hand, and the determination by this committee on conformity to the *Catechism*, on the other hand. This honors the role of the bishop of a diocese. However, the conformity/nonconformity decisions of this committee strongly influence the diocesan bishops. The lens through which all catechetical texts and series are judged is not the New Testament, nor is it the theological traditions of the western church. The lens is narrowly a conformity to a particular catechism.

reformers by restating what they considered a more correct understanding of Augustine. Moreover, the Catholic bishops and theologians at Trent were also deeply trained in both the Dominican and the Franciscan intellectual traditions. In many sessions of the Council of Trent, specific Thomistic or Scotistic positions were defended by the tridentine bishops, which caused the papal legate who chaired the session to squelch such a debate between the two mendicant theologies. We are here, the legate would say, not to settle the scholastic divisions but to refute the reformers.

At the end of the thirteenth century and the beginning of the fourteenth century, the Dominican Friars formally selected the teachings of Thomas Aquinas as the intellectual center of their theological formation and educational institutions. This formal move guaranteed a long life for the Dominican intellectual tradition. Shortly after, the Franciscans followed this pattern by selecting both Bonaventure and John Duns Scotus as the intellectual center of their formation and educational institutions. From AD 1300 to 1563 (the conclusion of the Council of Trent) the intellectual traditions of the two mendicant orders became far more popular than the Augustinian intellectual tradition.

All three of the major intellectual traditions in the Western church—Augustinian, Dominican, and Franciscan—are based on the same foundations, namely: holy scripture, holy tradition, and holy doctrine. None of these three intellectual traditions, however, started as a *creatio ex nihilo*, a creation from nothing. All three of these traditions inherited philosophical theologies of the past on which they continued to build. All three traditions were even more fundamentally based on the Christian faith. In other words, the basis for all three traditions remained identical, namely, the revealed Word of God as expressed in holy scripture, holy tradition, and holy doctrine. Differences among the three traditions are based on the various philosophical and theological ways in which the three traditions express the implications of the revealed Word of God and on the interfacing of spirituality and theology.[56]

---

56. Kenan Osborne, *The Franciscan Intellectual Tradition: Tracing Its Origins and Identifying Its Central Components* (St. Bonaventure, NY: Franciscan Institute, 2003).

In the Roman Catholic Church, there has never been a *single* theology; hence a better designation for Catholic theology would be Catholic theologies. Nor has there ever been a *single* Christology; hence the better term is plural—Christologies. Nor has there been a *single* theology of the Triune God; hence the better term is plural—theologies of God/Trinity. Anyone conversant with the patristic period of the church cannot help but be amazed at the varieties of trinitarian and christological thought. Each of these theologies of the Triune God and of Jesus Christ was developed through a lengthy process. Over time, some of the early theologies and Christologies became nonrelevant. Others, however, are still operative today. Most of those that are still operative continue to remain in process, since they are being further developed and more carefully honed by contemporary theologians.

If one includes the Eastern churches in this overview, the extent of the different Christologies and different theologies becomes even more dramatic, since the several Eastern theologies of the Trinity and of Jesus are also quite diverse. The theologies of the Eastern churches are based on the same three foundations we have in the West: holy scripture, holy tradition, and holy doctrine.

Over the past two thousand years, the world has never experienced a theological golden age, that is, an age by which all subsequent theological ages are to be judged. This means that there is in the Roman Catholic Church no single theology, no single Christology, nor even a single ecclesiology that is definitive. Rather, there are and have been many theologies, Christologies, and ecclesiologies, all of which are based on the same foundation of God's revealed Word. To understand and to live the Word of God, revealed in both creation and incarnation, has been and will be a continual task for Christians. The schools of theology that developed in the thirteenth century must be seen against this background.

By limiting the theological approach to a literal presentation of the text of the *Catechism*, the three main theological traditions in the Western church—Augustinian, Dominican, and Franciscan—are relegated to a historical footnote. Even the Thomism that is quite evident in the *Catechism* does not precisely represent the teaching of Thomas Aquinas. Rather, the Kantian-Cartesian

203

Thomism in the *Catechism* is simply a preferred Thomism among the many Thomisms that have been prevalent for the last hundred years.[57]

This ecclesial situation affects the permanent deacon, since in such a formation of permanent deacons, it is not the New Testament that dominates as the norm, nor are the documents of Vatican II seen as foundationally normative. Rather, the *Catechism* is, in certain dioceses, presented as a standard that shapes the formation programs of the permanent deacon in a very strong way. This has a negative effect: namely, deacons who accept this mononormative role of the *Catechism* begin to show disdain for any and all other theological positions and any and all other catechetical positions. Western theology has a richness in its diversity, as we have seen, and to jettison this theological diversity indicates that one does not understand the richness of the Roman Catholic Church at all. Theology, however, guides much of one's pastoral work, and again to jettison the theologically diverse underpinnings of pastoral ministry indicates that one does not understand the richness of the interplay between theology and pastoral activity.

These three negative issues will not go away as the permanent diaconate at the beginning of the third millennium charts out its hopes and dreams. It is hoped that the reader will not take it amiss that I have begun this section on a negative note. The reality must be acknowledged.

---

57. See Thomas O'Meara, *Thomas Aquinas Theologian* (Notre Dame, IN: University of Notre Dame Press, 1997), 152–200, for a clear presentation of the terms *Thomism* and *Thomistic theology*. The Thomism that is rampant in the Roman Catholic Church today is a contemporary form of some major Thomistic ideas and some major philosophical ideas from the Enlightenment.

FINAL OBSERVATIONS

The future of the diaconate depends deeply on how we dream today. At the heart of our dreaming we must return again and again to the Deacon Jesus.[58] His form of *diakonia* is the motive for all ministry, mission, and leadership in the church. To meditate on the Deacon Jesus is to delve into the very source of a theology of deacon. Meditation and theology are intricately united, and thus meditation on the Deacon Jesus and a theology of the diaconate are also intricately united. To meditate on the Deacon Jesus also enriches diaconal pastoral ministry. When deacons, in their pastoral activities, radiate the Deacon Jesus, then, and only then, are they truly sharing in the mission, ministry, and leadership of the Lord. The pastoral works of each and every deacon become convincing and enabling when Jesus, the *Lumen gentium*, is in a lunar way reexpressed in what the deacon does and says. To meditate on the Deacon Jesus is also basic for a deacon's personal identity as a minister of the gospel. In one's interior reflection on the deaconing of Jesus, one finds the qualities and values of one's own deaconing. In many ways, it is this interior meditation on the Deacon Jesus in comparison with one's own identity as deacon that makes the diaconal ministry a joy. A deacon truly finds himself and his own spiritual identity only when in both prayer and action he sees himself in some small way a sacrament of the one deacon, Jesus himself. The icon of Jesus washing the feet of his own disciples is the icon that the deacon himself tries to be. The words "I have not come to be served but to serve" become the guiding principle of diaconal theology, diaconal pastoral work, and diaconal identity. Only Jesus the deacon can make the future of the permanent diaconate a future of grace, compassion, and gospel life.

---

58. See Cummings, "Jesus the Deacon," in *Deacons and the Church*, 22–29.

BIBLIOGRAPHY

For a further understanding and appreciation of the permanent diaconate, I offer the following list of books together with a brief comment on each of them. Naturally, many other books could be included, but I offer this list of books that I think are of special interest for further reading by those who are preparing for or who are in the permanent diaconate.

On the Issue of Context and Theology

Bevans, Stephen B. *Models of Contextual Theology*. Rev. Ed. Maryknoll, NY: Orbis Books, 2002.

Schreiter, Robert J. *Constructing Local Theologies*. Maryknoll, NY: Orbis Books, 1985.

———.*The New Catholicity: Theology between the Global and the Local*. Maryknoll, NY: Orbis Books, 1997.

These three volumes present in English some of the best work today on the issue of theology and the context of globalization.

On a Post–Vatican II Church

Alberigo, Giuseppe, Jean-Pierre Jossua, and Joseph A. Komonchak, eds. *The Reception of Vatican II*. Washington, DC: Catholic University of America Press, 1987. The essays in this volume present in a very clear way the various responses and acceptance of the Vatican II documents. This small book is a gold mine for information on why and how Vatican II has or has not been accepted in the current Roman Catholic Church.

Phan, Peter, ed. *The Gift of the Church*. Collegeville, MN: Liturgical Press, 2000. Although many essays in this volume deal with the church prior to Vatican II, this volume is one of the best books on a theology of church that has appeared in the last ten years.

On Ministry

O'Meara, Thomas. *Theology of Ministry*. Rev. ed. New York: Paulist Press, 1999. This is a "must book" for all Catholics who are working in ecclesial ministry. O'Meara's revised edition provides a solid theological background on the meaning of ministry in today's post–Vatican II church.

Lakeland, Paul. *The Liberation of the Laity: In Search of an Accountable Church*. New York: Continuum, 2004. Lakeland's book focuses on the layperson in church ministry, but permanent deacons would do well to study this volume, since most of their diaconal work is done in conjunction with lay ministers.

On the Diaconate

Barnett, James Monroe. *The Diaconate: A Full and Equal Order*. Rev. ed. Valley Forge, PA: Trinity Press International, 1995. Barnett offers a detailed but readable discussion of the diaconate in the early period of church history. He helps the reader understand the origins and first developments of the diaconate in the Christian church. He also includes in his history of the diaconate, the deacon in the Orthodox churches and in Protestant churches.

Bulson, Michael E. *Believe What You Read: Timeless Homilies for Deacons—Liturgical Cycle C*. Mahwah, NJ: Paulist Press, 2006.
———. *Preach What You Believe: Timeless Homilies for Deacons—Liturgical Cycle B*. Mahwah, NJ: Paulist Press, 2005.

Collins, John N. *Diakonia: Re-interpreting the Ancient Sources*. New York: Oxford University Press, 1990. Collins offers a solid and well-researched book on the meaning of the term *diakonia* in the Greco-Roman world. Deacons would find this book very helpful for understanding the meaning of *deacon* as used in the New Testament and the early church writers.

Cummings, Owen F. *Deacons and the Church*. Mahwah, NJ: Paulist Press, 2004.

———.*Saintly Deacons*, Mahwah, NJ: Paulist Press, 2005.

Cummings, Owen F., William T. Ditewig, and Richard Gaillardetz. *Theology of the Diaconate: The State of the Question*. Mahwah, NJ: Paulist Press, 2005.

Ditewig, William T. *101 Questions and Answers on Deacons*. Mahwah, NJ: Paulist Press, 2004.

Echlin, Edward. *The Deacon in the Church: Past and Present*. Staten Island, NY: Alba House, 1971. Even though this is a somewhat older book, Echlin presents in a very readable way the early history of the diaconate, and he offers some excellent considerations regarding the permanent diaconate today based on the historical material.

United States Conference of Catholic Bishops. *National Directory for the Formation, Ministry, and Life of Permanent Deacons in the United States, including the Secondary Documents Basic Standards for Readiness and Visit of Consultation Teams to Diocesan Permanent Diaconate Formation Programs*. Washington, DC: USCCB, 2005.

Author Index

Alberigo, Giuseppe, 16, 22, 24, 25, 207
Albert the Great, 63, 186
Alexander of Hales, 63, 136, 186, 187
Ante, Oscar, 9
Arbuckle, Gerald, 10
Athanasius, St., 183
Augustine, St., 120, 201, 202

Barnett, James Monroe, 5, 94, 208
Bauer, J. B., 123
Bellarmine, Robert, 21
Bellitto, Chris, 16
Bevans, Stephen, 9, 11, 12, 14, 207
Billot, Louis, 21
Bleichner, Howard, 91
Bligh, John, 95
Boff, Leonardo, 119
Bonaventure, St., 38, 63, 65, 90, 120, 136, 186, 187, 202
Bord, J. B., 179, 190
Boudinhon, A., 179
Bradshaw, Paul, 145, 171, 173
Brockman, Norbert, 95
Brown, Raymond, 168
Bruno, P. G., 123
Bucer, Martin, 133

Bulson, Michael, 95, 208

Cachia, Nicholas, 21
Caesar of Arles, 183
Calvin, John, 64, 133, 201
Chavasse, A., 179, 180, 181, 190
Chenu, Marie-Dominique, 4
Cohalan, Florence D., 21
Collins, John, 95, 208
Congar, Yves M. -J., 4, 23, 42, 123
Cote, Richard, 10
Cummings, Owen, 95, 144, 205, 209
Cunningham, Agnes, 173, 174

D'Alès, Aldémar, 21
Daniélou, Jean, 4, 123
Dauvillier, J., 180
De Augustinis, Aemilius, 21
De Coninck, Giles, 21
De Franch, Sugranyes, 41
De la Taille, Maurice, 21
De Lubac, Henri, 4
De Mesa, José, 13
De Valencia, Gregorio, 21
Del Molino, A., 29
Diekamp, Wilhelm, 21
Ditewig, William, 95, 151, 209
Doronzo, Emmanuel, 21